flights:

Readings in Magic, Mysticism, Fantasy, and Myth

flights:
Readings in Magic, Mysticism, Fantasy, and Myth

DAVID ADAMS LEEMING
University of Connecticut

HARCOURT BRACE JOVANOVICH, INC.
New York   Chicago   San Francisco   Atlanta

ISBN: 0-15-527556-9

Library of Congress Catalog Card Number: 73-13029

Printed in the United States of America

FOR PAMELA, MARGARET, AND JULIET

Copyrights and Acknowledgments

For permission to use the selections reprinted in this book, the author is grateful to the following publishers and copyright holders:

CHARLES BOER   For *The Bacchae* by Euripides, translated by Charles Boer and reprinted with his permission.

THE CHURCH OF SATAN   For "The Black Mass" from *The Satanic Bible* by Anton Szandor LaVey. Reprinted by permission of The Church of Satan.

DELACORTE PRESS   For "Harrison Bergeron" from *Welcome to the Monkey House* by Kurt Vonnegut, Jr. Copyright © 1961 by Kurt Vonnegut, Jr. A Seymour Lawrence Book/Delacorte Press. Reprinted by permission of the publisher. Originally appeared in *Fantasy and Science Fiction*.

THE DIAL PRESS   For "Going to Meet the Man" from the book, *Going to Meet the Man*, copyright © 1965 by James Baldwin. Reprinted by permission of The Dial Press.

DOUBLEDAY & COMPANY, INC.   For "The Myth of Objective Consciousness" from *The Making of a Counter Culture*, copyright © 1968, 1969 by Theodore Roszak. Reprinted by permission of Doubleday & Company, Inc.

E.P. DUTTON & CO., INC.   For "What is Mysticism?" from the book *Practical Mysticism* by Evelyn Underhill. Copyright, 1915 by E.P. Dutton & Co., Inc. Renewed, 1943, by Evelyn Underhill. Published by E.P. Dutton & Co., Inc. and used with their permission.

FABER AND FABER LTD.   For "Crow's Fall" from *Crow* by Ted Hughes. Reprinted by permission of Faber and Faber Ltd.

Acknowledgments and picture credits to be continued on page 386.

preface

The human mind has always sensed the existence of an active and conscious unknown—a state of reality separate from but dominant over earthly life. At times, it has ignored or even denied supernatural and occult powers, while at other times, it has actively sought knowledge of or union with them. At present, we are experiencing a period of the latter sort. In nearly every intellectual discipline, as well as in most areas of popular culture, that which is "beyond the material"—literally "out of sight"—is being explored or exploited.

This book, through a varied group of selections and through commentary, attempts to define and analyze this new interest. Four basic paths into the unknown are treated: magic, mysticism, fantasy, and myth. Many of the examples in each section are currently popular, some are more esoteric. There are three types of examples within each section: theoretical, practical, and literary. In Part One, for instance, the Hughes and Macfarlane selections are theoretical; the Black Elk, Jung, Castaneda, LaVey, and Hart selections, in the sense that they describe actual occurrences, are practical; and the rest are literary. These categories, however, are not mutually exclusive. For example, the Black Elk piece is also literary, and the Castaneda one contains a theoretical discussion.

All the selections have literary merit and have been chosen to provide examples of as many genres and forms as possible. There is a complete Greek tragedy, a rich selection of poetry, several complete stories, and even a long essay that could serve as a model for a research paper. In some cases, lack of space has prevented the inclusion of otherwise appropriate selections. Complete short works have been given precedence over excerpts from longer ones. The suggestions for further reading provide directions for expansion of knowledge on the given subject, and longer works are, of course, mentioned there. At the end of each of the four major sections, there is a commentary that interprets the collected material, suggests approaches to it, and points out connections between the various sections.

The audience to which the book is addressed is necessarily varied. This book will interest not only students but anyone concerned with the unknown—anyone who has begun the voyage into the collective being that is man's ultimate Self.

D. A. L.

contents

PREFACE   v

introduction: the revolution of the spirit   1

part one magic: shamans and witches   12

SHAMANISM: DEFINITIONS   13

Ted Hughes
FROM "Secret Ecstasies"   13

THE SHAMAN AND HIS APPRENTICE   16

Carlos Castaneda
FROM *The Teachings of Don Juan: A Yaqui Way of Knowledge*   16

THE SHAMANISTIC FLIGHT OF AN AMERICAN INDIAN   26

John G. Neihardt
FROM *Black Elk Speaks*   26

CONTENTS

THE SHAMANISTIC FLIGHT IN FOLKLORE ·   32

Stith Thompson
FROM *Tales of the North American Indians*   32

THE SHAMANISTIC FLIGHT OF THE POET   38

Samuel Taylor Coleridge
Kubla Khan   38

William Butler Yeats
Sailing to Byzantium   40

Ted Hughes
Crow's Fall   41

Gene Fowler
Shaman Song #12   42

THE SHAMANISTIC FLIGHT OF A MODERN PSYCHIATRIST   44

Carl Gustav Jung
FROM *Memories, Dreams, Reflections*   44

WITCHCRAFT: DEFINITIONS   49

Alan Macfarlane
FROM *Witchcraft in Tudor and Stuart England*   49

THE BLACK MASS   58

Anton Szandor LaVey
FROM *The Satanic Bible*   58

THE SALEM WITCH TRIALS   64

Roger Hart
FROM *Witchcraft*   64

WITCHCRAFT IN FICTION   73

Nathaniel Hawthorne
Young Goodman Brown   73

WITCHES IN POETRY   86

Robert Frost
Two Witches   86

COMMENTARY: The Witch and the Shaman: The Diabolist and the Visionary   94

part two mysticism   101

MYSTICISM: DEFINITIONS   103

Evelyn Underhill
FROM *Practical Mysticism*   103

THE TAO: THE GREAT WAY   109

Richard Wilhelm, translator
FROM *The Secret of the Golden Flower* 109

EASTERN MYSTICISM AND MODERN WESTERN MAN   114

Alan Watts
"Beat Zen, Square Zen, Zen"   114

MYSTICISM AND THE VISIONARY EXPERIENCE 134

FROM *The Old Testament*   134

CONTENTS

x   **MYSTICISM AND THE POETIC EXPERIENCE**   138

William Blake
The Mental Traveller   138
Walt Whitman
A Noiseless Patient Spider   142
Francis Thompson
The Hound of Heaven   143
Thomas Merton
Elegy for the Monastery Barn   148

MYSTICISM IN DRAMA   151

William Butler Yeats
The Shadowy Waters   151

MYSTICISM IN FICTION   167

Herman Hesse
FROM *Siddhartha*   167

COMMENTARY: The World as a Mandala   173

part three   fantasy   177

FANTASY: DEFINITIONS   179

G. K. Chesterton
FROM "The Ethics of Elfland"   179

THE FAIRY TALE   187

Jacob Ludwig Carl Grimm and Wilhelm Carl Grimm
The Frog Prince   187

THE FAIRY TALE IN POETRY   192

James Scully
Facing Up   192

Stevie Smith
The Frog Prince   193

THE FANTASY CLASSIC   197

Lewis Carroll
FROM *Alice's Adventures in Wonderland*   197

THE WEIRD TALE   203

Edgar Allan Poe
The Tell-Tale Heart   203

SCIENCE FICTION   210

Kurt Vonnegut, Jr.
Harrison Bergeron   210

FANTASY AND THE REALIST WRITER   217

F. Scott Fitzgerald
The Diamond as Big as the Ritz   217

COMMENTARY: Fantasy and Reality   258

part four   myth and symbol   263

MYTH AND SYMBOL: DEFINITIONS   265

Joseph Campbell
FROM *The Hero with a Thousand Faces*   265

CONTENTS

xii   MYTH, SCIENCE, AND MODERN MAN   272

      Theodore Roszak
      FROM *The Making of a Counter Culture*   272

    MYTH AND LITERARY THEORY   280

      Northrop Frye
      "The Archetypes of Literature"   280

    MYTH AND ANCIENT DRAMA   297

      Euripides
      The Bacchae   297

    MYTH AND POETRY   343

      John Keats
      Ode to Psyche   343

    MYTH AND MODERN FICTION   346

      James Baldwin
      Going to Meet the Man   346

    COMMENTARY: Myth and the Discovery of Self   364

    SUGGESTIONS FOR FURTHER READING   369

introduction:

the revolution of the spirit

a bishop of the Episcopal Church communicates, through a medium, with his dead son, and he does so on television. A student at a major university is granted permission to do an independent project on "Taoism, the Yin and the Yang, Jung, Alan Watts, Carlos Castaneda and 'all that'." A group of young people who were political activists now join a commune called the "Brotherhood of the Spirit." In Michigan, a teenage girl is tortured and killed by a group called "Satan's Satanic Servants." In London, a young woman convinces her fiancé that her unexpected pregnancy is the result of the attentions of a helmeted, leather-jacketed, motorcycle-riding being from another planet. A university dean speaks seriously of the "spaced-out" state of a student. The renewed interest in magic, mysticism, fantasy, and mythology, not to mention the interest in such things as ESP and drug-induced hallucinations, is part of a current revolution of the spirit.

The young person of ten years ago was happy enough to believe in what many students of today might call the "fantasy of reason." Human problems, whether general or individual, were complex and could be solved best by reason and technology. Religion played a role for many, but even religion fulfilled a need that modern psychology could rationalize. And clergymen tended to cooperate by emphasizing the reasonableness of faiths and the historicity of prophets and gods.

Suddenly however, reason and technology are being questioned. Clergymen (when they maintain contact with the new revolutionaries) are being told that liberal interpretations of the great religious texts, historical proof of the existence of prophets, and the

3

4   deritualization of worship have only increased the gap between what we pretend to be and the nearly smothered spirit within. "Put aside objectivity," cries the new revolutionary. "Turn to magic and strange rites, to mystical experience; turn to Hesse's *Siddhartha,* Indries Shah's *The Sufis,* Castaneda's *Don Juan,* Pauwels' and Bergier's *Morning of the Magicians,* Alan Watts' *The Book,* Tolkien's *Lord of the Rings.*" "Objective consciousness," writes Theodore Roszak, "is alienated life promoted to its most honorific status as the scientific method."[1] The "Jesus freak" asks his "successful" father in suburbia, "What does it profit a man that he should gain the whole world, but lose his soul?"

To be sure, the majority of young people today continue to strive for the goals of their fathers, for the things we have learned to associate with material success, but a growing number will never again accept those goals with the old peace of mind. The revolution of the spirit, the general movement from the known to the unknown, from the objective to the subjective, continues to gather momentum. As they see that technocracy leaves us with a heritage of gadgets and pollution, that new, "exotic" forms of death take the place of the old diseases that have been scientifically eradicated, that material success does not provide a viable alternative to dropping-out and copping-out, the disillusioned young turn increasingly to the world of the spirit—the world of flights. They now recognize what has always been clear to saints and visionaries —that blind faith in reason and the material world leaves us with a dangerous emptiness. C. G. Jung writes:

> Modern man does not understand how much his "rationalism" (which has destroyed his capacity to respond to numinous symbols and ideas) has put him at the mercy of the psychic "underworld." He has freed himself from "superstition" (or so he believes), but in the process he has lost his spiritual values to a positively dangerous degree. His moral and spiritual tradition has disintegrated, and he is now paying the price for this break-up in world-wide disorientation and dissociation."[2]

[1] Theodore Roszak, *The Making of a Counter Culture* (New York: Doubleday & Co., Inc., 1969), p. 232.

[2] Carl Gustav Jung and others, *Man and his Symbols* (New York: Dell Books, 1971), p. 84.

At its best, the revolution of the spirit has spoken to these problems and led to a new consideration of man's inner needs. At its worst, it has spawned pop-fads, escapism, and even justification for the excessive use of drugs and for cult crimes. Therefore, the observer who sees the validity of the revolutionaries' complaints but abhors many of their practices would do well to read the revolutionary texts and to ask such questions as: What and who is real, and what and who is false? Is there a difference between Alan Watts' idea of spiritual freedom and that of the cult murderer? What do magic, mysticism, fantasy, and myth have to do with the "normal" human being of the here and now? In order to begin to answer these questions, we must first consider the revolution against the background of history, and we must consider the relation of its components to the physcial sciences, which are at the very center of what we think of as modern, civilized, realistic life.

Today's revolution of the spirit is, of course, not the first. At various times, the major religions have found it necessary to condemn "mystery" cults and mystical offshoots considered threatening to the survival of the orthodox, established faith. Such groups as the Sufis, Rosicrucians, Gnostics, and Zen Buddhists have been persecuted, physically or intellectually, for their faith in the direct and positive knowledge of spiritual truth and for their serious study of such "occult" practices and texts as astrology, alchemy, the *Kabala*, and the *I Ching*. Occasionally, large-scale spiritual revolutions have developed, as, for example, during the late nineteenth century, which experienced one analagous to our own. Respectable people joined such hermetic and mystical—often secret—societies as The Golden Dawn, the Theosophists, and the Rosicrucians. These societies had been previously considered off limits to serious men and women of intellect. Certain people, such as Macgregor Mathers, and, later, Aleister Crowley—both theoreticians of magic—became cult figures with large followings. In addition, Indian *gurus* became popular, as is also the case today.

It should be noted here that periods of revolutionary scientific discovery often coincide with revolutions of the spirit, and that both kinds of activity frequently arouse repressive reactions. This should not be surprising, as the greatest scientific discoveries are actually voyages into the unknown that always have a profoundly disturbing effect upon the rationalized *status quo*. Thus, in the late nineteenth century, when the scientific academies were particularly

6   repressive, claiming that science had essentially discovered all there was to discover, when a respected chemist could write, "From now on there is no mystery about the Universe," certain extraordinary findings that we now take for granted were dismissed on much the same grounds as was the work of the mystics and magicians.[3] Professor Samuel Pierpont Langley was dismissed from the Smithsonian Institution for suggesting the possibility of flying machines propelled by the newly invented internal combustion engine. James Maxwell was considered mad because of his work on the channeling of electricity, as was Ferdinand von Zeppelin for his work on dirigibles. Louis Pauwels suggests that Henri Poincaré would have discovered the theory of relativity were it not for the repressive air of a scientific establishment bent on denying the existence of any mystery whatsoever.[4] The fact that scientific repression during our present revolution does not appear to exist on anything like the scale that it did in the nineteenth century, is a measure of the power of the current revolution and an indication of an essential aspect of its nature. It is a revolution of immense potential because one of its as yet generally unrecognized supporters—one is tempted to say its major or most meaningful supporter—is modern science itself.

The spaceship can serve as an emblem of the scientific aspect of the revolution of the spirit—an aspect that, in its ultimate ramifications, is tied rather closely to such older aspects as magic and traditional mysticism. It may be argued that today the truly modern mystic and mythologist—the real explorer of the unknown—is the scientist. He expresses and explores the mysteries—the mystical and fantastical unknown—by way of the actual myth of our times—the scientific myth. Louis Pauwels writes:

> The modern disciples of Einstein recognize nothing but the eternal present, which was also what the ancient mystics believed. If the future exists already, then precognition is a fact. The whole trend of advanced knowledge is to place the laws of physics, and biology and psychology as well, in a four-dimensional continuum—that is to say, in the eternal

---

[3] Louis Pauwels and Jacques Bergier, *The Morning of the Magicians* (New York: Avon Books, 1972), p. 34.

[4] *Ibid.*, p. 39.

present. Past, present and future *are*. Perhaps it is only our consciousness that moves. For the first time, consciousness is admitted in its own right into the equations of theoretical physics. In this eternal present, matter appears as a slender thread stretched between past and future. Along this thread glides human consciousness. By what means is it able to modify the tensions of this thread so as to have an influence on events? One day we shall know, and psychology will then become a branch of physics.[5]

Pauwels speaks of the "poetry of science," the language of "fantastic realism," in which such terms as "strangeness quantum number" or "absolute elsewhere" are now heard. A chair, once thought to be a piece of dead, solid matter is seen, by our new scientific mystic, as "suspended energy," as a magic object moving in space in regular patterns within patterns, each of which and all of which express a total pattern that is expressed, in turn, by the universe and by existence itself. In a quantum theory textbook we read:

> . . . the world can not be analyzed correctly into distinct parts; instead, it must be regarded as an individual unit in which separate parts appear as valid approximations only in the classical limit. . . . Thus, at the quantum level of accuracy, an object does not have any "intrinsic" properties (for instance, wave or particle) belonging to itself alone; instead, it shares all its properties mutually and indivisibly with the systems with which it interacts.[6]

Erwin Schrödinger, a biophysicist, writes:

> . . . inconceivable as it seems to ordinary reason, you—and all other conscious beings as such—are all in all. Hence this life of yours which you are living is not merely a piece of the entire existence, but is in a certain sense the whole; only this whole is not so constituted that it can be surveyed in one single glance.[7]

[5] *Ibid.*, p. 46.
[6] David Bohm, *Quantum Theory* (New Jersey: Prentice-Hall, Inc., 1958), p. 161.
[7] Erwin Schrödinger, *My View of the World* (New York: Cambridge University Press, 1964), p. 22.

8

These are the terms of magic, mysticism, fantasy, and myth. Modern philosophers such as Teilhard de Chardin and Alan Watts tell us that reality, at the cosmic level, is what we would normally call fantasy, and that human phenomena, to be seen realistically, must be measured against the cosmic scale. For Alan Watts:

> The individual may be understood neither as an isolated person nor as an expendable, humanoid working-machine. He may be seen, instead, as one particular focal point at which the whole universe expresses itself—as an incarnation of the Self, of the Godhead, or whatever one may choose to call IT.

> . . . your essential Self, is the whole cosmos as it is centered around the particular time, place, and activity called John Doe.

> . . . each organism is the universe expressing itself in endless variety.[8]

Our modern scientists and those modern philosophers and theologians who do not feel threatened by the marriage of science and mystery are, in a sense, telling us that, all along, the true realists have not been the cynics and sceptics but rather the magicians, mystics, dreamers, and myth-makers. They tell us not to look for the unknown in the void, but to look for it, instead, in the "being" that we are—in the great material pattern of which we are a microcosmic expression. "Artists who seek for the fantastic outside reality in the clouds, lack imagination."[9] Magic, mysticism, fantasy, and myth are alive and real in the very chair in which one sits. The point to be stressed here is that modern science has, albeit to a great extent unconsciously, corroborated what the visionaries have always told us.

The whole question of the relationship between science and the unknown has become increasingly important in recent years, as the revolution of the spirit has led people to an increased awareness of the magic and mystery around us. But, the modern rationalist will

[8] Alan Watts, *The Book: On the Taboo Against Knowing Who You Are* (New York: Collier Books, 1968), pp. 63, 73, and 113.
[9] Pauwels and Bergier, *op. cit.*, p. xxvi.

ask what effect this has on us and our everyday lives. To this, the new revolutionary will answer that the unknown is alive in all aspects of our environment, and thus has everything to do with us. It is precisely this faith, for instance, that can and does give the ecological movement a spiritual basis. One need not be a pantheist to feel what D. H. Lawrence called the "spirit of place." In addition, the word *environment,* as used here, does not refer merely to flowers and trees, mountains and rivers; it also includes pots and pans, nuts and bolts. The revolutionary of the spirit tells us we must learn to rediscover the magic—the state of being—in all things. C. G. Jung, one of whose hobbies was cooking, talked to his cooking utensils as he used them. The rational, technologically oriented world considers this sort of behavior—especially in a man of science —quaint, if not neurotic. For Jung, however, it was simply realistic— his way of acknowledging and feeling community with an object whose vitality, as now confirmed by the nuclear physicist, was as real as his own. If we could respect the being in all things, we might think twice before littering our planet with discarded matter. We might also have less difficulty in discovering the magic—the unknown—within ourselves. Those who discard things lightly, say the revolutionaries of the spirit, find it easy enough, finally, to discard people and to ignore the sacred universal Self within.

The essential point the revolutionaries are making, whether they approach the unknown by way of the physical sciences, psychology, or the more traditional forms of religion and the occult, is that we must put aside the veil of rational prejudice in order to experience the flights that can lead us to true reality. It is the image of flight, therefore, that serves as the connecting theme of this book, in which four basic paths to the unknown are explored. By way of magic, the witch and the shaman are able to circumvent the illusory barriers of reason and matter. The witch's flight, although most commonly directed toward a union with the negative forces of the universe, does free him from the physical restrictions of this world. The shaman's essential identity lies in his ability to make flights to the "other world"—to break through death itself to reach the "absolute elsewhere." The mystic has traditionally sought to move beyond the illusory aspects of the physical in order to achieve a higher state of union with the unknown. Fantasy, which involves flights of the imagination, is also an attempt to manifest a level of reality beyond

10   the illusory natural law. Finally, myths are expressions of man's religious and psychic flights, of his eternal quest for the universal principles—for the ultimate reality that activates us all.

The magician, the mystic, the creator of fantasy, and the myth-maker, then, have much in common. Each attempts to escape the illusion of the purely temporal, physical life, which, to each of them is, at least in some sense, false. Each thinks of reality as existing in what most people in the modern world have learned to think of as the unknown and unknowable. Each, therefore, explains and reveals otherwise intangible and ineffable regions of existence. Each moves toward what might be called a vision of God in the person of the universal, unmasked Self. Finally, each has been rediscovered, in our own time, by the revolutionaries of the spirit.

PART ONE

MAGIC: shamans and witches

A ceremonial mask from the island of New Ireland (New Guinea)

shamanism: definitions

TED HUGHES (1930–)

Ted Hughes is a contemporary British poet who believes that some element of shamanism is basic to the poetic experience. In this selection, a review of Mircea Eliade's definitive work, *Shamanism: Archaic Techniques of Ecstasy,* he defines the essential characteristics of the shaman, including his ability to take flight—to achieve a state of ecstasy in which the soul, free of the restrictions of the body, is able to communicate with the unknown.

FROM "SECRET ECSTASIES"

Traces and variations of Shamanism are found all over the world, but it has developed its purest or most characteristic procedures in north-eastern and central Asia. The word 'shaman' comes from the Tungus. Shamanism is not a religion, but a technique for moving in a state of ecstasy among the various spiritual realms, and for generally dealing with souls and spirits, in a practical way, in some practical crisis. It flourishes alongside and within the prevailing religion. For instance, some Tibetan Lamas occasionally shamanize. And whereas religions may differ fundamentally, the inner experiences and techniques and application of shamanism spring into shape

14 everywhere similar, as if the whole activity were something closer to biological inevitability than to any merely cultural tradition—though obviously cultural traditions influence it a good deal too, in detail. The Buddhist influence on Asiatic shamanism is strong.

The vital function shamanizing can take on, even in a colossally formed religion like Buddhism, may be seen in the *Bardo Thodol*, the Tibetan 'Book of the Dead'. In the *Bardo Thodol* the geography and furnishings of the afterworld are Buddhist, but the main business of the work as a whole, which is to guide a dead soul to its place in death, or back into life—together with the principal terrific events, and the flying accompaniment of descriptive songs, exhortations to the soul, threats, and the rest—are all characteristically shaman. This huge, formal work has long ago lost contact with any shaman, but its origins seem clear.

The shaman is 'chosen' in a number of ways. In some regions, commonly among the North American Indians, the aspirant inflicts on himself extraordinary solitary ordeals of fasting and self-mutilation, until a spirit, usually some animal, arrives, and becomes henceforth his liaison with the spirit world. In other regions, the tribe chooses the man—who may or may not, under the initiation ordeals, become a shaman. But the most common form of election comes from the spirits themselves: they approach the man in a dream. At the simplest, these dreams are no more than a vision of an eagle, as among the Buryats, or a beautiful woman (who marries them), as among the Goldi. But at the other extreme, the dreams are long and complicated, and dramatize in full the whole psychological transformation that any shaman, no matter how he has been initially chosen, must undergo. The central episode in this full-scale dream, just like the central episode in the rites where the transformation is effected forcibly by the tribe, is a magical death, then dismemberment, by a demon or equivalent powers, with all possible variants of boiling, devouring, burning, stripping to the bones. From this nadir, the shaman is resurrected with new insides, a new body created for him by the spirits. When he recovers from this—the dream may hold him in a dead trance for several days—he begins to study under some shaman, learning the great corpus of mythological, medical, and technical lore of the particular cultural line of shamanism he is in: this stage takes several years.

Some shamans shamanize to amuse themselves, but usually the

performance is public and to some public purpose. The prepara- 15
tions are elaborate, the shamanizing prolonged and spectacular, as
the shaman dances, drums, leaps—in regalia hung with mirrors and
iron emblems often weighing more than fifty pounds—and sings
himself into ecstasy, entering the spirit realm. In this condition he
can handle fire, be stabbed and not bleed, and do incredible feats
of strength and agility. His business is usually to guide some soul to
the underworld, or bring back a sick man's lost soul, or deliver
sacrifices to the dead, or ask the spirits the reason for an epidemic,
or the whereabouts of game or a man lost. The structure of these
spirit realms is universally fairly consistent, and familiar figures re-
cur as consistently: the freezing river, the clashing rocks, the dog
in the cave-entrance, the queen of animals, the holy mountain, and
so on. The results, when the shaman returns to the living, are some
display of healing power, or a clairvoyant piece of information. The
cathartic effect on the audience, and the refreshing of their religious feeling, must be profound. These shamanizings are also
entertainments, full of buffoonery, mimicry, dialogue, and magical
contortions. The effect on the shaman himself is something to wonder about. One main circumstance in becoming a shaman, in the
first place, is that once you've been chosen by the spirits, and
dreamed the dreams, there is no other life for you, you must shamanize or die: this belief seems almost universal.

The initiation dreams, the general schema of the shamanic flight,
and the figures and adventures they encounter, are not a shaman
monopoly: they are, in fact, the basic experience of the poetic
temperament we call 'romantic'. In a shamanizing society, 'Venus
and Adonis', some of Keats's longer poems, 'The Wanderings of
Oisin', 'Ash Wednesday', would all qualify their authors for the
magic drum; while the actual flight lies perceptibly behind many
of the best fairy tales, and behind myths such as those of Orpheus
and Herakles, and behind the epics of Gilgamesh and Odysseus. It
is the outline, in fact, of the Heroic Quest. The shamans seem to
undergo, at will and at phenomenal intensity, and with practical
results, one of the main regenerating dramas of the human psyche:
the fundamental poetic event.

the shaman
and
his apprentice

CARLOS CASTANEDA (1925–   )

Carlos Castaneda, an anthropologist from California, and
Don Juan, a Yaqui Indian medicine man from Sonora,
Mexico, have become major figures in the revolution of the
spirit. In the course of several years, which are recorded in
three books by Castaneda, Don Juan taught the anthropologist the uses of peyote and other hallucinogenic plants,
and, more important, he directed him on shamanistic flights
toward a "nonordinary reality."

FROM the teachings of don juan: a yaqui way of knowledge

My last encounter with Mescalito was a cluster of four sessions
which took place within four consecutive days. Don Juan called
this long session a *mitote*. It was a peyote ceremony for *peyoteros*
and apprentices. There were two older men, about don Juan's age,
one of whom was the leader, and five younger men including
myself.

16

The ceremony took place in the state of Chihuahua, Mexico, near the Texas border. It consisted of singing and of ingesting peyote during the night. In the daytime women attendants, who stayed outside the confines of the ceremony site, supplied each man with water, and only a token of ritual food was consumed each day.

Saturday, September 12, 1964

During the first night of the ceremony, Thursday, September 3, I took eight peyote buttons. They had no effect on me, or if they did, it was a very slight one. I kept my eyes closed most of the night. I felt much better that way. I did not fall asleep, nor was I tired. At the very end of the session the singing became extraordinary. For a brief moment I felt uplifted and wanted to weep, but as the song ended the feeling vanished.

We all got up and went outside. The women gave us water. Some of the men gargled it; others drank it. The men did not talk at all, but the women chatted and giggled all day long. The ritual food was served at midday. It was cooked corn.

At sundown on Friday, September 4, the second session began. The leader sang his peyote song, and the cycle of songs and intake of peyote buttons began once again. It ended in the morning with each man singing his own song, in unison with the others.

When I went out I did not see as many women as had been there the day before. Someone gave me water, but I was no longer concerned with my surroundings. I had ingested eight buttons again, but the effect had been different.

It must have been toward the end of the session that the singing was greatly accelerated, with everybody singing at once. I perceived that something or somebody outside the house wanted to come in. I couldn't tell whether the singing was done to prevent "it" from bursting in, or to lure it inside.

I was the only who did not have a song. They all seemed to look at me questioningly, especially the young men. I grew embarrassed and closed my eyes.

Then I realized I could perceive what was going on much better if I kept my eyes closed. This idea held my undivided attention.

I closed my eyes, and saw the men in front of me. I opened my eyes, and the image was unchanged. The surroundings were exactly the same for me, whether my eyes were open or closed.

Suddenly everything vanished, or crumbled, and there emerged in its place the manlike figure of Mescalito I had seen two years before. He was sitting some distance away with his profile toward me. I stared fixedly at him, but he did not look at me; not once did he turn.

I believed I was doing something wrong, something that kept him away. I got up and walked toward him to ask him about it. But the act of moving dispelled the image. It began to fade, and the figures of the men I was with were superimposed upon it. Again I heard the loud, frantic singing.

I went into the nearby bushes and walked for a while. Everything stood out very clearly. I noticed I was seeing in the darkness, but it mattered very little this time. The important point was, why did Mescalito avoid me?

I returned to join the group, and as I was about to enter the house I heard a heavy rumbling and felt a tremor. The ground shook. It was the same noise I had heard in the peyote valley two years before.

I ran into the bushes again. I knew that Mescalito was there, and that I was going to find him. But he was not there. I waited until morning, and joined the others just before the session ended.

The usual procedure was repeated on the third day. I was not tired, but I slept during the afternoon.

In the evening of Saturday, September 5, the old man sang his peyote song to start the cycle once more. During this session I chewed only one button and did not listen to any of the songs, nor did I pay attention to anything that went on. From the first moment my whole being was uniquely concentrated on one point. I knew something terribly important for my well-being was missing.

While the men sang I asked Mescalito, in a loud voice, to teach me a song. My pleading mingled with the men's loud singing. Immediately I heard a song in my ears. I turned around and sat with my back to the group and listened. I heard the words and the tune over and over, and I repeated them until I had learned the whole song. It was a long song in Spanish. Then I sang it to the group several times. And soon afterward a new song came to my ears. By morning I had sung both songs countless times. I felt I had been renewed, fortified.

After the water was given to us, don Juan gave me a bag, and we all went into the hills. It was a long, strenuous walk to a low mesa. There I saw several peyote plants. But for some reason I did not want to look at them. After we had crossed the mesa, the group broke up. Don Juan and I walked back, collecting peyote buttons just as we had done the first time I helped him.

We returned in the late afternoon of Sunday, September 6. In the evening the leader opened the cycle again. Nobody had said a word but I knew perfectly well it was the last gathering. This time the old man sang a new song. A sack with fresh peyote buttons was passed around. This was the first time I had tasted a fresh button. It was pulpy but hard to chew. It resembled a hard, green fruit, and was sharper and more bitter than the dried buttons. Personally, I found the fresh peyote infinitely more alive.

I chewed fourteen buttons. I counted them carefully. I did not finish the last one, for I heard the familiar rumble that marked the presence of Mescalito. Everybody sang frantically, and I knew that don Juan, and everybody else, had actually heard the noise. I refused to think that their reaction was a response to a cue given by one of them merely to deceive me.

At that moment I felt a great surge of wisdom engulfing me. A conjecture I had played with for three years turned then into a certainty. It had taken me three years to realize, or rather to find out, that whatever is contained in the cactus *Lophophora williamsii* had nothing to do with me in order to exist as an entity; it existed by itself out there, at large. I knew it then.

I sang feverishly until I could no longer voice the words. I felt as if my songs were inside my body, shaking me uncontrollably. I needed to go out and find Mescalito, or I would explode. I walked toward the peyote field. I kept on singing my songs. I knew they were individually mine—the unquestionable proof of my singleness. I sensed each one of my steps. They resounded on the ground; their echo produced the indescribable euphoria of being a man.

Each one of the peyote plants on the field shone with a bluish, scintillating light. One plant had a very bright light. I sat in front of it and sang my songs to it. As I sang Mescalito came out of the plant—the same manlike figure I had seen before. He looked at me.

With great audacity, for a person of my temperament, I sang to him. There was a sound of flutes, or of wind, a familiar musical vibration. He seemed to have said, as he had two years before, "What do you want?"

I spoke very loudly. I said that I knew there was something amiss in my life and in my actions, but I could not find out what it was. I begged him to tell me what was wrong with me, and also to tell me his name so that I could call him when I needed him. He looked at me, elongated his mouth like a trumpet until it reached my ear, and then told me his name.

Suddenly I saw my own father standing in the middle of the peyote field; but the field had vanished and the scene was my old home, the home of my childhood. My father and I were standing by a fig tree. I embraced my father and hurriedly began to tell him things I had never before been able to say. Every one of my thoughts was concise and to the point. It was as if we had no time, really, and I had to say everything at once. I said staggering things about my feelings toward him, things I would never have been able to voice under ordinary circumstances.

My father did not speak. He just listened and then was pulled, or sucked, away. I was alone again. I wept with remorse and sadness.

I walked through the peyote field calling the name Mescalito had taught me. Something emerged from a strange, starlike light on a peyote plant. It was a long shiny object—a stick of light the size of a man. For a moment it illuminated the whole field with an intense yellowish or amber light; then it lit up the whole sky above, creating a portentous, marvelous sight. I thought I would go blind if I kept on looking; I covered my eyes and buried my head in my arms.

I had a clear notion that Mescalito told me to eat one more peyote button. I thought, "I can't do that because I have no knife to cut it."

"Eat one from the ground," he said to me in the same strange way.

I lay on my stomach and chewed the top of a plant. It kindled me. It filled every corner of my body with warmth and directness. Everything was alive. Everything had exquisite and intricate detail, and yet everything was so simple. I was everywhere; I could see up and down and around, all at the same time.

This particular feeling lasted long enough for me to become aware of it. Then it changed into an oppressive terror, terror that did not come upon me abruptly, but somehow swiftly. At first my marvelous world of silence was jolted by sharp noises, but I was not concerned. Then the noises became louder and were uninterrupted, as if they were closing in on me. And gradually I lost the feeling of floating in a world undifferentiated, indifferent, and beautiful. The noises became gigantic steps. Something enormous was breathing and moving around me. I believed it was hunting for me.

I ran and hid under a boulder, and tried to determine from there what was following me. At one moment I crept out of my hiding place to look, and whoever was my pursuer came upon me. It was like sea kelp. It threw itself on me. I thought its weight was going to crush me, but I found myself inside a pipe or a cavity. I clearly saw that the kelp had not covered all the ground surface around me. There remained a bit of free ground underneath the boulder. I began to crawl underneath it. I saw huge drops of liquid falling from the kelp. I "knew" it was secreting digestive acid in order to dissolve me. A drop fell on my arm; I tried to rub off the acid with dirt, and applied saliva to it as I kept on digging. At one point I was almost vaporous. I was being pushed up toward a light. I thought the kelp had dissolved me. I vaguely detected a light which grew brighter; it was pushing from under the ground until finally it erupted into what I recognized as the sun coming out from behind the mountains.

Slowly I began to regain my usual sensorial processes. I lay on my stomach with my chin on my folded arm. The peyote plant in front of me began to light up again, and before I could move my eyes the long light emerged again. It hovered over me. I sat up. The light touched my whole body with quiet strength, and then rolled away out of sight.

I ran all the way to the place where the other men were. We all returned to town. Don Juan and I stayed one more day with don Roberto, the peyote leader. I slept all the time we were there. When we were about to leave, the young men who had taken part in the peyote sessions came up to me. They embraced me one by

22   one, and laughed shyly. Each one of them introduced himself. I talked with them for hours about everything except the peyote meetings.

Don Juan said it was time to leave. The young men embraced me again. "Come back," one of them said. "We are already waiting for you," another one added. I drove away slowly trying to see the older men, but none of them was there.

Thursday, September 10, 1964

To tell don Juan about an experience always forced me to recall it step by step, to the best of my ability. This seemed to be the only way to remember everything.

Today I told him the details of my last encounter with Mescalito. He listened to my story attentively up to the point when Mescalito told me his name. Don Juan interrupted me there.

"You are on your own now," he said. "The protector has accepted you. I will be of very little help to you from now on. You don't have to tell me anything more about your relationship with him. You know his name now; and neither his name, nor his dealings with you, should ever be mentioned to a living being."

I insisted that I wanted to tell him all the details of the experience, because it made no sense to me. I told him I needed his assistance to interpret what I had seen. He said I could do that by myself, that it was better for me to start thinking on my own. I argued that I was interested in hearing his opinions because it would take me too long to arrive at my own, and I did not know how to proceed.

I said, "Take the songs for instance. What do they mean?"

"Only you can decide that," he said. "How could I know what they mean? The protector alone can tell you that, just as he alone can teach you his songs. If I were to tell you what they mean, it would be the same as if you learned someone else's songs."

"What do you mean by that, don Juan?"

"You can tell who are the phonies by listening to people singing the protector's songs. Only the songs with soul are his and were taught by him. The others are copies of other men's songs. People are sometimes as deceitful as that. They sing someone else's songs without even knowing what the songs say."

I said that I had meant to ask for what purpose the songs were used. He answered that the songs I had learned were for calling the protector, and that I should always use them in conjunction with his name to call him. Later Mescalito would probably teach me other songs for other purposes, don Juan said.

I asked him then if he thought the protector had accepted me fully. He laughed as if my question were foolish. He said the protector had accepted me and had made sure I knew that he had accepted me by showing himself to me as a light, twice. Don Juan seemed to be very impressed by the fact that I had seen the light twice. He emphasized that aspect of my encounter with Mescalito.

I told him I could not understand how it was possible to be accepted by the protector, yet terrified by him at the same time.

He did not answer for a very long time. He seemed bewildered. Finally he said, "It is so clear. What he wanted is so clear that I don't see how you can misunderstand."

"Everything is still incomprehensible to me, don Juan."

"It takes time really to see and understand what Mescalito means; you should think about his lessons until they become clear."

Friday, September 11, 1964

Again I insisted upon having don Juan interpret my visionary experiences. He stalled for a while. Then he spoke as if we had already been carrying on a conversation about Mescalito.

"Do you see how stupid it is to ask if he is like a person you can talk to?" don Juan said. "He is like nothing you have ever seen. He is like a man, but at the same time he is not at all like one. It is difficult to explain that to people who know nothing about him and want to know everything about him all at once. And then, his lessons are as mysterious as he is himself. No man, to my knowledge, can predict his acts. You ask him a question and he shows you the way, but he does not tell you about it in the same manner you and I talk to each other. Do you understand now what he does?"

"I don't think I have trouble understanding that. What I can't figure out is his meaning."

"You asked him to tell you what's wrong with you, and he gave you the full picture. There can be no mistake! You can't claim you did not understand. It was not conversation—and yet it was. Then you asked him another question, and he answered you in exactly the same manner. As to what he meant, I am not sure I understand it, because you chose not to tell me what your question was."

I repeated very carefully the questions I remembered having asked; I put them in the order in which I had voiced them: "Am I doing the right thing? Am I on the right path? What should I do with my life?" Don Juan said the questions I had asked were only words; it was better not to voice the questions, but to ask them from within. He told me the protector meant to give me a lesson; and to prove that he meant to give me a lesson and not to scare me away, he showed himself as a light twice.

I said I still could not understand why Mescalito terrorized me if he had accepted me. I reminded don Juan that, according to his statements, to be accepted by Mescalito implied that his form was constant and did not shift from bliss to nightmare. Don Juan laughed at me again and said that if I would think about the question I had had in my heart when I talked to Mescalito, then I myself would understand the lesson.

To think about the question I had had in my "heart" was a difficult problem. I told don Juan I had had many things in my mind. When I asked if I was on the right path, I meant: Do I have one foot in each of two worlds? Which world is the right one? What course should my life take?

Don Juan listened to my explanations and concluded that I did not have a clear view of the world, and that the protector had given me a beautifully clear lesson.

He said, "You think there are two worlds for you—two paths. But there is only one. The protector showed you this with unbelievable clarity. The only world available to you is the world of men, and that world you cannot choose to leave. You are a man! The protector showed you the world of happiness where there is no difference between things because there is no one there to ask about the difference. But that is not the world of men. The protector shook you out of it and showed you how a man thinks and fights. *That*

is the world of man! And to be a man is to be condemned to that 25
world. You have the vanity to believe you live in two worlds, but
that is only your vanity. There is but one single world for us. We
are men, and must follow the world of men contentedly.

"I believe that was the lesson."

the shamanistic flight of an american indian

JOHN G. NEIHARDT (1881–   )

Black Elk was a Sioux Indian holy man who, through John G. Neihardt and *Black Elk Speaks,* was able to "save his Great Vision for men." Black Elk's vision was that of the shaman—a messianic vision based on his ability to fly to and know the "Other World." Like the *peyoteros* of Don Juan, Black Elk experienced his vision in a trancelike song. This song is an indication of the close relationship that exists between shamanism and poetry.

FROM Black elk speaks

So I dressed myself in a sacred manner, and before the dance began next morning I went among the people who were standing around the withered tree. Good Thunder, who was a relative of my father and later married my mother, put his arms around me and took me to the sacred tree that had not bloomed, and there he offered up a prayer for me. He said: "Father, Great Spirit, behold this boy! Your ways he shall see!" Then he began to cry.

I thought of my father and my brother and sister who had left us, and I could not keep the tears from running out of my eyes. I raised my face up to keep them back, but they came out just the same. I cried with my whole heart, and while I cried I thought of my people in despair. I thought of my vision, and how it was promised me that my people should have a place in this earth where they could be happy every day. I thought of them on the wrong road now, but maybe they could be brought back into the hoop again and to the good road.

Under the tree that never bloomed I stood and cried because it had withered away. With tears on my face I asked the Great Spirit to give it life and leaves and singing birds, as in my vision.

Then there came a strong shivering all over my body, and I knew that the power was in me.

Good Thunder now took one of my arms, Kicking Bear the other, and we began to dance. The song we sang was like this:

> "Who do you think he is that comes?
> It is one who seeks his mother!"

It was what the dead would sing when entering the other world and looking for their relatives who had gone there before them.

As I danced, with Good Thunder and Kicking Bear holding my arms between them, I had the queer feeling that I knew and I seemed to be lifted clear off the ground. I did not have a vision all that first day. That night I thought about the other world and that the Wanekia himself was with my people there and maybe the holy tree of my vision was really blooming yonder right then, and that it was there my vision had already come true. From the center of the earth I had been shown all good and beautiful things in a great circle of peace, and maybe this land of my vision was where all my people were going, and there they would live and prosper where no Wasichus were or could ever be.

Before we started dancing next day, Kicking Bear offered a prayer, saying: "Father, Great Spirit, behold these people! They shall go forth to-day to see their relatives, and yonder they shall be happy, day after day, and their happiness will not end."

Then we began dancing, and most of the people wailed and cried as they danced, holding hands in a circle; but some of them laughed with happiness. Now and then some one would fall down like dead, and others would go staggering around and panting before they would fall. While they were lying there like dead they were having

28   visions, and we kept on dancing and singing, and many were crying for the old way of living and that the old religion might be with them again.

After awhile I began to feel very queer. First, my legs seemed to be full of ants. I was dancing with my eyes closed, as the others did. Suddenly it seemed that I was swinging off the ground and not touching it any longer. The queer feeling came up from my legs and was in my heart now. It seemed I would glide forward like a swing, and then glide back again in longer and longer swoops. There was no fear with this, just a growing happiness.

I must have fallen down, but I felt as though I had fallen off a swing when it was going forward, and I was floating head first through the air. My arms were stretched out, and all I saw at first was a single eagle feather right in front of me. Then the feather was a spotted eagle dancing on ahead of me with his wings fluttering, and he was making the shrill whistle that is his. My body did not move at all, but I looked ahead and floated fast toward where I looked.

There was a ridge right in front of me, and I thought I was going to run into it, but I went right over it. On the other side of the ridge I could see a beautiful land where many, many people were camping in a great circle. I could see that they were happy and had plenty. Everywhere there were drying racks full of meat. The air was clear and beautiful with a living light that was everywhere. All around the circle, feeding on the green, green grass, were fat and happy horses; and animals of all kinds were scattered all over the green hills, and singing hunters were returning with their meat.

I floated over the tepees and began to come down feet first at the center of the hoop where I could see a beautiful tree all green and full of flowers. When I touched the ground, two men were coming toward me, and they wore holy shirts made and painted in a certain way. They came to me and said: "It is not yet time to see your father, who is happy. You have work to do. We will give you something that you shall carry back to your people, and with it they shall come to see their loved ones."

I knew it was the way their holy shirts were made that they wanted me to take back. They told me to return at once, and then I was out in the air again, floating fast as before. When I came right over the dancing place, the people were still dancing, but it seemed they were not making any sound. I had hoped to see the withered tree in bloom, but it was dead.

Then I fell back into my body, and as I did this I heard voices all around and above me, and I was sitting on the ground. Many were crowding around, asking me what vision I had seen. I told them just what I had seen, and what I brought back was the memory of the holy shirts the two men wore.

That evening some of us got together at Big Road's tepee and decided to use the ghost shirts I had seen. So the next day I made ghost shirts all day long and painted them in the sacred manner of my vision. As I made these shirts, I thought how in my vision everything was like old times and the tree was flowering, but when I came back the tree was dead. And I thought that if this world would do as the vision teaches, the tree could bloom here too.

I made the first shirt for Afraid-of-Hawk and the second for the son of Big Road.

In the evening I made a sacred stick like that I had seen in my first vision and painted it red with the sacred paint of the Wanekia. On the top of it I tied one eagle feather, and this I carried in the dance after that, wearing the holy shirt as I had seen it.

Because of my vision and the power they knew I had, I was asked to lead the dance next morning. We all stood in a straight line, facing the west, and I prayed: "Father, Great Spirit, behold me! The nation that I have is in despair. The new earth you promised you have shown me. Let my nation also behold it."

After the prayer we stood with our right hands raised to the west, and we all began to weep, and right there, as they wept, some of them fainted before the dance began.

As we were dancing I had the same queer feeling I had before, as though my feet were off the earth and swinging. Kicking Bear and Good Thunder were holding my arms. Afterwhile it seemed they let go of me, and once more I floated head first, face down, with arms extended, and the spotted eagle was dancing there ahead of me again, and I could hear his shrill whistle and his scream.

I saw the ridge again, and as I neared it there was a deep, rumbling sound, and out of it there leaped a flame. But I glided right over it. There were six villages ahead of me in the beautiful land that was all clear and green in living light. Over these in turn

30   I glided, coming down on the south side of the sixth village. And as I touched the ground, twelve men were coming towards me, and they said: "Our Father, the two-legged chief, you shall see!"

Then they led me to the center of the circle where once more I saw the holy tree all full of leaves and blooming.

But that was not all I saw. Against the tree there was a man standing with arms held wide in front of him. I looked hard at him, and I could not tell what people he came from. He was not a Wasichu and he was not an Indian. His hair was long and hanging loose, and on the left side of his head he wore an eagle feather. His body was strong and good to see, and it was painted red. I tried to recognize him, but I could not make him out. He was a very fine-looking man. While I was staring hard at him, his body began to change and became very beautiful with all colors of light, and around him there was light. He spoke like singing: "My life is such that all earthly beings and growing things belong to me. Your father, the Great Spirit, has said this. You too must say this."

Then he went out like a light in a wind.

The twelve men who were there spoke: "Behold them! Your nation's life shall be such!"

I saw again how beautiful the day was—the sky all blue and full of yellow light above the greening earth. And I saw that all the people were beautiful and young. There were no old ones there, nor children either—just people of about one age, and beautiful.

Then there were twelve women who stood in front of me and spoke: "Behold them! Their way of life you shall take back to earth." When they had spoken, I heard singing in the west, and I learned the song I heard.

Then one of the twelve men took two sticks, one painted white and one red, and, thrusting them in the ground, he said: "Take these! You shall depend upon them. Make haste!"

I started to walk, and it seemed as though a strong wind went under me and picked me up. I was in the air, with outstretched arms, and floating fast. There was a fearful dark river that I had to go over, and I was afraid. It rushed and roared and was full of angry foam. Then I looked down and saw many men and women who were trying to cross the dark and fearful river, but they could not. Weeping, they looked up to me and cried: "Help us!" But I could not stop gliding, for it was as though a great wind were under me.

Then I saw my earthly people again at the dancing place, and fell back into my body lying there. And I was sitting up, and people were crowding around me to ask what vision I had seen.

I told my vision through songs, and the older men explained them to the others. I sang a song, the words of which were those the Wanekia spoke under the flowering tree, and the air of it was that which I heard in the West after the twelve women had spoken. I sang it four times, and the fourth time all the people began to weep together because the Wasichus had taken the beautiful world away from us.

I thought and thought about this vision. The six villages seemed to represent the Six Grandfathers that I had seen long ago in the Flaming Rainbow Tepee, and I had gone to the sixth village, which was for the Sixth Grandfather, the Spirit of the Earth, because I was to stand for him in the world. I wondered if the Wanekia might be the red man of my great vision, who turned into a bison, and then into the four-rayed herb, the daybreak-star herb of understanding. I thought the twelve men and twelve women were for the moons of the year.

the shamanistic flight in folklore

STITH THOMPSON (1885–   )

In this tale of the Tlingit Indians, the shamanistic flight to the other world is expressed metaphorically. An important function of the shaman was to retrieve loved ones from the dead. It is precisely this function that is represented here by the Indian boy's rescuing of his playmate.

FROM tales of the north american indians

The Arrow Chain

Two very high-caste boys were chums. The father of one was town chief and had his house in the middle of the village, but the house of the other boy's father stood at one end. These boys would go alternately to each other's houses and make great quantities of arrows which they would play with until all were broken up.

One time both of the boys made a great quantity of arrows to see which could have the more. Just back of their village was a hill on the top of which was a smooth grassy place claimed by the boys as their playground, and on a certain fine, moonlight night they started thither. As they were going along the lesser chief's son, who was ahead, said, "Look here, friend. Look at that moon. Don't you think that the shape of that moon is the same as that of my mother's labret and that the size is the same, too?" The other answered, "Don't: You must not talk that way of the moon."

Then suddenly it became very dark about them and presently the head chief's son saw a ring about them just like a rainbow. When it disappeared his companion was gone. He called and called to him but did not get any answer and did not see him. He thought, "He must have run up the hill to get away from that rainbow." He looked up and saw the moon in the sky. Then he climbed the hill, and looked about, but his friend was not there. Now he thought, "Well! the moon must have gone up with him. That circular rainbow must have been the moon."

The boy thus left alone sat down and cried, after which he began to try the bows. He put strings on them one after the other and tried them, but every one broke. He broke all of his own bows and all of his chum's except one which was made of very hard wood. He thought, "Now I am going to shoot that star next to the moon." In that spot was a large and very bright one. He shot an arrow at this star and sat down to watch, when, sure enough, the star darkened. Now he began shooting at that star from the big piles of arrows he and his chum had made, and he was encouraged by seeing that the arrows did not come back. After he had shot for some time he saw something hanging down very near him and, when he shot up another arrow, it stuck to this. The next did likewise, and at last the chain of arrows reached him. He put a last one on to complete it.

Now the youth felt badly for the loss of his friend and, lying down under the arrow chain, he went to sleep. After a while he awoke, found himself sleeping on that hill, remembered the arrows he had shot away, and looked up. Instead of the arrows there was a long ladder reaching right down to him. He arose and looked so as to make sure. Then he determined to ascend. First, however, he took various kinds of bushes and stuck them into the knot of hair he wore on his head. He climbed up his ladder all day and camped at nightfall upon it, resuming his journey the following morning. When he awoke early on the second morning his head felt very

34 heavy. Then he seized the salmon berry bush that was in his hair, pulled it out, and found it was loaded with berries. After he had eaten the berries off, he stuck the branch back into his hair and felt very much strengthened. About noon of the same day he again felt hungry, and again his head was heavy, so he pulled out a bush from the other side of his head and it was loaded with blue huckle-berries. It was already summer there in the sky. That was why he was getting berries. When he resumed his journey next morning his head did not feel heavy until noon. At that time he pulled out the bush at the back of his head and found it loaded with red huckle-berries.

By the time he had reached the top the boy was very tired. He looked round and saw a large lake. Then he gathered some soft brush and some moss and lay down to sleep. But, while he slept, some person came to him and shook him saying, "Get up. I am after you." He awoke and looked around but saw no one. Then he rolled over and pretended to go to sleep again but looked out through his eyelashes. By and by he saw a very small but hand-some girl coming along. Her skin clothes were very clean and neat, and her leggings were ornamented with porcupine quills. Just as she reached out to shake him he said, "I have seen you already."

Now the girl stood still and said, "I have come after you. My grandmother has sent me to bring you to her house." So he went with her, and they came to a very small house in which was an old woman. The old woman said, "What is it you came way up here after, my grandson?" and the boy answered, "On account of my playmate who was taken up hither." "Oh!" answered the old woman, "He is next door, only a short distance away. I can hear him crying every day. He is in the moon's house."

Then the old woman began to give him food. She would put her hand up to her mouth, and a salmon or whatever she was going to give would make its appearance. After the salmon she gave him berries and then meat, for she knew that he was hungry from his long journey. After that she gave him a spruce cone, a rose bush, a piece of devil's club, and a small piece of whetstone to take along.

As the boy was going toward the moon's house with all of these things he heard his playmate screaming with pain. He had been put up on a high place near the smoke hole, so, when his rescuer came to it, he climbed on top, and, reaching down through the smoke hole, pulled him out. He said, "My friend, come. I am here to help you." Putting the spruce cone down where the boy had been, he told it to imitate his cries, and he and his chum ran away.

After a while, however, the cone dropped from the place where it had been put, and the people discovered that their captive had escaped. Then the moon started in pursuit. When the head chief's son discovered this, he threw behind them the devil's club he had received from the old woman, and a patch of devil's club arose which the moon had so much trouble in getting through that they gained rapidly on him. When the moon again approached, the head chief's son threw back the rose bushes, and such a thicket of roses grew there that the moon was again delayed. When he approached them once more, they threw back the grindstone, and it became a high cliff from which the moon kept rolling back. It is on account of this cliff that people can say things about the moon nowadays with impunity. When the boys reached the old woman's house they were very glad to see each other, for before this they had not had time to speak.

The old woman gave them something to eat, and, when they were through, she said to the rescuer, "Go and lie down at the place where you lay when you first came up. Don't think of anything but the playground you used to have." They went there and lay down, but after some time the boy who had first been captured thought of the old woman's house and immediately they found themselves there. Then the old woman said, "Go back and do not think of me any more. Lie there and think of nothing but the place where you used to play." They did so, and, when they awoke, they were lying on their playground at the foot of the ladder.

As the boys lay in that place they heard a drum beating in the head chief's house, where a death feast was being held for them, and the head chief's son said, "Let us go," but the other answered, "No, let us wait here until that feast is over." Afterward the boys went down and watched the people come out with their faces all blackened. They stood at a corner, but, as this dance is always given in the evening, they were not seen.

Then the head chief's son thought, "I wish my younger brother would come out," and sure enough, after all of the other people had gone, his younger brother came out. He called to his brother saying, "Come here. It is I," but the child was afraid and ran into

36   the house instead. Then the child said to his mother, "My brother and his friend are out here." "Why do you talk like that?" asked his mother. "Don't you know that your brother died some time ago?" And she became very angry. The child, however, persisted, saying, "I know his voice, and I know him." His mother was now very much disturbed, so the boy said, "I am going to go out and bring in a piece of his shirt." "Go and do so," said his mother. "Then I will believe you."

When the boy at last brought in a piece of his brother's shirt his mother was convinced, and they sent word into all of the houses, first of all into that of the second boy's parents, but they kept both with them so that his parents could come there and rejoice over him. All of the other people in that village also came to see them.

The Sorcerer, Paleolithic Cave Painting
(French Pyrenees)

the shamanistic flight of the poet

In ancient times, the poet was often considered a priest-prophet—a kind of medium between men and the unknown. His actual poetry was believed to be the expression of a trancelike state of flight in which, like the shaman, the poet had been granted a vision of the other world. This parallel to the shamanistic flight is still evident in the works of many modern poets. Coleridge's "Kubla Khan" was inspired by an actual opium trance. In "Sailing to Byzantium," Yeats is the artist-seer visualizing the eternal. Hughes' crow is a symbol of the poetic-shamanistic flight itself. Finally, Fowler's contemporary "Shaman Song #12" is a song of a shaman "grounded" by the modern, spiritless world.

SAMUEL TAYLOR COLERIDGE (1772–1874)

kubla khan

In Xanadu did Kubla Khan
    A stately pleasure dome decree:
Where Alph, the sacred river, ran
Through caverns measureless to man
    Down to a sunless sea.
So twice five miles of fertile ground
With walls and towers were girdled round:
And here were gardens bright with sinuous rills,

5

Where blossomed many an incense-bearing tree,   10
And here were forests ancient as the hills,
Enfolding sunny spots of greenery.

But oh! that deep romantic chasm which slanted
Down the green hill athwart a cedarn cover!
A savage place; as holy and enchanted
As e'er beneath a waning moon was haunted   15
By woman wailing for her demon lover!
And from this chasm, with ceaseless turmoil seething,
As if this earth in fast thick pants were breathing,
A mighty fountain momently was forced,
Amid whose swift half-intermitted burst   20
Huge fragments vaulted like rebounding hail,
Or chaffy grain beneath the thresher's flail:
And 'mid these dancing rocks at once and ever
It flung up momently the sacred river.
Five miles meandering with a mazy motion   25
Through wood and dale the sacred river ran,
Then reached the caverns measureless to man,
And sank in tumult to a lifeless ocean:
And 'mid this tumult Kubla heard from far
Ancestral voices prophesying war!   30

    The shadow of the dome of pleasure
    Floated midway on the waves;
    Where was heard the mingled measure
    From the fountain and the caves.
It was a miracle of rare device,   35
A sunny pleasure dome with caves of ice!

    A damsel with a dulcimer
    In a vision once I saw:
    It was an Abyssinian maid,
    And on her dulcimer she played,   40
    Singing of Mount Abora.
    Could I revive within me
    Her symphony and song,
    To such a deep delight 'twould win me,
That with music loud and long,   45

40   I would build that dome in air,
That sunny dome! those caves of ice!
And all who heard should see them there,
And all should cry, Beware! Beware!
His flashing eyes, his floating hair!   **50**
Weave a circle round him thrice,
And close your eyes with holy dread,
For he on honey-dew hath fed,
And drunk the milk of Paradise.

WILLIAM BUTLER YEATS (1865–1939)

SAILING TO BYZANTIUM

I

That is no country for old men. The young
In one another's arms, birds in the trees
—Those dying generations—at their song,
The salmon-falls, the mackerel-crowded seas,
Fish, flesh, or fowl, commend all summer long   5
Whatever is begotten, born, and dies.
Caught in that sensual music all neglect
Monuments of unageing intellect.

II

An aged man is but a paltry thing,
A tattered coat upon a stick, unless   10
Soul clap its hands and sing, and louder sing
For every tatter in its mortal dress,
Nor is there singing school but studying
Monuments of its own magnificence;

And therefore I have sailed the seas and come   15   **41**
To the holy city of Byzantium.

III

O sages standing in God's holy fire
As in the gold mosaic of a wall,
Come from the holy fire, perne in a gyre,
And be the singing-masters of my soul.   20
Consume my heart away; sick with desire
And fastened to a dying animal
It knows not what it is; and gather me
Into the artifice of eternity.

IV

Once out of nature I shall never take   25
My bodily form from any natural thing,
But such a form as Grecian goldsmiths make
Of hammered gold and gold enamelling
To keep a drowsy Emperor awake;
Or set upon a golden bough to sing   30
To lords and ladies of Byzantium
Of what is past, or passing, or to come.

TED HUGHES (1930–   )

CROW'S FALL

When Crow was white he decided the sun was too white.
He decided it glared much too whitely.
He decided to attack it and defeat it.

42   He got his strength flush and in full glitter.
He clawed and fluffed his rage up.   5
He aimed his beak direct at the sun's centre.

He laughed himself to the centre of himself

And attacked.

At his battle cry trees grew suddenly old,
Shadows flattened.   10

But the sun brightened—
It brightened, and Crow returned charred black.

He opened his mouth but what came out was charred black.

"Up there," he managed,
"Where white is black and black is white, I won."   15

GENE FOWLER (1931–   )

shaman song # 12

We have made hawks
that fly
where no hawks have flown.

We have made hard sky
and look out at the rain.   5

We have made warm hides
from no animal yet slain.

We have made horses   **43**
that stride
as no horses ever known.   10

      But, we are weak.
      On our wounded plains, we are alone.

We have forgotten
the shame and cry of our bellies.

We have forgotten   15
the dances of our own faces,
the songs of our own voices.

We have forgotten
the chants of the souls
in our running feet.   20

      Now, we remember.
      In our weeping tents, we are alone.

the shamanistic flight of a modern psychiatrist

CARL GUSTAV JUNG (1875–1961)

It may well be that modern man's dependency on psychiatry reflects a continuing need for shamanism. The Swiss psychiatrist C. G. Jung did feel this need because, like the shaman, he recognized the danger involved in unlocking the gates of the unknown. In this incident from his autobiography, *Memories, Dreams, Reflections,* Jung experiences what appears to be a shamanic vision and flight and also projects such a flight onto his doctor.

FROM MEMORIES, DREAMS, REFLECTIONS

At the beginning of 1944 I broke my foot, and this misadventure was followed by a heart attack. In a state of unconsciousness I experienced deliriums and visions which must have begun when I hung on the edge of death and was being given oxygen and camphor injections. The images were so tremendous that I myself concluded that I was close to death. My nurse afterward told me, "It was as if you were surrounded by a bright glow." That was a phenomenon she had sometimes observed in the dying, she added. I had reached the outermost limit, and do not know whether I was

in a dream or an ecstasy. At any rate, extremely strange things
began to happen to me.

It seemed to me that I was high up in space. Far below I saw
the globe of the earth, bathed in a gloriously blue light. I saw the
deep blue sea and the continents. Far below my feet lay Ceylon,
and in the distance ahead of me the subcontinent of India. My field
of vision did not include the whole earth, but its global shape was
plainly distinguishable and its outlines shone with a silvery gleam
through that wonderful blue light. In many places the globe seemed
colored, or spotted dark green like oxydized silver. Far away to the
left lay a broad expanse—the reddish-yellow desert of Arabia; it
was as though the silver of the earth had there assumed a reddish-
gold hue. Then came the Red Sea, and far, far back—as if in the
upper left of a map—I could just make out a bit of the Mediter-
ranean. My gaze was directed chiefly toward that. Everything else
appeared indistinct. I could also see the snow-covered Himalayas,
but in that direction it was foggy or cloudy. I did not look to the
right at all. I knew that I was on the point of departing from the
earth.

Later I discovered how high in space one would have to be to
have so extensive a view—approximately a thousand miles! The
sight of the earth from this height was the most glorious thing I
had ever seen.

After contemplating it for a while, I turned around. I had been
standing with my back to the Indian Ocean, as it were, and my
face to the north. Then it seemed to me that I made a turn to the
south. Something new entered my field of vision. A short distance
away I saw in space a tremendous dark block of stone, like a
meteorite. It was about the size of my house, or even bigger. It was
floating in space, and I myself was floating in space.

I had seen similar stones on the coast of the Gulf of Bengal. They
were blocks of tawny granite, and some of them had been hollowed
out into temples. My stone was one such gigantic dark block. An
entrance led into a small antechamber. To the right of the entrance,
a black Hindu sat silently in lotus posture upon a stone bench. He
wore a white gown, and I knew that he expected me. Two steps
led up to this antechamber, and inside, on the left, was the gate to
the temple. Innumerable tiny niches, each with a saucer-like con-
cavity filled with coconut oil and small burning wicks, surrounded
the door with a wreath of bright flames. I had once actually seen

46   this when I visited the Temple of the Holy Tooth at Kandy in Ceylon; the gate had been framed by several rows of burning oil lamps of this sort.

As I approached the steps leading up to the entrance into the rock, a strange thing happened: I had the feeling that everything was being sloughed away; everything I aimed at or wished for or thought, the whole phantasmagoria of earthly existence, fell away or was stripped from me—an extremely painful process. Nevertheless something remained; it was as if I now carried along with me everything I had ever experienced or done, everything that had happened around me. I might also say: it was with me, and I was it. I consisted of all that, so to speak. I consisted of my own history, and I felt with great certainty: this is what I am. "I am this bundle of what has been, and what has been accomplished."

This experience gave me a feeling of extreme poverty, but at the same time of great fullness. There was no longer anything I wanted or desired. I existed in an objective form; I was what I had been and lived. At first the sense of annihilation predominated, of having been stripped or pillaged; but suddenly that became of no consequence. Everything seemed to be past; what remained was a *fait accompli,* without any reference back to what had been. There was no longer any regret that something had dropped away or been taken away. On the contrary: I had everything that I was, and that was everything.

Something else engaged my attention: as I approached the temple I had the certainty that I was about to enter an illuminated room and would meet there all those people to whom I belong in reality. There I would at last understand—this too was a certainty—what historical nexus I or my life fitted into. I would know what had been before me, why I had come into being, and where my life was flowing. My life as I lived it had often seemed to me like a story that has no beginning and no end. I had the feeling that I was a historical fragment, an excerpt for which the preceding and succeeding text was missing. My life seemed to have been snipped out of a long chain of events, and many questions had remained unanswered. Why had it taken this course? Why had I brought these particular assumptions with me? What had I made of them? What will follow? I felt sure that I would receive an answer to all these questions as soon as I entered the rock temple. There I would learn why everything had been thus and not otherwise. There I would meet the people who knew the answer to my question about what had been before and what would come after.

While I was thinking over these matters, something happened that caught my attention. From below, from the direction of Europe, an image floated up. It was my doctor, Dr. H.—or, rather, his likeness—framed by a golden chain or a golden laurel wreath. I knew at once: "Aha, this is my doctor, of course, the one who has been treating me. But now he is coming in his primal form, as a *basileus* of Kos.[1] In life he was an avatar of this *basileus*, the temporal embodiment of the primal form, which has existed from the beginning. Now he is appearing in that primal form."

Presumably I too was in my primal form, though this was something I did not observe but simply took for granted. As he stood before me, a mute exchange of thought took place between us. Dr. H. had been delegated by the earth to deliver a message to me, to tell me that there was a protest against my going away. I had no right to leave the earth and must return. The moment I heard this, the vision ceased.

I was profoundly disappointed, for now it all seemed to have been for nothing. The painful process of defoliation had been in vain, and I was not to be allowed to enter the temple, to join the people in whose company I belonged.

In reality, a good three weeks were still to pass before I could truly make up my mind to live again. I could not eat because all food repelled me. The view of city and mountains from my sickbed seemed to me like a painted curtain with black holes in it, or a tattered sheet of newspaper full of photographs that meant nothing. Disappointed, I thought, "Now I must return to the 'box system' again." For it seemed to me as if behind the horizon of the cosmos a three-dimensional world had been artificially built up, in which each person sat by himself in a little box. And now I should have to convince myself all over again that this was important! Life and the whole world struck me as a prison, and it bothered me beyond measure that I should again be finding all that quite in order. I had been so glad to shed it all, and now it had come about that I— along with everyone else—would again be hung up in a box by a thread. While I floated in space, I had been weightless, and there

---

[1] *Basileus* = king. Kos was famous in antiquity as the site of the temple of Asklepios, and was the birthplace of Hippocrates.

48 had been nothing tugging at me. And now all that was to be a thing of the past!

I felt violent resistance to my doctor because he had brought me back to life. At the same time, I was worried about him. "His life is in danger, for heaven's sake! He has appeared to me in his primal form! When anybody attains this form it means he is going to die, for already he belongs to the 'greater company'!" Suddenly the terrifying thought came to me that Dr. H. would have to die in my stead. I tried my best to talk to him about it, but he did not understand me. Then I became angry with him. "Why does he always pretend he doesn't know he is a *basileus* of Kos? And that he has already assumed his primal form? He wants to make me believe that he doesn't know!" That irritated me. My wife reproved me for being so unfriendly to him. She was right; but at the same time I was angry with him for stubbornly refusing to speak of all that had passed between us in my vision. "Damn it all, he ought to watch his step. He has no right to be so reckless! I want to tell him to take care of himself." I was firmly convinced that his life was in jeopardy.

In actual fact I was his last patient. On April 4, 1944—I still remember the exact date—I was allowed to sit up on the edge of my bed for the first time since the beginning of my illness, and on this same day Dr. H. took to his bed and did not leave it again. I heard that he was having intermittent attacks of fever. Soon afterward he died of septicemia. He was a good doctor; there was something of the genius about him. Otherwise he would not have appeared to me as a prince of Kos.

During those weeks I lived in a strange rhythm. By day I was usually depressed. I felt weak and wretched, and scarcely dared to stir. Gloomily, I thought, "Now I must go back to this drab world." Toward evening I would fall asleep, and my sleep would last until about midnight. Then I would come to myself and lie awake for about an hour, but in an utterly transformed state. It was as if I were in an ecstasy. I felt as though I were floating in space, as though I were safe in the womb of the universe—in a tremendous void, but filled with the highest possible feeling of happiness. "This is eternal bliss," I thought. "This cannot be described; it is far too wonderful!"

witchcraft: definitions

ALAN MACFARLANE (1941–   )

Alan Macfarlane is a leading anthropologist and authority on witchcraft. The definitions presented here are based on his studies of African and English witches, but they are of a general enough nature to provide an understanding of the organization of American witches as well. It is important to note that the witch and the shaman are related in that both overcome rational and physical barriers, but that they are also very different, as the shaman works for the good of his society, while, most frequently, the witch uses his power for diabolical purposes.

FROM witchcraft in tudor and stuart england

Organization of witches

Witches are sometimes believed to act alone; sometimes they are part of an organization. 'Night-witches (among the Lovedu) form a sort of fraternity; they all know one another and meet at night

49

50   to drum and dance for amusement.' Witches among the Gusii do
not operate alone but in a group. In other societies witches can
operate alone *or* in company. Thus witches among the Nyakusa attack either singly or in covens. While some witches practise alone,
others share in their necrophagous feasts among the Kaguru and
are organized locally. Finally, there are societies where witches are
lone individuals. Among the Gisu 'Witchcraft is performed by individuals against other individuals, not by a group against an individual nor by an individual against a group.' Witchcraft is similarly
the activity of individuals working alone among the Dinka. If
witches do co-operate there is often some kind of hierarchy amongst
them. The Azande believe that there is 'status and leadership among
witches' and that 'experience must be obtained under the tuition of
elder witches before a man is qualified to kill his neighbours.' Proceedings at night witch meetings, the Navaho say, are directed by
a chief witch who, with his leading helpers, is thought of as rich,
but they are assisted by a class of menial 'helpers' and these are
said to be poor. Essex witchcraft, with the exception of the 1645
cases, appears to be closer to the individual, solitary witch pattern.

How the power of witchcraft is acquired

The three principal ways of acquiring witchcraft are by birth, by
purchase, and by training. Usually at least two of these methods
are combined—thus, among the Mbugwe, witches must both be instructed in the secret art of harming people and given a special con-
stitutional trait by committing incest with a witch relative, and
among the Lovedu witchcraft is said to be imbibed with the
mother's milk, but also involves a strenuous course of learning. The
most usual way of combining the hereditary and teaching principles
is by saying, as do the Gusii, that witchcraft is an acquired art
which is usually handed down from parent to child. Thus witches
among the Mandari teach their children how to dance at night.
Essex witches, it seems, usually acquired their witchcraft later in
life, though there was a strong contemporary belief that witchcraft
was also hereditary, and up to 10 per cent of the accusations may
have been against daughters of known witches.

Witches are often cannibals, feeding either on the living souls and bodies, or necrophagous, as they are among the Mandari. They kill people by eating their souls among the Tallensi. Another method favoured by witches is some unclean act—defecating or urinating into a person's house or food, for instance. A witch may thus secretly defecate or urinate into a victim's water, beer, or food among the Kaguru, a certain type of witch among the Lugbara vomits blood or defecates near doorways, and the same is said of Dinka witches.

Daytime witches favour pointing gestures and staring. Among the Lovedu, to point at a man in a menacing way, or to say the words, 'You will see,' suffices, should evil befall him, as ground for an accusation of witchcraft, and among the Gisu the evil eye is supposed to harm by excessive admiration or staring. Essex witches, we have seen, tended either to use the spoken word—cursing or praising—or sent their familiars to harm their victims.

Types of injury caused by witches

Though, in theory, any kind of misfortune is likely to be ascribed to witchcraft among certain peoples, in fact this explanation is invoked only in certain situations. For instance, general disasters are not usually believed to be caused by witchcraft. Crop failure over a wide area or epidemics are said to result from the anger of the ancestors among the Gisu. Local drought among the Mandari is blamed on witches—universal misfortunes are acts of God, to be met by sacrifice and prayers; widespread misfortunes among the Kaguru are likewise thought to be caused by the anger of ancestors owing to some person's having broken a clan rule, while the misfortunes of *individuals* are thought to be owing to witches. Witchcraft and religious rituals therefore serve different purposes as responses to individual and collective disaster.

Witches usually attack human beings, but they do not attack all classes of humanity, nor do they bring certain kinds of death or illness. Often very young children are excepted from their attack:

thus among the Azande the 'deaths of babies from certain diseases are attributed vaguely to the Supreme Being,' while among the Lele the deaths of women in childbirth and deaths of infants are not considered to be caused by sorcery. This is related to Evans-Pritchard's observation that 'it is the social situation' which indicates the relevant cause of misfortune: to ascribe the very frequent deaths of children in a primitive society to witchcraft would be to overload the concept. Sometimes the determining factor is the type of disease; thus sudden sickness is attributed to sorcery and magic, not to witchcraft, among the Azande, for it is slow, wasting disease that is caused by witchcraft. On the other hand, among the Nupe, accusations were formed around some unexplained *sudden* death or rapid deadly illness—not always mysterious, but always sudden.

Witches wither and stunt crops, dry up milking cows, cause women to be barren and miscarry and in other ways hinder essential fertility among the Mandari. Physical beauty, outstanding gardens or cattle, are the most likely to be attacked among the Dinka, where they also set light to the thatch of byres and huts. Misfortune in hunting is attributed to witchcraft among the Mbugwe, and witches make love potions among the Kaguru as among other peoples. In Essex, we have seen, they principally attacked human beings, but also farm stock and equipment.

Other activities of witches

The witch is the archetype of evil, and horror is piled on horror in the creation of this mysterious mythical figure: 'he embodies those appetites and passions in every man which, if ungoverned, would destroy any moral law.' His behaviour 'is inverted, physically, socially and morally,' and if we are careful we can learn much about the values he is supposed pervertedly to reflect.

Witches travel in curious ways. Firstly, they defy the laws of gravity—a concept necessary to explain how they strike so secretly at a distance. Sometimes they just run very fast, with the help of human flesh, among the Gusii. Usually, however, they fly as among the Cewa, the Tallensi, and Nyakusa. When they walk or stand around they often do this in a peculiar fashion; among the Kaguru they walk around upside-down on their hands, and Amba witches pass leisure moments in their hectic lives standing on their heads or resting hanging upside-down from limbs of trees. Both in their journeys and their meetings they are often naked. Among the Navaho they are naked at their nightly meetings, except for masks and jewellery. Witches among the Amba, and the Gusii, to mention only two cases, travel around naked.

They indulge in various forbidden and revolting activities at their meetings. They eat human flesh—preferably the corpses of victims—among the Gisu, the Cewa, and Nyakusa. This seems to be a very general feature. They are often extremely greedy, stealing milk from their neighbours' cows, as they do among the Nyakusa, or sitting in a circle surrounded by piles or baskets of corpse flesh among the Navaho. Their eating habits are generally eccentric: for instance, they eat salt to quench their thirst among the Amba. Another common feature of the witchmeetings is sexual obscenity. Witches meet at night to have intercourse with dead women among the Navaho; they perform obscene rites at their saturnalia among the Mbugwe. They are often said to commit incest, fornication, and adultery among the Lugbara, while among the Pondo they indulge in sexual relations with hairy familiars.

Essex witches, in comparison with their African counterparts, lived an austere and blameless life, neither flying, dancing, feasting on human flesh, nor indulging in sexual perversions.

The supposed motives of witches

Witches among the Lovedu try to harm people from motives of jealousy, revenge, frustration, or anger. Similarly, a Zande witch attacks a man when motivated by hatred, envy, jealousy, and greed. All witchcraft and sorcery comes from jealousy, anger, and spite, the Gisu say, and jealousy is believed to be the foundation of the witch's character among the Mandari. There seems to be an important distinction between witches, whose acts are prompted by unappeasable motives—lust for food or sex, hatred of all the normal human values—and sorcerers, who act because of a specific grievance which they have really suffered. The idea that the witch's heart can be softened by kindness and an appeal to mercy, or by reparation for an injury received, which is held by the Amba and the Lugbara, seems likely to lead to the conclusion that a man who is bewitched or 'ensorcelled' is partly to blame for it—a concept which the Lugbara do indeed have. The Cewa also sometimes imply that the witches' victim often gets his deserts. The twin concepts could be stated differently. On the one hand, it is usually believed that 'even a witch does not injure or kill someone unknown to him and from whose sickness and death he will not derive some benefit', as the Gisu point out. If one is going to pin witchcraft on to certain individuals they must have had some reason for acting; therefore, when witchcraft is suspected among this tribe both victim and diviner look for some motive of witchcraft: someone injured or insulted, an obligation unfulfilled or some favour refused. This places the responsibility of conflict on both accuser and accused, though this may not be openly recognized. Witches among the Nyakusa select as victims those against whom they have a grudge; 'they act illegally and immorally but not without cause'. There has to be a motive and a will of evil before latent witchcraft takes effect among the Azande. But in other instances the motive may not be connected with the activities of the victim. The Pondo seem to conceive of witches as acting without a particular cause, thus breaking the link between misfortune and morality. The activities of Amba witches are ultimately inexplicable to their countrymen, for they are motivated by an abnormal desire for human flesh. As we have seen with the Pondo, this leads to a state of hopelessness, since one cannot take logical action against illogical activity. The motives of Essex witches, we have seen, were clearly understood. They sought revenge for unneighbourly acts done against them.

The relationship of witches to other evil agents

Witches are often one of a number of supernatural agents which bring misfortune on a people. Others are ancestors, sorcerers, ghosts, and spirits. Which agent is blamed usually depends on the amount of injury done and whether the attack is considered to be justified. It has been said that 'witchcraft attacks the virtuous, ancestors attack the wicked', and this is certainly true among the Gusii. But some societies do not make this division, and believe that ancestors can act wrongly, and on these occasions show anger against them. Kin, prophets, sacred chiefs, and others may all cause injury similar to witchcraft among the Dinka, but in their case it is believed to be justified. As far as can be seen, Essex witches do not appear to have competed with so many other agents of misfortune. Ghosts, ancestors, evil fairies appear to have played little part as bringers of affliction.

The personality and physical characteristics of the witch

Usually those actually accused are not as ugly, antisocial, or perverted as might be expected from the witch 'legends'. The stereotype of the witch is often far from the reality. But the stereotype is, nevertheless, important. Witches are often thought of as old—the older the witch among the Azande 'the more potent his witchcraft and the more unscrupulous his use of it'. Another feature which is often given in the myth is the sex of the witch; thus men and women are equally witches among the Azande. Night-witches among the Mandari are invariably male and, though both men and women may become witches among the Navaho, male witches are thought to be considerably more numerous. On the other hand, the Lovedu and Gusii agree that, though a witch can be of either sex, the great majority are female.

Beliefs vary as to the outward and inward physical attributes of witchcraft. Some people believe that though there are no outward signs, witchcraft is a substance, discoverable by autopsy, in the body of witches. Night-witches are said to be white or grey in colour among the Lugbara, and similarly to smear themselves white with ashes among the Kaguru. But, like the small tail which they are supposed to have among the Dinka, these outward signs are kept so secret that they are no help in actually finding who is bewitching one. On the whole, it seems to be believed that witches do not have any special stigmata or outward signs which mark them off from other people. When there is an ideal type, this is in keeping with the antisocial motives we have noted earlier. Thus the Kaguru describe a witch 'as an ugly person with dark skin and red eyes', but, like the Mandari, whose witches are ideally ugly, deformed, and dirty, observation shows that those accused are often the very opposite. It is true that a person with an unpleasant face

56   is often thought of as a witch among the Lovedu, even though nothing has definitely been attributed to him, but it is ultimately on his behaviour that a witch is detected—behaviour arising from the motives we have studied earlier. The same appears to be true of Essex. Though the witch's 'mark' might be important in proving a person a witch, it was her behaviour that led to the suspicions and accusations.

The Witches' Sabbath, Francisco de Goya

the Black mass

ANTON SZANDOR LAVEY (1930–   )

Anton LaVey is often called "The Black Pope" by his followers in the Church of Satan. Here, in the Bible of that
church, he defends Satanic witchcraft on the grounds that
what it stands for is real, while the teachings of the Christian
Church are hypocritical and alien to human nature.

FROM the satanic Bible

No other single device has been associated with Satanism as much
as the black mass. To say that the most blasphemous of all religious ceremonies is nothing more than a literary invention is certainly a statement which needs qualifying—but nothing could be
truer.

The popular concept of the black mass is thus: a defrocked
priest stands before an altar consisting of a nude woman, her legs
spread-eagled and vagina thrust open, each of her outstretched
fists grasping a black candle made from the fat of unbaptized
babies, and a chalice containing the urine of a prostitute (or blood)
reposing on her belly. An inverted cross hangs above the altar, and
triangular hosts of ergot-laden bread or black-stained turnip are
methodically blessed as the priest dutifully slips them in and out of

the altar-lady's labia. Then, we are told, an invocation to Satan and various demons is followed by an array of prayers and psalms chanted backwards or interspersed with obscenities . . . all performed within the confines of a "protective" pentagram drawn on the floor. If the Devil appears he is invariably in the form of a rather eager man wearing the head of a black goat upon his shoulders. Then follows a potpourri of flagellation, prayer-book burning, cunnilingus, fellatio, and general hindquarters kissing— all done to a background of ribald recitations from the Holy Bible, and audible expectorations on the cross! If a baby can be slaughtered during the ritual, so much the better; for as everyone knowns, this is the favorite sport of the Satanist!

If this sounds repugnant, then the success of the reports of the black mass, in keeping the devout in church, is easy to understand. No "decent" person could fail to side with the inquisitors when told of these blasphemies. The propagandists of the church did their job well, informing the public at one time or another of the heresies and heinous acts of the Pagans, Cathars, Bogomils, Templars and others who, because of their dualistic philosophies and sometimes Satanic logic, had to be eradicated.

The stories of unbaptized babies being stolen by Satanists for use in the mass were not only effective propaganda measures, but also provided a constant source of revenue for the Church, in the form of baptism fees. No Christian mother would, upon hearing of these diabolical kidnappings, refrain from getting her child properly baptized, post haste.

Another facet of man's nature was apparent in the fact that the writer or artist with lewd thoughts could exercise his most obscene predilections in the portrayal of the activities of heretics. The censor who views all pornography so that he will know what to warn others of is the modern equivalent of the medieval chronicler of the obscene deeds of the Satanists (and, of course, their modern journalist counterparts). It is believed that the most complete library of pornography in the world is owned by the Vatican!

The kissing of the Devil's behind during the traditional black mass is easily recognized as the forerunner of the modern term used to describe one who will, through appealing to another's ego, gain materially from him. As all Satanic ceremonies were performed toward very real or material goals, the *oscularum infame* (or kiss of shame) was considered a symbolic requisite towards earthly, rather than spiritual, success.

The usual assumption is that the Satanic ceremony or service is always called a black mass. A black mass is *not* the magical ceremony practiced by Satanists. The Satanist would only employ the use of a black mass as a form of psychodrama. Furthermore, a black mass does not necessarily imply that the performers of such are Satanists. A black mass is essentially a parody on the religious service of the Roman Catholic Church, but can be loosely applied to a satire on any religious ceremony.

To the Satanist, the black mass, in its blaspheming of orthodox rites, is nothing more than a redundancy. The services of all established religions are actually parodies of old rituals performed by the worshippers of the earth and the flesh. In attempts to de-sexualize and de-humanize the Pagan beliefs, later men of spiritual faith whitewashed the honest meanings behind the rituals into the bland euphemisms now considered to be the "true mass." Even *if* the Satanist were to spend each night performing a black mass, he would no more be performing a travesty than the devout church-goer who unwittingly attends his own "black mass"—*his* spoof on the honest and emotionally-sound rites of Pagan antiquity.

Any ceremony considered a black mass must effectively shock and outrage, as this seems to be the measure of its success. In the Middle Ages, blaspheming the holy church was shocking. Now, however, the Church does not present the awesome image it did during the inquisition. The traditional black mass is no longer the outrageous spectacle to the dilettante or renegade priest that it once was. If the Satanist wishes to create a ritual to blaspheme an accepted institution, for the purpose of psychodrama, he is careful to choose one that is not in vogue to parody. Thus, he is truly stepping on a sacred cow.

A black mass, today, would consist of the blaspheming of such "sacred" topics as Eastern mysticism, psychiatry, the psychedelic movement, ultra-liberalism, etc. Patriotism would be championed, drugs and their gurus would be defiled, acultural militants would be deified, and the decadence of ecclesiastical theologies might even be given a Satanic boost.

The Satanic magus has always been the catalyst for the dichotomy necessary in molding popular beliefs, and in this case a ceremony in the nature of black mass may serve a far-reaching magical purpose.

In the year 1666, some rather interesting events occurred in France. With the death of François Mansart, the architect of the trapezoid, whose geometrics were to become the prototype of the haunted house, the Palace of Versailles was being constructed, in accordance with his plans. The last of the glamorous priestesses of Satan, Jeanne-Marie Bouvier (Madame Guyon) was to be over-shadowed by a shrewd opportunist and callous business-woman named Catherine Deshayes, otherwise known as LaVoisin. Here was an erstwhile beautician who, while dabbling in abortions and purveying the most efficient poisons to ladies desirous of eliminating unwanted husbands or lovers, found in the lurid accounts of the "messes noir" a proverbial brainstorm.

It is safe to say that 1666 was the year of the first "commerical" black mass! In the region south of St. Denis, which is now called LaGarenne, a great walled house was purchased by LaVoisin and fitted with dispensaries, cells, laboratories, and . . . a chapel. Soon it became *de rigueur* for royalty and lesser dilettantes to attend and participate in the very type of service mentioned earlier in this chapter. The organized fraud perpetrated in these ceremonies has become indelibly marked in history as the "true black mass."

When LaVoisin was arrested on March 13, 1679 (in the Church of Our Blessed Lady of Good Tidings, incidentally), the die had already been cast. The degraded activities of LaVoisin had stifled the majesty of Satanism for many years to come.

The Satanism-for-fun-and-games fad next appeared in England in the middle 18th Century in the form of Sir Francis Dash-wood's Order of the Medmanham Franciscans, popularly called The Hell-Fire Club. While eliminating the blood, gore, and baby-fat candles of the previous century's masses, Sir Francis managed to conduct rituals replete with good dirty fun, and certainly pro-vided a colorful and harmless form of psychodrama for many of the leading lights of the period. An interesting sideline of Sir Francis, which lends a clue to the climate of the Hell-Fire Club, was a group called the Dilettani Club, of which he was the founder.

It was the 19th Century that brought a whitewashing to Satan-ism, in the feeble attempts of "white" magicians trying to per-form "black" magic. This was a very paradoxical period for

Satanism, with writers such as Baudelaire and Huysmans who, despite their apparent obsession with evil, seemed nice enough fellows. The Devil developed his Luciferian personality for the public to see, and gradually evolved into a sort of drawing-room gentleman. This was the era of "experts" on the black arts, such as Éliphas Lévi and countless trance-mediums who, with their carefully bound spirits and demons, have also succeeded in binding the minds of many who call themselves parapsychologists to this day!

As far as Satanism was concerned, the closet outward signs of this were the neo-Pagan rites conducted by MacGregor Mathers' Hermetic Order of the Golden Dawn, and Aleister Crowley's later Order of the Silver Star (A ∴ A ∴ —Argentinum Astrum) and Order of Oriental Templars (O.T.O.), which paranoiacally denied any association with Satanism, despite Crowley's self-imposed image of the beast of revelation. Aside from some rather charming poetry and a smattering of magical bric-a-brac, when not climbing mountains Crowley spent most of his time as a poseur par excellence and worked overtime to be wicked. Like his contemporary, Rev.(?) Montague Summers, Crowley obviously spent a large part of his life with his tongue jammed firmly into his cheek, but his followers, today, are somehow able to read esoteric meaning into his every word.

Perennially concurrent with these societies were the sex clubs using Satanism as a rationale—that persists today, for which tabloid newspaper writers may give thanks.

If it appears that the black mass developed from a literary invention of the church, to a depraved commercial actuality, to a psychodrama for dilettantes and iconoclasts, to an ace in the hole for popular media . . . then *where* does it fit into the true nature of Satanism—and *who* was practicing Satanic magic in those years beyond 1666?

The answer to this riddle lies in another. Is the person generally considered to be a Satanist really practicing Satanism *in its true sense,* or rather from the point of view taken by the opinion-makers of heavenly persuasion? It has often been said, and rightly so, that all of the books about the Devil have been written by the agents of God. It is, therefore, quite easy to understand how a certain breed of devil worshippers was created through the inventions of theologians. This erstwhile "evil" character is not necessarily practicing *true* Satanism. Nor is he a living embodiment of the element of untrammeled pride or majesty of self which gave the post-Pagan world the churchman's definition of evil. He is instead the by-product of later and more elaborate propaganda.

The pseudo-Satanist has always managed to appear throughout modern history, with his black masses of varying degrees of blasphemy; but the *real* Satanist is not quite so easily recognized as such.

It would be an over-simplification to say that every successful man and woman on earth is, without knowing it, a practicing Satanist; but the thirst for earthly success and its ensuing realization are certainly grounds for Saint Peter turning thumbs down. If the rich man's entry into heaven seems as difficult as the camel's attempt to go through the eye of a needle; if the love of money is the root of all evil; then we must at least assume the most powerful men on earth to be the most Satanic. This applies to financiers, industrialists, popes, poets, dictators, and all assorted opinion-makers and field marshals of the world's activities.

Occasionally, through "leakages," one of the enigmatic men or women of earth will be found to have "dabbled" in the black arts. These, of course, are brought to light as the "mystery men" of history. Names like Rasputin, Zaharoff, Cagliostro, Rosenberg and their ilk are links—clues, so to speak, of the true legacy of Satan . . . a legacy which transcends ethnic, racial and economic differences and temporal ideologies, as well. The Satanist has always ruled the earth . . . and always will, by whatever name he is called.

One thing stands sure: the standards, philosophy and practices set forth on these pages are those employed by the most self-realized and powerful humans on earth. In the secret thoughts of each man and woman, still motivated by sound and unclouded minds, resides the potential of the Satanist, as always has been. The sign of the horns shall appear to many, now, rather than the few; and the magician will stand forth that he may be recognized.

the salem witch trials

ROGER HART

Witchcraft has always inspired fear—fear, which has, at various times, exploded into what we know of, even in contemporary political life, as the "witch-hunt." One of the most famous American witch-hunts was that of the Salem witch trials of the seventeenth century, described here by an Englishman of our own time.

FROM witchcraft

Perhaps no single witch hunt has attracted so much popular attention as that which took place at Salem, in New England, in the year 1692. This American witch hunt was remarkable, not merely on account of the large number of people found guilty (Salem was a small community), but also because of the late date at which it took place. No one had been executed for witchcraft in England, for example, since 1684. But above all, the Salem affair has generally been seen as a fascinating microcosm of the whole Western witchcraft delusion.

Witchcraft had existed in New England many years before Salem. In 1656, for example, Anne Hibbins "was hanged for a witch only for having more wit than her neighbours. It was his very expression; she having, as he explained it, unhappily guessed that two of her persecutors, whom she saw talking in the street, were talking of her. This cost her her life, despite all he could do to the contrary, as he himself told us." In other words, Anne Hibbins was the unfortunate victim of mere village gossip.

In New England, as elsewhere, hysteria was a common characteristic of the accusers. Cases of hysterical fits were known years before Salem. One such was that of Anne Cole in Hartford, Connecticut, in 1662: "Extremely violent bodily motions she many times had, even to the hazard of her life in the fears of those who saw them. And very often she gave great disturbance in the public worship of God to two other women, who had also strange fits. Once especially, on a day of prayer kept on that account, the motion and noise of the afflicted was so terrible that a godly person fainted at the appearance of it." It was popularly imagined that Anne Cole was bewitched, or possessed by devils. In the Puritan society of seventeenth-century America, the devil was every bit as real a person as God.

This hysteria, so often associated with witchcraft trials, has been the subject of much argument. Was it some kind of religious frenzy, or was it a medical condition? A modern writer has described medical hysteria as beginning "with a pain or a strange sensation situated at such or such a point of the body . . . it often begins in the lower part of the abdomen [and] seems to ascend and to spread to other organs. For instance, it very often spreads to the epigastrium, to the breasts, then to the throat. There it assumes rather an interesting form, which was for a very long time considered as quite characteristic of hysteria. The patient has the sensation of too big an object, as it were, a ball, rising in her throat and choking her."

This medical description of hysteria has strong points of similarity with contemporary accounts. This one was given by the Boston minister Cotton Mather (1662–1728) in the case of the Goodwin children of Boston, in 1688: "Sometimes they would be deaf, sometimes dumb, and sometimes blind, and often all this at once. One while their tongues would be drawn down their throats; another while they would be pulled out upon their chins to a pro-

ROGER HART

66   digious length. They would have their mouths opened so wide that
their jaws went out of joint, and they would at once clap together
again with a force like that of a strong spring-lock.

"The same would happen to their shoulder blades, and their
elbows, and hand wrists, and several of their joints. They would at
times lie in a benumbed condition and be drawn together like those
who are tied neck and heels, and presently be stretched out, yea,
drawn backwards to such an extent that it was feared the very
skin of their bellies would have cracked. They would make most
piteous outcries that they were cut with knives, and struck with
blows that they could not bear."

A modern historian has written of Salem in 1692: "The primary
causes should now be clear. There was an outbreak of epidemic
hysteria in Salem Village which originated in experiments with the
occult. And the hysterical hallucinations of the afflicted persons
were confirmed by some concrete evidence of actual witchcraft
and by many confessions, the majority of them also hysterical."

But such explanations were foreign to New Englanders of the
time. A sincere and devout man, Cotton Mather believed that
witches must be fervently hunted down as evil monsters: "The
devils, after a most preternatural manner, by the dreadful judgment of heaven, took a bodily possession of many people in Salem,
and the adjacent places; and the houses of the poor people began
to be filled with the horrid cries of persons tormented by evil
spirits. There seemed to be an execrable witchcraft in the foundation of this wonderful affliction. Many persons, of divers characters,
were accused, apprehended, prosecuted, upon the visions of the
afflicted." Cotton Mather was perhaps the most influential and
active of the Massachusets Bay Colony witch hunters.

It has been said of Salem: "The year 1692 seems to have been a
particularly troubled one in New England. It was a time of political
uncertainty, with Increase Mather at the English court, seeking clari-
fication of the colony's government. The French were waging war,
and the Indians were on the warpath. Taxes were intolerable (in
1691 the colonial government had demanded £1,346), the winter
was cruel, pirates were attacking commerce, and smallpox was
raging. In addition, the ingrown irritations of a small village, where
ownership of land and boundaries were in dispute, increased the

tensions. To men and women brought up in a restricting evangelical world, the troubles of 1692 were caused by the Devil."

A contemporary, John Hale, expressed the common fear of the people of Salem. The witches' "design was to destroy Salem Village, and to begin at the minister's house, and to destroy the Church of God, and to set up Satan's kingdom." It has been pointed out that Massachusetts was not a monarchy or a republic, but a theocracy. Witchcraft—treason against God—was therefore treason against the state. Witchcraft seemed to threaten the very basis of the religious society in which the people of Salem lived: and the people of Salem took their religion very seriously.

In these circumstances, the local people were appalled to find that witchcraft was apparently being practised in the home of their minister, the Reverend Samuel Parris. Certain young women, including his own daughter Elizabeth (aged nine) and her cousin Abigail Williams (aged eleven), used to spend their evenings with Tituba, the family's slave. Tituba would tell them lurid tales of the West Indies, fillled with superstition which fired their ripe imaginations. Perhaps the girls were feverish or hysterical; perhaps they gave way to a terrible reaction against their strict Puritan background. Whatever the reality, to the people of Salem there could only be one explanation: witchcraft. The young girls, brought up in devout homes, were undeniably bewitched.

Elizabeth and Abigail deeply frightened their elders with their apparent bewitchment and they soon became the center of local attention. Not surprisingly, they were joined by other impressionable girls, some of them rather older. The girls who indulged in this "sport," as it was called, included Elizabeth Parris, Abigail Williams, Ann Putnam (twelve), Elizabeth Hubbard (seventeen), Mary Walcott (sixteen), Elizabeth Proctor (twenty), Mercy Lewis (nineteen), Susan Sheldon (eighteen), Elizabeth Booth (eighteen), and others.

But if they were bewitched, who was responsible? In response to the earnst questions of adults, the girls were quick to single out their unfortunate victims, perhaps out of fear of recanting, perhaps out of childish spite. The game had begun and must be played out to its terrible end. One by one the girls made their sworn depositions. Elizabeth Booth, for example, accused a neighbour, John

Proctor: "The deposition of Elizabeth Booth, aged eighteen years, who testifieth and saith that since I have been afflicted, I have been most grievously tormented by my neighbour, John Proctor, senior, or his appearance [spectre]. Also I have seen John Proctor, senior, or his appearance [spectre] most grievously torment and afflict Mary Walcott, Mercy Lewis, and Ann Putnam, junior, by pinching, twisting, and almost choking them."

On this "evidence," John Proctor was later convicted of witchcraft and hanged.

Similarly, Mary Walcott accused Abigail Faulkner of being a witch: "The deposition of Mary Walcott, who testifieth and saith that about the 9th August, 1692, I was most dreadfully afflicted by a woman that told me her name was Abigail Faulkner. But on the 11th of August, being the day of the examination of Abigail Faulkner, she did most dreadfully afflict me during the time of her examination. I saw Abigail Faulkner, or her appearance [spectre], most grievously afflict and torment Sarah Phelps and Ann Putnam. And I verily believe in my heart that Abigail Faulkner is a witch, and that she has often afflicted me and the aforesaid persons by acts of witchcraft."

It has been said that "there can be no mitigation of the crimes of the Salem girls. Never at any time, even during the hangings, was the slightest compunction or contrition shown, with the possible exception of Sarah Churchill and Mary Warren. They knew exactly what they were doing. Their acts during 1692 imply a state of utter delinquency, causing death without rhyme or reason, for sport. On 28th March, at Ingersoll's inn, one girl said she saw Mrs. Proctor afflicting her. Mrs. Ingersol 'told the girl she told a lie, for there was nothing.' Then the girl said she did it for sport. 'They must have some sport.'"

In the tense, unnatural atmosphere, virtually anything would be believed by the public. If witchcraft was the cause of the young peoples' conduct, then it must be ruthlessly eliminated—no matter who was implicated. The trouble was, that in the trials which were held late in 1692, the accusers were so anxious to locate the "guilty" parties, that elementary rules of evidence were ignored. The girls' imaginative evidence was believed almost entirely, and often without corroboration.

Worse still, even if a victim could prove an alibi, it was claimed that his "spectre" had appeared before the girls, and bewitched them. It seems extraordinary that any credence could be lent to this "spectral evidence" at so late a date. But it was a central part of the Salem trials, that a man could be condemned for what his "spectre" did.

Cotton Mather believed in spectres, but did not think that spectral evidence should be admissible in court: "When there is not further evidence against a person but only this, that a spectre in their shape does afflict a neighbour, that evidence is not enough to convict the person of witchcraft. That the devils have a natural power which makes them capable of exhibiting what shape they please, I suppose nobody doubts. And I have no absolute promise of God that they shall not exhibit *mine*. It is the opinion, generally, of all Protestant writers that the Devil may thus abuse the innocent. . . ." But if Cotton Mather opposed spectral evidence, most people were only too willing to believe it, if the result was the desired conviction and punishment.

The Salem trials had much in common both with English and Continental witchcraft. The legend of flying witches, promoted by tradition, was confirmed by Mrs. Anne Foster at the Salem trials: "She and Martha Carrier did both ride on a stick or pole when they went to the witch meeting at Salem Village, and that the stick broke as they were carried in the air above the tops of the trees, and they fell. But she did hang fast about the neck of Goody Carrier and were presently at the village, that she was then much hurt of her leg."

Other evidence mentioned familiars, bewitchment, acts of *maleficium* or petty spite such as killing pigs, and possession by devils. One or two of the girls even claimed to have seen the accused writing their names in the "devil's book," but the Salem magistrates were unwilling to believe in this, at least.

Increase Mather (1639–1723)—the President of Harvard—was one New Englander to advise caution: "It were better that ten suspected witches should escape than that one honest person should be condemned . . . It is better a guilty person should be absolved, than that he should without ground of conviction be condemned. I had rather judge a witch to be an honest woman, than judge an honest woman as a witch." But his advice was scarcely heeded; and in any case he believed in witchcraft as much as anyone.

The trials continued. The depositions of the girls were taken, the spectral evidence believed; the religious fears of the Puritan community inflated. Dozens of victims were thrown into jail. The Salem prisoners were badly treated: "An especially shocking detail about these trials is that the accused had to pay for their maintenance in jail, even when acquitted! A reprieve cost a fee, a discharge another. The relatives paid the hangman's fee for the execution. Many remained in prison after the general jail delivery because their possessions had been sold to maintain their families in the meantime. Sarah Dustin was acquitted in January, 1693, but, having no one to come to her aid, died in prison. Margaret Jacobs was acquited, but the property of her parents had been seized and she was kept in jail until at length a generous stranger (a Mr. Gammon) heard of her plight and bought her freedom. William Buckley spent his last shilling paying £10 to release his wife and daughter."

Some of the Salem "witches" deeply impressed the crowd at their executions: "They protested their innocence as in the presence of the great God whom forthwith they were to appear before. They wished, and declared their wish, that their blood might be the last innocent blood shed upon that account. With great affection [emotion] they entreated Mr. Cotton Mather to pray with them. They prayed that God would discover that witchcrafts were among us. They spoke without reflection on jury and judges for bringing them in guilty and condemning them.

"They prayed earnestly for pardon for all other sins and for an interest in the precious blood of our dear Redeemer. They seemed to be very sincere, upright, and sensible of their circumstances on all account, especially Proctor and Willard, whose whole management of themselves from the jail to the gallows and whilst at the gallows was very affecting and melting to the hearts of some considerable spectators."

Another victim, the Reverend George Burroughs, was obviously innocent: "Mr. Burroughs was carried in a cart with the others through the streets of Salem to execution. When he was upon the ladder he made a speech for the clearing of his innocence, with such solemn and serious expressions as were to the admiration of all present. His prayer (which he concluded by repeating the Lord's Prayer) was so well worded, and uttered with such composedness, and such (at least seeming) fervency of spirit, as was very affecting and drew tears from many. Indeed, it seemed to some that the spectators would hinder the execution." Burroughs was hanged on 19th August, 1692.

But despite scenes such as this, the superstition at Salem in 1692 seemed indestructible. At the execution of Samuel Wardwell on 22nd September, 1692, "while he was speaking to the people protesting his innocence, the executioner was at the same time smoking tobacco, and the smoke coming in his face interrupted his discourse; those accusers said the Devil hindered him with smoke."

All in all, the toll of Salem, a township of a hundred-odd households, was enormous. "During the hysteria, almost 150 people were arrested. A search of all the court records would no doubt add to this number. Because of the time taken to convict each prisoner, only thirty-one were tried in 1692, not including Sarah Churchill and Mary Warren, two accusers who briefly recanted. The court of Oyer and Terminer (hear and determine) sentenced to death all thirty-one, of whom six were men. Nineteen were hanged. Of the remaining twelve, two (Sarah Osborne and Ann Foster) died in jail; one (Giles Cory) was pressed to death; one (Tituba) was held indefinitely in jail without trial. Two (Abigail Faulkner and Elizabeth Proctor) postponed execution by pleading pregnancy and lived long enough to be reprieved. One (Mary Bradbury) escaped from jail after sentencing; and five made confessions which secured reprieves for them."

The historian George Lincoln Burr declared that "the New England panic at Salem was but a last bright flicker of the ghastly glare which had so long made hideous the European night." Another great student of witchcraft wrote of the Salem witch hunt: "Error is seldom overthrown by mere reasoning. It yields only to the logic of events. No power of learning or wit would have rooted the witchcraft superstition out of the minds of men. Nothing short of a demonstration of their deformities, follies, and horrors, such as here was held up to the view of the world, could have given their death blow. This was the final cause of Salem witchcraft, and makes it one of the great landmarks in the world's history."

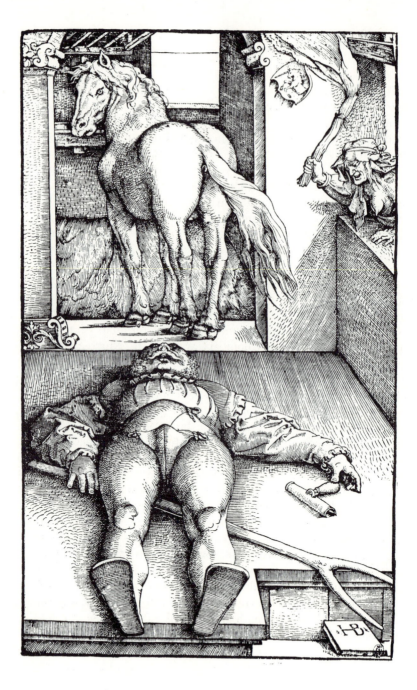

The Bewitched Groom, Hans Baldung

witchcraft in fiction

NATHANIEL HAWTHORNE (1804–1864)

In "Young Goodman Brown," which is set in Salem, Nathaniel Hawthorne recreates the powers of witchcraft in emotional terms. Through fiction, he provides a personal perspective for the historical viewpoint of the previous selection.

young goodman brown

Young Goodman Brown came forth at sunset into the street of Salem village; but put his head back, after crossing the threshold, to exchange a parting kiss with his young wife. And Faith, as the wife was aptly named, thrust her own pretty head into the street, letting the wind play with the pink ribbons of her cap while she called to Goodman Brown.

"Dearest heart," whispered she, softly and rather sadly, when her lips were close to his ear, "prithee put off your journey until sunrise and sleep in your own bed to-night. A lone woman is troubled with such dreams and such thoughts that she's afeared of herself sometimes. Pray tarry with me this night, dear husband, of all nights in the year."

"My love and my Faith," replied young Goodman Brown, "of

all nights in the year, this one night must I tarry away from thee. My journey, as thou callest it, forth and back again, must needs be done 'twixt now and sunrise. What, my sweet, pretty wife, dost thou doubt me already, and we but three months married?"

"Then God bless you!" said Faith, with the pink ribbons; "and may you find all well when you come back."

"Amen!" cried Goodman Brown. "Say thy prayers, dear Faith, and go to bed at dusk, and no harm will come to thee."

So they parted; and the young man pursued his way until, being about to turn the corner by the meeting house, he looked back and saw the head of Faith still peeping after him with a melancholy air, in spite of her pink ribbons.

"Poor little Faith!" thought he, for his heart smote him. "What a wretch am I to leave her on such an errand! She talks of dreams, too. Methought as she spoke there was trouble in her face, as if a dream had warned her what work is to be done to-night. But no, no; 'twould kill her to think it. Well, she's a blessed angel on earth; and after this one night I'll cling to her skirts and follow her to heaven."

With this excellent resolve for the future, Goodman Brown felt himself justified in making more haste on his present evil purpose. He had taken a dreary road, darkened by all the gloomiest trees of the forest, which barely stood aside to let the narrow path creep through, and closed immediately behind. It was all as lonely as could be; and there is this peculiarity in such a solitude, that the traveller knows not who may be concealed by the innumerable trunks and thick boughs overhead; so that with lonely footsteps he may yet be passing through an unseen multitude.

"There may be a devilish Indian behind every tree," said Goodman Brown to himself; and he glanced fearfully behind him as he added, "What if the devil himself should be at my very elbow!"

His head being turned back, he passed a crook of the road, and, looking forward again, beheld the figure of a man, in grave and decent attire, seated at the foot of an old tree. He arose at Goodman Brown's approach and walked onward side by side with him.

"You are late, Goodman Brown," said he. "The clock of the Old South was striking as I came through Boston; and that is full fifteen minutes agone."

"Faith kept me back a while," replied the young man, with a

tremor in his voice, caused by the sudden appearance of his companion, though not wholly unexpected.

It was now deep dusk in the forest, and deepest in that part of it where these two were journeying. As nearly as could be discerned, the second traveller was about fifty years old, apparently in the same rank of life as Goodman Brown, and bearing a considerable resemblance to him, though perhaps more in expression than features. Still they might have been taken for father and son. And yet, though the elder person was as simply clad as the younger and as simple in manner too, he had an indescribable air of one who knew the world, and who would not have felt abashed at the governor's dinner table or in King William's court, were it possible that his affairs should call him thither. But the only thing about him that could be fixed upon as remarkable was his staff, which bore the likeness of a great black snake, so curiously wrought that it might almost be seen to twist and wriggle itself like a living serpent. This, of course, must have been an ocular deception, assisted by the uncertain light.

"Come, Goodman Brown," cried his fellow-traveller, "this is a dull pace for the beginning of a journey. Take my staff, if you are so soon weary."

"Friend," said the other, exchanging his slow pace for a full stop, "having kept covenant by meeting thee here, it is my purpose now to return whence I came. I have scruples touching the matter thou wot'st of."

"Sayest thou so?" replied he of the serpent, smiling apart. "Let us walk on, nevertheless, reasoning as we go; and if I convince thee not thou shalt turn back. We are but a little way in the forest yet."

"Too far! too far!" exclaimed the goodman, unconsciously resuming his walk. "My father never went into the woods on such an errand, nor his father before him. We have been a race of honest men and good Christians since the days of the martyrs; and shall I be the first of the name of Brown that ever took this path and kept——"

"Such company, thou wouldst say," observed the elder person, interpreting his pause. "Well said, Goodman Brown! I have been as well acquainted with your family as with ever a one among the Puritans; and that's no trifle to say. I helped your grandfather, the constable, when he lashed the Quaker woman so smartly through the streets of Salem; and it was I that brought your father a pitch-pine knot, kindled at my own hearth, to set fire to an Indian village, in King Philip's war. They were my good friends, both; and many a pleasant walk have we had along this path, and returned merrily after midnight. I would fain be friends with you for their sake."

"If it be as thou sayest," replied Goodman Brown, "I marvel they never spoke of these matters; or, verily, I marvel not, seeing that the least rumor of the sort would have driven them from New England. We are a people of prayer, and good works to boot, and abide no such wickedness."

"Wickedness or not," said the traveller with the twisted staff, "I have a very general acquaintance here in New England. The deacons of many a church have drunk the communion wine with me; the selectmen of divers towns make me their chairman; and a majority of the Great and General Court are firm supporters of my interest. The governor and I, too——But these are state secrets."

"Can this be so?" cried Goodman Brown, with a stare of amazement at his undisturbed companion. "Howbeit, I have nothing to do with the governor and council; they have their own ways, and are no rule for a simple husbandman like me. But, were I to go on with thee, how should I meet the eye of that good old man, our minister, at Salem village? O, his voice would make me tremble both Sabbath day and lecture day."

Thus far the elder traveller had listened with due gravity; but now burst into a fit of irrepressible mirth, shaking himself so violently that his snakelike staff actually seemed to wriggle in sympathy.

"Ha! ha! ha!" shouted he again and again; then composing himself. "Well, go on, Goodman Brown, go on; but, prithee, don't kill me with laughing."

"Well, then, to end the matter at once," said Goodman Brown, considerably nettled, "there is my wife, Faith. It would break her dear little heart; and I'd rather break my own."

"Nay, if that be the case," answered the other, "e'en go thy ways, Goodman Brown. I would not for twenty old women like the one hobbling before us that Faith should come to any harm."

As he spoke, he pointed his staff at a female figure on the path, in whom Goodman Brown recognized a very pious and exemplary dame, who had taught him his catechism in youth, and was still his moral and spiritual adviser, jointly with the minister and Deacon Gookin.

"A marvel, truly, that Goody Cloyse should be so far in the wilderness at nightfall," said he. "But, with your leave, friend, I shall take a cut through the woods until we have left this Christian woman behind. Being a stranger to you, she might ask whom I was consorting with and whither I was going."

"Be it so," said his fellow-traveller. "Betake you to the woods, and let me keep the path."

Accordingly the young man turned aside, but took care to watch his companion, who advanced softly along the road until he had come within a staff's length of the old dame. She, meanwhile, was making the best of her way, with singular speed for so aged a woman, and mumbling some indistinct words—a prayer, doubtless —as she went. The traveller put forth his staff and touched her withered neck with what seemed the serpent's tail.

"The devil!" screamed the pious old lady.

"Then Goody Cloyse knows her old friend?" observed the traveller, confronting her and leaning on his writhing stick.

"Ah, forsooth, and is it your worship indeed?" cried the good dame. "Yea, truly is it, and in the very image of my old gossip, Goodman Brown, the grandfather of the silly fellow that now is. But—would your worship believe it?—my broomstick hath strangely disappeared, stolen, as I suspect, by that unhanged witch, Goody Cory, and that, too, when I was all anointed with the juice of smallage, and cinquefoil, and wolf's bane——"

"Mingled with fine wheat and the fat of a new-born babe," said the shape of old Goodman Brown.

"Ah, your worship knows the recipe," cried the old lady, cackling aloud. "So, as I was saying, being all ready for the meeting, and no horse to ride on, I made up my mind to foot it; for they tell me there is a nice young man to be taken into communion to-night. But now your good worship will lend me your arm, and we shall be there in a twinkling."

"That can hardly be," answered her friend. "I may not spare you my arm, Goody Cloyse; but here is my staff, if you will."

So saying, he threw it down at her feet, where, perhaps, it assumed life, being one of the rods which its owner had formerly lent to the Egyptian magi. Of this fact, however, Goodman Brown could not take cognizance. He had cast up his eyes in astonishment, and, looking down again, beheld neither Goody Cloyse nor the serpentine staff, but his fellow-traveller alone, who waited for him as calmly as if nothing had happened.

"That old woman taught me my catechism," said the young man; and there was a world of meaning in this simple comment.

They continued to walk onward, while the elder traveller exhorted his companion to make good speed and persevere in the path, discoursing so aptly that his arguments seemed rather to spring up in the bosom of his auditor than to be suggested by himself. As they went, he plucked a branch of maple to serve for a walking stick, and began to strip it of the twigs and little boughs, which were wet with evening dew. The moment his fingers touched them they became strangely withered and dried up as with a week's sunshine. Thus the pair proceeded, at a good free pace, until suddenly, in a gloomy hollow of the road, Goodman Brown sat himself down on the stump of a tree and refused to go any farther.

"Friend," said he, stubbornly, "my mind is made up. Not another step will I budge on this errand. What if a wretched old woman do choose to go to the devil when I thought she was going to heaven: is that any reason why I should quit my dear Faith and go after her?"

"You will think better of this by and by," said his acquaintance, composedly. "Sit here and rest yourself a while; and when you feel like moving again, there is my staff to help you along."

Without more words, he threw his companion the maple stick, and was as speedily out of sight as if he had vanished into the deepening gloom. The young man sat a few moments by the roadside, applauding himself greatly, and thinking with how clear a conscience he should meet the minister in his morning walk, nor shrink from the eye of good old Deacon Gookin. And what calm sleep would be his that very night, which was to have been spent so wickedly, but so purely and sweetly now, in the arms of Faith! Amidst these pleasant and praiseworthy meditations, Goodman Brown heard the tramp of horses along the road, and deemed it advisable to conceal himself within the verge of the forest, conscious of the guilty purpose that had brought him thither, though now so happily turned from it.

On came the hoof tramps and the voices of the riders, two grave old voices, conversing soberly as they drew near. These mingled sounds appeared to pass along the road, within a few yards of the young man's hidingplace; but, owing doubtless to the depth of the gloom at that particular spot, neither the travellers nor their steeds were visible. Though their figures brushed the small boughs by the wayside, it could not be seen that they intercepted, even for a moment, the faint gleam from the strip of bright sky athwart which they must have passed. Goodman Brown alternately crouched and stood on tiptoe, pulling aside the branches and thrusting forth his head as far as he durst without discerning so much as a shadow. It vexed him the more, because he could have sworn, were such a thing possible, that he recognized the voices of the minister and Deacon Gookin, jogging along quietly, as they were wont to do, when bound to some ordination or ecclesiastical council. While yet within hearing, one of the riders stopped to pluck a switch.

"Of the two, reverend sir," said the voice like the deacon's, "I had rather miss an ordination dinner than to-night's meeting. They tell me that some of our community are to be here from Falmouth and beyond, and others from Connecticut and Rhode Island, besides several of the Indian powwows, who, after their fashion, know almost as much deviltry as the best of us. Moreover, there is a goodly young woman to be taken into communion."

"Mighty well, Deacon Gookin!" replied the solemn old tones of the minister. "Spur up, or we shall be late. Nothing can be done, you know, until I get on the ground."

The hoofs clattered again; and the voices, talking so strangely in the empty air, passed on through the forest, where no church had ever been gathered or solitary Christian prayed. Whither, then, could these holy men be journeying so deep into the heathen wilderness? Young Goodman Brown caught hold of a tree for support, being ready to sink down on the ground, faint and over-burdened with the heavy sickness of his heart. He looked up to the sky, doubting whether there really was a heaven above him. Yet there was the blue arch, and the stars brightening in it.

"With heaven above and Faith below, I will yet stand firm against the devil!" cried Goodman Brown.

While he still gazed upward into the deep arch of the firmament and had lifted his hands to pray, a cloud, though no wind was stirring, hurried across the zenith and hid the brightening stars. The blue sky was still visible except directly overhead, where this black mass of cloud was sweeping swiftly northward. Aloft in the air, as if from the depths of the cloud, came a confused and doubtful sound of voices. Once the listener fancied that he could distinguish the accents of townspeople of his own, men and women, both pious and ungodly, many of whom he had met at the communion table, and had seen others rioting at the tavern. The next moment, so indistinct were the sounds, he doubted whether he had heard aught but the murmur of the old forest, whispering without a wind. Then came a stronger swell of those familiar tones, heard daily in the sunshine at Salem village, but never until now from a cloud of night. There was one voice, of a young woman, uttering lamentations, yet with an uncertain sorrow, and entreating for some favor, which, perhaps, it would grieve her to obtain; and all the unseen multitude, both saints and sinners, seemed to encourage her onward.

"Faith!" shouted Goodman Brown, in a voice of agony and desperation; and the echoes of the forest mocked him, crying, "Faith! Faith!" as if bewildered wretches were seeking her all through the wilderness.

The cry of grief, rage, and terror was yet piercing the night, when the unhappy husband held his breath for a response. There was a scream, drowned immediately in a louder murmur of voices, fading into far-off laughter, as the dark cloud swept away, leaving the clear and silent sky above Goodman Brown. But something fluttered lightly down through the air and caught on the branch of a tree. The young man seized it, and beheld a pink ribbon.

"My Faith is gone!" cried he, after one stupefied moment. "There is no good on earth; and sin is but a name. Come, devil; for to thee is this world given."

And, maddened with despair, so that he laughed loud and long, did Goodman Brown grasp his staff and set forth again, at such a rate that he seemed to fly along the forest path rather than to walk or run. The road grew wilder and drearier and more faintly traced, and vanished at length, leaving him in the heart of the dark wilderness, still rushing onward with the instinct that guides mortal man to evil. The whole forest was peopled with frightful sounds— the creaking of the trees, the howling of wild beasts, and the yell of Indians; while sometimes the wind tolled like a distant church bell, and sometimes gave a broad roar around the traveller, as if all Nature were laughing him to scorn. But he was himself the chief horror of the scene, and shrank not from its other horrors.

"Ha! ha! ha!" roared Goodman Brown when the wind laughed at him. "Let us hear which will laugh loudest. Think not to frighten me with your deviltry. Come witch, come wizard, come Indian powwow, come devil himself, and here comes Goodman Brown. You may as well fear him as he fear you."

In truth, all through the haunted forest there could be nothing more frightful than the figure of Goodman Brown. On he flew among the black pines, brandishing his staff with frenzied gestures, now giving vent to an inspiration of horrid blasphemy, and now shouting forth such laughter as set all the echoes of the forest laughing like demons around him. The fiend in his own shape is less hideous than when he rages in the breast of man. Thus sped the demoniac on his course, until, quivering among the trees, he saw a red light before him, as when the felled trunks and branches of a clearing have been set on fire, and throw up their lurid blaze against the sky, at the hour of midnight. He paused, in a lull of the tempest that had driven him onward, and heard the swell of what seemed a hymn, rolling solemnly from a distance with the weight of many voices. He knew the tune; it was a familiar one in the choir of the village meeting house. The verse died heavily away, and was lengthened by a chorus, not of human voices, but of all the sounds of the benighted wilderness pealing in awful harmony together. Goodman Brown cried out; and his cry was lost to his own ear by its unison with the cry of the desert.

In the interval of silence he stole forward until the light glared full upon his eyes. At one extremity of an open space, hemmed in by the dark wall of the forest, arose a rock, bearing some rude, natural resemblance either to an altar or a pulpit, and surrounded by four blazing pines, their tops aflame, their stems untouched, like candles at an evening meeting. The mass of foliage that had overgrown the summit of the rock was all on fire, blazing high into the night and fitfully illuminating the whole field. Each pendent twig and leafy festoon was in a blaze. As the red light arose and fell, a numerous congregation alternately shone forth, then disappeared in shadow, and again grew, as it were, out of the darkness, peopling the heart of the solitary woods at once.

"A grave and dark-clad company," quoth Goodman Brown.

In truth they were such. Among them, quivering to and fro between gloom and splendor, appeared faces that would be seen next day at the council board of the province, and others which, Sabbath after Sabbath, looked devoutly heavenward, and benignantly over the crowded pews, from the holiest pulpits in the land. Some affirm that the lady of the governor was there. At least there were high dames well known to her, and wives of honored husbands, and widows, a great multitude, and ancient maidens, all of excellent repute, and fair young girls, who trembled lest their mothers should espy them. Either the sudden gleams of light flashing over the obscure field bedazzled Goodman Brown, or he recognized a score of the church members of Salem village famous for their especial sanctity. Good old Deacon Gookin had arrived, and waited at the skirts of that venerable saint, his reverend pastor. But, irreverently consorting with these grave, reputable, and pious people, these elders of the church, these chaste dames and dewy virgins, there were men of dissolute lives and women of spotted fame, wretches given over to all mean and filthy vice, and suspected even of horrid crimes. It was strange to see that the good shrank not from the wicked, nor were the sinners abashed by the saints. Scattered also among their palefaced enemies were the Indian priests, or powwows, who had often scared their native forest with more hideous incantations than any known to English witchcraft.

"But where is Faith?" thought Goodman Brown, and, as hope came into his heart, he trembled.

Another verse of the hymn arose, a slow and mournful strain, such as the pious love, but joined to words which expressed all that our nature can conceive of sin, and darkly hinted at far more. Unfathomable to mere mortals is the lore of fiends. Verse after verse was sung; and still the chorus of the desert swelled between like the deepest tone of a mighty organ; and with the final peal of that dreadful anthem there came a sound, as if the roaring wind, the rushing streams, the howling beasts, and every other voice of the unconverted wilderness were mingling and according with the voice of guilty man in homage to the prince of all. The four blazing pines threw up a loftier flame, and obscurely discovered shapes and visages of horror on the smoke wreaths above the impious assembly. At the same moment the fire on the rock shot redly forth and formed a glowing arch above its base, where now appeared a

figure. With reverence be it spoken, the figure bore no slight simili-
tude, both in garb and manner, to some grave divine of the New
England churches.

"Bring forth the converts!" cried a voice that echoed through the
field and rolled into the forest.

At the word, Goodman Brown stepped forth from the shadow of
the trees and approached the congregation, with whom he felt a
loathful brotherhood by the sympathy of all that was wicked in his
heart. He could have well nigh sworn that the shape of his own
dead father beckoned him to advance, looking downward from a
smoke wreath, while a woman, with dim features of despair, threw
out her hand to warn him back. Was it his mother? But he had no
power to retreat one step, nor to resist, even in thought, when the
minister and good old Deacon Gookin seized his arms and led him
to the blazing rock. Thither came also the slender form of a veiled
female, led between Goody Cloyse, that pious teacher of the catechism, and Martha Carrier, who had received the devil's promise
to be queen of hell. A rampant hag was she. And there stood the
proselytes beneath the canopy of fire.

"Welcome, my children," said the dark figure, "to the communion
of your race. Ye have found thus young your nature and your destiny. My children, look behind you!"

They turned; and flashing forth, as it were, in a sheet of flame,
the fiend worshippers were seen; the smile of welcome gleamed
darkly on every visage.

"There," resumed the sable form, "are all whom ye have rever-
enced from youth. Ye deemed them holier than yourselves, and
shrank from your own sin, contrasting it with their lives of right-
eousness and prayerful aspirations heavenward. Yet here are they
all my worshipping assembly. This night it shall be granted you
to know their secret deeds; how hoarybearded elders of the church
have whispered wanton words to the young maids of their households; how many a woman, eager for widows' weeds, has given her
husband a drink at bedtime and let him sleep his last sleep in her
bosom; how beardless youths have made haste to inherit their
fathers' wealth; and how fair damsels—blush not, sweet ones—have
dug little graves in the garden, and bidden me, the sole guest, to
an infant's funeral. By the sympathy of your human hearts for sin
ye shall scent out all the places—whether in church, bed chamber,

street, field, or forest—where crime has been committed, and shall exult to behold the whole earth one stain of guilt, one mighty blood spot. Far more than this. It shall be yours to penetrate, in every bosom, the deep mystery of sin, the fountain of all wicked arts, and which inexhaustibly supplies more evil impulses than human power —than my power at its utmost—can make manifest in deeds. And now, my children, look upon each other."

They did so; and, by the blaze of the hell-kindled torches, the wretched man beheld his Faith, and the wife her husband, trembling before that unhallowed altar.

"Lo, there ye stand, my children," said the figure, in a deep and solemn tone, almost sad with its despairing awfulness, as if his once angelic nature could yet mourn for our miserable race. "Depending upon one another's hearts, ye had still hoped that virtue were not all a dream. Now are ye undeceived. Evil is the nature of mankind. Evil must be your only happiness. Welcome again, my children, to the communion of your race."

"Welcome," repeated the fiend worshippers, in one cry of despair and triumph.

And there they stood, the only pair, as it seemed, who were yet hesitating on the verge of wickedness in this dark world. A basin was hollowed, naturally, in the rock. Did it contain water, reddened by the lurid light? or was it blood? or, perchance, a liquid flame? Herein did the shape of evil dip his hand and prepare to lay the mark of baptism upon their foreheads, that they might be partakers of the mystery of sin, more conscious of the secret guilt of others, both in deed and thought, than they could now be of their own. The husband cast one look at his pale wife, and Faith at him. What polluted wretches would the next glance show them to each other, shuddering alike at what they disclosed and what they saw!

"Faith! Faith!" cried the husband, "look up to heaven, and resist the wicked one."

Whether Faith obeyed, he knew not. Hardly had he spoken when he found himself amid calm night and solitude, listening to a roar of the wind which died heavily away through the forest. He staggered against the rock, and felt it chill and damp; while a hanging twig, that had been all on fire, besprinkled his cheek with the coldest dew.

The next morning young Goodman Brown came slowly into the

street of Salem village, staring around him like a bewildered man. The good old minister was taking a walk along the graveyard to get an appetite for breakfast and meditate his sermon, and bestowed a blessing, as he passed, on Goodman Brown. He shrank from the venerable saint as if to avoid an anathema. Old Deacon Gookin was at domestic worship, and the holy words of his prayer were heard through the open window. "What God doth the wizard pray to?" quoth Goodman Brown. Goody Cloyse, that excellent old Christian, stood in the early sunshine at her own lattice, catechizing a little girl who had brought her a pint of morning's milk. Goodman Brown snatched away the child as from the grasp of the fiend himself. Turning the corner by the meeting house, he spied the head of Faith, with the pink ribbons, gazing anxiously forth, and bursting into such joy at sight of him that she skipped along the street and almost kissed her husband before the whole village. But Goodman Brown looked sternly and sadly into her face, and passed on without a greeting.

Had Goodman Brown fallen asleep in the forest and only dreamed a wild dream of a witch meeting?

Be it so, if you will; but, alas; it was a dream of evil omen for young Goodman Brown. A stern, a sad, a darkly meditative, a distrustful, if not a desperate, man did he become from the night of that fearful dream. On the Sabbath day, when the congregation were singing a holy psalm, he could not listen, because an anthem of sin rushed loudly upon his ear and drowned all the blessed strain. When the minister spoke from the pulpit, with power and fervid eloquence and with his hand on the open Bible, of the sacred truths of our religion, and of saintlike lives and triumphant deaths, and of future bliss or misery unutterable, then did Goodman Brown turn pale, dreading lest the roof should thunder down upon the gray blasphemer and his hearers. Often, awaking suddenly at midnight, he shrank from the bosom of Faith; and at morning or eventide, when the family knelt down at prayer, he scowled, and muttered to himself, and gazed sternly at his wife, and turned away. And when he had lived long, and was borne to his grave, a hoary corpse, followed by Faith, an aged woman, and children and grandchildren, a goodly procession, besides neighbors not a few, they carved no hopeful verse upon his tombstone; for his dying hour was gloom.

witches in poetry

ROBERT FROST (1874–1963)

In this poem, witches come to life in a way that they
have not in the previous selections. By their own words, they
convey what it is to be possessed.

two witches

I. The Witch of Coös

I stayed the night for shelter at a farm
Behind the mountain, with a mother and son,
Two old-believers. They did all the talking.

MOTHER.   Folks think a witch who has familiar spirits
She could call up to pass a winter evening,   5
But won't, should be burned at the stake or something.
Summoning spirits isn't "Button, button,
Who's got the button," I would have them know.

SON.   Mother can make a common table rear
And kick with two legs like an army mule.   10

MOTHER.   And when I've done it, what good have I done?
Rather than tip a table for you, let me
Tell you what Ralle the Sioux Control once told me.
He said the dead had souls, but when I asked him
How could that be—I thought the dead were souls—   15
He broke my trance. Don't that make you suspicious
That there's something the dead are keeping back?
Yes, there's something the dead are keeping back.

SON.   You wouldn't want to tell him what we have
Up attic, mother?

MOTHER.   Bones—a skeleton.   20

SON.   But the headboard of mother's bed is pushed
Against the attic door: the door is nailed.
It's harmless. Mother hears it in the night,
Halting perplexed behind the barrier
Of door and headboard. Where it wants to get   25
Is back into the cellar where it came from.

MOTHER.   We'll never let them, will we, son? We'll never!

SON.   It left the cellar forty years ago
And carried itself like a pile of dishes
Up one flight from the cellar to the kitchen,   30
Another from the kitchen to the bedroom,
Another from the bedroom to the attic,
Right past both father and mother, and neither stopped it.
Father had gone upstairs; mother was downstairs.
I was a baby: I don't know where I was.   35

MOTHER.   The only fault my husband found with me—
I went to sleep before I went to bed,
Especially in winter when the bed
Might just as well be ice and the clothes snow.
The night the bones came up the cellar stairs   40
Toffile had gone to bed alone and left me,

88 But left an open door to cool the room off
So as to sort of turn me out of it.
I was just coming to myself enough
To wonder where the cold was coming from, 45
When I heard Toffile upstairs in the bedroom
And thought I heard him downstairs in the cellar.
The board we had laid down to walk dry-shod on
When there was water in the cellar in spring
Struck the hard cellar bottom. And then someone 50
Began the stairs, two footsteps for each step,
The way a man with one leg and a crutch,
Or a little child, comes up. It wasn't Toffile:
It wasn't anyone who could be there.
The bulkhead double doors were double-locked 55
And swollen tight and buried under snow.
The cellar windows were banked up with sawdust
And swollen tight and buried under snow.
It was the bones. I knew them—and good reason.
My first impulse was to get to the knob 60
And hold the door. But the bones didn't try
The door; they halted helpless on the landing,
Waiting for things to happen in their favor.
The faintest restless rustling ran all through them.
I never could have done the thing I did 65
If the wish hadn't been too strong in me
To see how they were mounted for this walk.
I had a vision of them put together
Not like a man, but like a chandelier.
So suddenly I flung the door wide on him. 70
A moment he stood balancing with emotion,
And all but lost himself. (A tongue of fire
Flashed out and licked along his upper teeth.
Smoke rolled inside the sockets of his eyes.)
Then he came at me with one hand outstretched, 75
The way he did in life once; but this time
I struck the hand off brittle on the floor,
And fell back from him on the floor myself.
The finger-pieces slid in all directions.
(When did I see one of those pieces lately? 80

Hand me my button box—it must be there.)
I sat up on the floor and shouted, "Toffile,
It's coming up to you." It had its choice
Of the door to the cellar or the hall.
It took the hall door for the novelty,
And set off briskly for so slow a thing,
Still going every which way in the joints, though,
So that it looked like lightning or a scribble,
From the slap I had just now given its hand.
I listened till it almost climbed the stairs
From the hall to the only finished bedroom,
Before I got up to do anything;
Then ran and shouted, "Shut the bedroom door,
Toffile, for my sake!" "Company?" he said,
"Don't make me get up; I'm too warm in bed."
So lying forward weakly on the handrail
I pushed myself usptairs, and in the light
(The kitchen had been dark) I had to own
I could see nothing. "Toffile, I don't see it.
It's with us in the room, though. It's the bones."
"What bones?" "The cellar bones—out of the grave."
That made him throw his bare legs out of bed
And sit up by me and take hold of me.
I wanted to put out the light and see
If I could see it, or else mow the room,
With our arms at the level of our knees,
And bring the chalk-pile down. "I'll tell you what—
It's looking for another door to try.
The uncommonly deep snow has made him think
Of his old song, 'The Wild Colonial Boy,'
He always used to sing along the tote road.
He's after an open door to get outdoors.
Let's trap him with an open door up attic."
Toffile agreed to that, and sure enough,
Almost the moment he was given an opening,
The steps began to climb the attic stairs.
I heard them. Toffile didn't seem to hear them.
"Quick!" I slammed to the door and held the knob.
"Toffile, get nails." I made him nail the door shut

85

90

95

100

105

110

115

90   And push the headboard of the bed against it.   120
Then we asked was there anything
Up attic that we'd ever want again.
The attic was less to us than the cellar.
If the bones liked the attic, let them have it.
Let them stay in the attic. When they sometimes   125
Come down the stairs at night and stand perplexed
Behind the door and headboard of the bed,
Brushing their chalky skull with chalky fingers,
With sounds like the dry rattling of a shutter,
That's what I sit up in the dark to say—   130
To no one anymore since Toffile died.
Let them stay in the attic since they went there.
I promised Toffile to be cruel to them
For helping them be cruel once to him.

SON.   We think they had a grave down in the cellar.   135

MOTHER.   We know they had a grave down in the cellar.

SON.   We never could find out whose bones they were.

MOTHER.   Yes, we could too, son. Tell the truth for once.
They were a man's his father killed for me.
I mean a man he killed instead of me.   140
The least I could do was help dig their grave.
We were about it one night in the cellar.
Son knows the story: but 'twas not for him
To tell the truth, suppose the time had come.
Son looks surprised to see me end a lie   145
We'd kept up all these years between ourselves
So as to have it ready for outsiders.
But tonight I don't care enough to lie—
I don't remember why I ever cared.
Toffile, if he were here, I don't believe   150
Could tell you why he ever cared himself. . . .

She hadn't found the finger-bone she wanted
Among the buttons poured out in her lap.

I verified the name next morning: Toffile.
The rural letter box said Toffile Lajway.   155

II. The Pauper Witch of Grafton

Now that they've got it settled whose I be,
I'm going to tell them something they won't like:
They've got it settled wrong, and I can prove it.
Flattered I must be to have two towns fighting
To make a present of me to each other.   5
They don't dispose me, either one of them,
To spare them any trouble. Double trouble's
Always the witch's motto anyway.
I'll double theirs for both of them—you watch me.
They'll find they've got the whole thing to do over,   10
That is, if facts is what they want to go by.
They set a lot (now don't they?) by a record
Of Arthur Amy's having once been up
For Hog Reeve in March Meeting here in Warren.
I could have told them any time this twelvemonth   15
The Arthur Amy I was married to
Couldn't have been the one they say was up
In Warren at March Meeting, for the reason
He wa'n't but fifteen at the time they say.
The Arthur Amy I was married to   20
Voted the only times he ever voted,
Which wasn't many, in the town of Wentworth.
One of the times was when 'twas in the warrant
To see if the town wanted to take over
The tote road to our clearing where we lived.   25
I'll tell you who'd remember—Heman Lapish.
Their Arthur Amy was the father of mine.
So now they've dragged it through the law courts once,
I guess they'd better drag it through again.
Wentworth and Warren's both good towns to live in,   30
Only I happen to prefer to live
In Wentworth from now on; and when all's said,
Right's right, and the temptation to do right

92   When I can hurt someone by doing it
Has always been too much for me, it has.   35
I know of some folks that'd be set up
At having in their town a noted witch:
But most would have to think of the expense
That even I would be. They ought to know
That as a witch I'd often milk a bat   40
And that'd be enough to last for days.
It'd make my position stronger, think,
If I was to consent to give some sign
To make it surer that I was a witch?
It wa'n't no sign, I s'pose, when Mallice Huse   45
Said that I took him out in his old age
And rode all over everything on him
Until I'd had him worn to skin and bones,
And if I'd left him hitched unblanketed
In front of one Town Hall, I'd left him hitched   50
In front of every one in Grafton County.
Some cried shame on me not to blanket him,
The poor old man. It would have been all right
If someone hadn't said to gnaw the posts
He stood beside and leave his trademark on them,   55
So they could recognize them. Not a post
That they could hear tell of was scarified.
They made him keep on gnawing till he whined.
Then that same smarty someone said to look—
He'd bet Huse was a cribber and had gnawed   60
The crib he slept in—and as sure's you're born
They found he'd gnawed the four posts of his bed,
All four of them to splinters. What did that prove?
Not that he hadn't gnawed the hitching posts
He said he had, besides. Because a horse   65
Gnaws in the stable ain't no proof to me
He don't gnaw trees and posts and fences too.
But everybody took it for a proof.
I was a strapping girl of twenty then.
The smarty someone who spoiled everything   70
Was Arthur Amy. You know who he was.
That was the way he started courting me.

He never said much after we were married,
But I mistrusted he was none too proud
Of having interfered in the Huse business.   75
I guess he found he got more out of me
By having me a witch. Or something happened
To turn him round. He got to saying things
To undo what he'd done and make it right,
Like, "No, she ain't come back from kiting yet.   80
Last night was one of her nights out. She's kiting.
She thinks when the wind makes a night of it
She might as well herself." But he liked best
To let on he was plagued to death with me:
If anyone had seen me coming home   85
Over the ridgepole, 'stride of a broomstick,
As often as he had in the tail of the night,
He guessed they'd know what he had to put up with.
Well, I showed Arthur Amy signs enough
Off from the house as far, as we could keep   90
And from barn smells you can't wash out of plowed ground
With all the rain and snow of seven years;
And I don't mean just skulls of Rogers' Rangers
On Moosilauke, but woman signs to man,
Only bewitched so I would last him longer.   95
Up where the trees grow short, the mosses tall,
I made him gather me wet snowberries
On slippery rocks beside a waterfall.
I made him do it for me in the dark.
And he liked everything I made him do.   100
I hope if he is where he sees me now
He's so far off he can't see what I've come to.
You *can* come down from everything to nothing.
All is, if I'd a-known when I was young
And full of it, that this would be the end,   105
It doesn't seem as if I'd had the courage
To make so free and kick up in folks' faces.
I might have, but it doesn't seem as if.

commentary: the witch and the shaman: the diabolist and the visionary

"Magick," wrote the English magician Aleister Crowley, "is the Science and Art of causing change to occur in conformity with the will." Changes that "normal" human beings appear to will and bring about are far removed from this definition. In fact, Crowley and other "believers" would be apt to say that modern man, in his superficial and material attempts to change the course of things, has merely frustrated himself, and that the real power lies in an inner will, long repressed by civilized man, but tapped by the magician.

Magic is an immense subject, and most of us are familiar only with the form it takes on the stage or in the drawing room. More profound and subtle forms of it exist and can be found in shamanism and witchcraft. Shamans and witches are special beings who have learned to recognize and make use of their inner willpower in order to gain control over spirits and forces of the unknown. They possess a great degree of freedom from material restrictions—a freedom that is denied to those of us who are committed to what we call the "real" world. Distinctions between shamans and witches are sometimes difficult to make, but it seems fair to say that the shaman is somehow mythic, and that he is marked by a visionary asceticism related to that of the mystic, while the witch is associated, in the minds of most of us, with black magic and with qualities that are more worldly than ascetic, more "self-ish" than visionary. If these distinctions are valid, Don Juan and Black Elk are certainly shamans, while Anton LaVey is a witch. The shaman, in his work for the whole tribe or for society, can be thought of as representing the forces of what we generally consider good, while the witch, with his (or her) "hexes" and solitary "ghoulishness," is thought of, in the conventional sense, as evil.

It is generally agreed that shamanism is a state of being and not a profession. The shaman is a man who has been called by the unknown to a certain way of life—a man literally "possessed" by the spirits. In the words of an old Sioux chieftain:

> To the Holy Man comes in youth the knowledge that he will be holy. The Great Mystery makes him know this. Sometimes it is the Spirits who tell him. The Spirits come not in sleep always, but also when man is awake. . . . With the Spirits the Holy Man may commune always, and they teach him holy things.

Shamans must prove and continually renew their calling by inflicting extreme self-denial upon themselves:

> The Holy Man goes apart to a lone tipi and fasts and prays. Or he goes to the hills in solitude. When he returns to men he teaches them and tells them what the Great Mystery has bidden him to tell.[1]

The life of the shaman is dangerous. Much of this danger comes from the shaman's role as a public figure much depended upon by his society. In fulfilling that role he must risk voyages to the most forbidden places. The primary duty of the shaman is to send his soul to the underworld—where it guides or retrieves the dead—and to the heavens—where it intercedes for the living. The extent of the danger is indicated by the fact that shamans sometimes fail to return from these flights. At this point, the rationalist will argue that the shaman has not really gone anywhere, that he has simply put himself into a trance—a state of extreme frenzy—and has somehow remained stuck there. When death results, the rationalist will continue, it is due to extreme self-induced shock. The obvious answer to this is that the shaman's voyage is real, in all but the physi-

---

[1] Natalie Curtis, *The Indians' Book* (New York: Harper & Row, Publishers, 1907), pp. 38–39.

cal sense, which might well be the least real sense of all. Objective consciousness fails to recognize the validity and reality of the shaman's visions and voyages because it has for so long repressed the unknown—the Great Mystery—which the shaman sees and to which he flies. The closest we can come to expressing the shamanistic flight, in our terms, is to say that it is a psychological flight and that psychological states are as real as physical ones.

One way to understand the essence of the shamanistic principle is to approach it through other disciplines and forms. Black Elk and Don Juan are real shamans: they are ascetics, they have visions, they make flights to the Other World, and they are concerned with the good of a society. Shamanism is not, however, confined to medicine men or holy men: it is also the basis for other more familiar aspects of our lives. To begin with, as Ted Hughes suggests, shamanism is the principle behind the traditional heroic quest. It is primarily this fact that gives the shaman his mythic quality. The world's great culture heroes are "super-shamans"—Jesus is a good example. From an early age, he felt the call of the Great Mystery. He was an ascetic who even experienced the shaman's ritualistic fasting in the wilderness. Like all shamans, he had visions, practiced magic, and knew the power of the Other World over that of the merely physical one. Consider this incident:

> Now in the morning as he [Jesus] returned into the city, he hungered.
> And when he saw a fig tree in the way, he came to it, and found nothing thereon, but leaves only, and said unto it, Let no fruit grow on thee henceforward forever. And presently the fig tree withered away
> And when the disciples saw it, they marvelled, saying, How soon is the fig tree withered away!
> Jesus answered and said unto them, Verily I say unto you, If ye have faith, and doubt not ye shall not only do this which is done to the fig tree, but also if ye shall say unto this mountain, Be thou removed, and be thou cast into the sea; it shall be done.[2]

But the shaman's main duty is to intervene for other human beings in the Other World. Thus, Jesus, like other culture heroes, such as

[2] Matt. 21:18–22.

Attis, Osiris, and Dionysus, is most a shaman during the events surrounding his death. He dies for the good of all, descends into Hell to retrieve Adam, returns from the underworld in his resurrection, and ascends into Heaven in a final shamanistic flight. Both the shaman and the hero risk direct confrontation with the Great Mystery in the Other World so that others may live. The "scapegoat act"—the great myth of death and resurrection—is the one most basic to the shaman and the hero. For the shaman/hero, death, whether ritualistic or real, is a creative act.

The heroic quest is actually a metaphor for our own journey through life. The hero—the collective shaman—does, in an extraordinary manner, what our psyches or souls must do during what Jung calls the "process of individuation." The hero is the externalization —the collective dream representation—of each of us, as we move from birth to childhood and adulthood, and, hopefully, through the barrier of death to some form of resurrection and ascension to a new life. In purely psychological terms, the shaman/hero's quest is our own quest for the great Self within which is an expression of the entire universe. In simple terms, the shaman/hero, through his trials and tribulations, literally "finds" himself, and, in so doing, he finds the essence of all existence as well. What could have more to do with us?

It should be said, at this point, that religious ceremony in general is shamanistic in nature. Like the activities of the shaman and the myths surrounding the hero, ritual is an expression of a psychic need to relate to the unknown. For the believing Catholic, bread and wine literally "become" the body and blood of Christ during the Mass. The fact that, physically, the bread and wine remain bread and wine, does not belie the miracle that the worshipper has experienced on a higher plane of reality. For a moment, he has become a shaman, for the shaman's role is literally to "raise the spirit."

Shamanism is also expressed in art. This has been suggested in Ted Hughes' definition and illustrated in the poems collected in this section, as well as in the Indian folk tale, which owes its plot to the ritual flight of the shaman. The poet, like the shaman, can concentrate his consciousness to such a degree as to be able to tap the unknown, or, in psychological terms, the collective unconscious, out of which both the shamanistic instinct and universal art motifs arise. Both the poet and the shaman, then, are literally "mediums."

98
Thus, the poems by Coleridge and Yeats presented in this section are shamanistic flights in metaphor, in which the consciousness of the poems moves beyond the illusory physical life to reach higher states of being.

The area in which shamanism is probably most evident today is psychology. The modern psychiatrist has taken over several of the "primitive" shaman's functions. In a real sense, he uses magic—the magic of dream and free association, for example—to raise spirits from the depths, from the unconscious, be it the individual unconscious of Freud or the even more magical collective unconscious of Jung. In the case of Jung, the shamanistic flight is psychologically real in an almost literal sense, as the selection here indicates. Jung had the extrasensory and visionary powers of the shaman, and, thus, he was able to do more than simply substitute psychology for shamanism—he could actually bring to bear on his patients powers of the unknown.

Witchcraft is, in some ways, more difficult to define than is shamanism. The major problem is the discrepancy between the reputation of witches, as illustrated by the Hawthorne and Hart selections, and the witches' views of themselves. Until recently, in Western cultures, it has been dangerous to admit to being a witch let alone to describe what it was like to be one. As Anton LaVey suggests, people tend to think of witches in terms of broomsticks, cannibalism, and black masses. Now that there is a renewed interest in witchcraft, and that society's fear of witches has been lessened, at least to the extent that such people as LaVey and Sybil Leek (*Diary of a Witch*) are able to tell their stories, we can hope that the truth about witchcraft will begin to emerge from centuries of deep-seated prejudice. Unfortunately, however, we can do no more than make a beginning. Although there are many public witch-related activities on the fringes of our culture today, and although covens are apparently springing up all over the Western world, the young witches themselves appear to be in wide disagreement as to what they are. One suspects that many use witchcraft to justify tendencies toward sadism, the use of drugs, and uncontrolled sexuality. Witches have also been involved in several cult crimes, as noted in the introduction to this book. But perhaps these young witches are themselves so affected by the prejudices about witchcraft that they become stereotypes of what people have always thought that witches were. It is a known fact that this actually did occur in England and America during the witch-hunts of the past.

The LaVey and Macfarlane selections, however, do give the sense of a more firmly based phenomenon. Where witchcraft is still seriously practiced and believed in by large portions of the population, where it still speaks to the soul of a society, it would seem, according to Macfarlane, to be very real. The witch, in this kind of a situation, is a magician, usually bent on doing harm to his enemies —a kind of negative shaman. The current Western witch revival is more esoteric. LaVey's comments on the Satanic Mass contain a general justification for the practices of witches and an attempt to whitewash their tarnished image. According to him, witches simply acknowledge and worship the most powerful universal force, the force that, if we but look around us, is quite obviously in control of the world. We are all satanists at heart, he says. Traditional religions and their ethics are not in keeping with what we are; they only encourage hypocrisy, since no one can possibly live up to them. In a sense, then, LaVey and the serious Western witches hold views that are not altogether unrelated to those of many respectable revolutionaries of the spirit who speak of the importance of communicating with the unknown and expressing the true being within. Most, however, would disagree with LaVey's view of the satanic nature of that being.

Perhaps the most important point to be made about witchcraft is that, psychologically, it represents a real aspect of what the American Indian shamans call the Great Mystery. The "primitive" tribes mentioned in the Macfarlane selection recognize this reality and deal with it through their belief in witchcraft. Instinctively, they realize that to ignore the evil spirits within us all and within the universe is to ignore the good. Without the interaction of the polar forces represented by the two—light and dark, God and Satan, night and day—life would disappear. Those aspects of the human psyche that are contained in the shaman's powers are superfluous without those that are contained in the witch's. The occult is all around us, and the tension created by the interaction of magical poles is the electricity that is life. Only when we have learned to accept the shaman *and* the witch can we begin to move to a fuller understanding of our ultimate Self.

part two
mysticism

端拱冥心圖

未到彼岸不能無法
既至彼岸又焉用法
頂中常放白毫光
痴人猶待問菩薩

遣照於外
宅神於內
冥心至趣
而與吉會

元君端拱坐玄都
三疊胎仙舞八隅
沒化純陽天地合
長生因此次工夫

無心於事
無事於心
超出萬幻
雖然一雲

*Meditation, Stage 3: Separation of the spirit-body
for independent existence*

mysticism: definitions

EVELYN UNDERHILL (1875–1941)

Evelyn Underhill is a leading authority on mysticism. Although her approach is essentially Christian, the definition at which she arrives in this selection is broad enough to convey a sense of the mystical experience in general. Basic to that experience is a belief in the possibility of achieving a state of union with a supersensible reality.

FROM practical mysticism

What is Mysticism?

Those who are interested in that special attitude towards the universe which is now loosely called "mystical," find themselves beset by a multitude of persons who are constantly asking—some with real fervour, some with curiosity, and some with disdain—"What *is* mysticism?" When referred to the writings of the mystics themselves, and to other works in which this question appears to be answered, these people reply that such books are wholly incomprehensible to them.

On the other hand, the genuine inquirer will find before long a number of self-appointed apostles who are eager to answer his

103

104 question in many strange and inconsistent ways, calculated to increase rather than resolve the obscurity of his mind. He will learn that mysticism is a philosophy, an illusion, a kind of religion, a disease; that it means having visions, performing conjuring tricks, leading an idle, dreamy, and selfish life, neglecting one's business, wallowing in vague spiritual emotions, and being "in tune with the infinite." He will discover that it emancipates him from all dogmas —sometimes from all morality—and at the same time that it is very superstitious. One expert tells him that it is simply "Catholic piety," another that Walt Whitman was a typical mystic; a third assures him that all mysticism comes from the East, and supports his statement by an appeal to the mango trick. At the end of a prolonged course of lectures, sermons, tea-parties, and talks with earnest persons, the inquirer is still heard saying—too often in tones of exasperation—"What *is* mysticism?"

I dare not pretend to solve a problem which has provided so much good hunting in the past. It is indeed the object of this little essay to persuade the practical man to the one satisfactory course: that of discovering the answer for himself. Yet perhaps it will give confidence if I confess at the outset that I have discovered a definition which to me appears to cover all the ground; or at least, all that part of the ground which is worth covering. It will hardly stretch to the mango trick; but it finds room at once for the visionaries and the philosophers, for Walt Whitman and the saints.

Here is the definition:—

Mysticism is the art of union with Reality. The mystic is a person who has attained that union in greater or less degree; or who aims at and believes in such attainment.

It is not expected that the inquirer will find great comfort in this sentence when first it meets his eye. The ultimate question, "What is Reality?"—a question, perhaps, which never occurred to him before—is already forming in his mind; and he knows that it will cause him infinite distress. Only a mystic can answer it: and he, in terms which other mystics alone will understand. Therefore, for the time being, the practical man may put it on one side. All that he is asked to consider now is this: that the word "union" represents not so much a rare and unimaginable operation, as something which he is doing, in a vague, imperfect fashion, at every moment of his conscious life; and doing with intensity and thoroughness in all the more valid moments of that life. We know a thing only by uniting with it; by assimilating it; by an interpenetration of it and ourselves. It gives itself to us, just in so far as we give ourselves to it; and it is because our outflow towards things is usually so perfunctory and so languid, that our comprehension of things is so perfunctory and languid too. The great Sūfi who said that "Pilgrimage to the place of the wise, is to escape the flame of separation" spoke the literal truth. Wisdom is the fruit of communion; ignorance the inevitable portion of those who "keep themselves to themselves," and stand apart, judging, analysing the things which they have never truly known.

Because he has surrendered himself to it, "united" with it, the patriot knows his country, the artist knows the subject of his art, the lover his beloved, the saint his God, in a manner which is inconceivable as well as unattainable by the looker-on. Real knowledge, since it always implies an intuitive sympathy more or less intense, is far more accurately suggested by the symbols of touch and taste than by those of hearing and sight. True, analytic thought follows swiftly upon the contact, the apprehension, the union: and we, in our muddle-headed way, have persuaded ourselves that this is the essential part of knowledge—that it is, in fact, more important to cook the hare than to catch it. But when we get rid of this illusion and go back to the more primitive activities through which our mental kitchen gets its supplies, we see that the distinction between mystic and non-mystic is not merely that between the rationalist and the dreamer, between intellect and intuition. The question which divides them is really this: What, out of the mass of material offered to it, shall consciousness seize upon—with what aspects of the universe shall it "unite"?

It is notorious that the operations of the average human consciousness unite the self, not with things as they really are, but with images, notions, aspects of things. The verb "to be," which he uses so lightly, does not truly apply to any of the objects amongst which the practical man supposes himself to dwell. For him the hare of Reality is always ready-jugged: he conceives not the living, lovely, wild, swift-moving creature which has been sacrificed in order that he may be fed on the deplorable dish which he calls "things as they really are." So complete, indeed, is the separation of his consciousness from the facts of being, that he feels no sense of loss. He is happy enough "understanding," garnishing, assimilating the carcass from which the principle of life and growth has been ejected, and whereof only the most digestible portions have been retained. He is not "mystical."

But sometimes it is suggested to him that his knowledge is not quite so thorough as he supposed. Philosophers in particular have a way of pointing out its clumsy and superficial character; of demonstrating the fact that he habitually mistakes his own private sensations for qualities inherent in the mysterious objects of the external world. From those few qualities of colour, size, texture, and the rest, which his mind has been able to register and classify, he makes a label which registers the sum of his own experiences. This he knows, with this he "unites"; for it is his own creature. It is neat, flat, unchanging, with edges well defined: a thing one can trust. He forgets the existence of other conscious creatures, provided with their own standards of reality. Yet the sea as the fish feels it, the borage as the bee sees it, the intricate sounds of the hedgerow as heard by the rabbit, the impact of light on the eager face of the primrose, the landscape as known in its vastness to the wood-louse and ant—all these experiences, denied to him for ever, have just as much claim to the attribute of Being as his own partial and subjective interpretations of things.

Because mystery is horrible to us, we have agreed for the most part to live in a world of labels; to make of them the current coin of experience, and ignore their merely symbolic character, the infinite gradation of values which they misrepresent. We simply do not attempt to unite with Reality. But now and then that symbolic character is suddenly brought home to us. Some great emotion, some devastating visitation of beauty, love, or pain, lifts us to another level of consciousness; and we are aware for a moment of the difference between the neat collection of discrete objects and experiences which we call the world, and the height, the depth, the breadth of that living, growing, changing Fact, of which thought, life, and energy are parts, and in which we "live and move and have our being." Then we realise that our whole life is enmeshed in great and living forces; terrible because unknown. Even the power which lurks in every coal-scuttle, shines in the electric lamp, pants in the motor-omnibus, declares itself in the ineffable wonders of reproduction and growth, is supersensual. We do but perceive its results. The more sacred plane of life and energy which seems to be manifested in the forces we call "spiritual" and "emotional"—in love, anguish, ecstasy, adoration—is hidden from us too. Symptoms, appearances, are all that our intellects can discern: sudden irresistible inroads from it, all that our hearts can apprehend. The material for an intenser life, a wider, sharper consciousness, a more profound understanding of our own existence, lies at our gates. But we are separated from it, we cannot assimilate it; except in abnormal moments, we hardly know that it is there.

We now begin to attach at least a fragmentary meaning to the statement that "mysticism is the art of union with Reality." We see that the claim of such a poet as Whitman to be a mystic lies in the fact that he has achieved a passionate communion with deeper levels of life than those with which we usually deal—has thrust past the current notion of the Fact: that the claim of such a saint as Teresa is bound up with her declaration that she has achieved union with the Divine Essence itself. The visionary is a mystic when his vision mediates to him an actuality beyond the reach of the senses. The philosopher is a mystic when he passes beyond thought to the pure apprehension of truth. The active man is a mystic when he knows his actions to be a part of a greater activity. Blake, Plotinus, Joan of Arc, and John of the Cross—there is a link which binds all these together: but if he is to make use of it, the inquirer must find that link for himself. All four exhibit different forms of the working of the contemplative consciousness; a faculty which is proper to all men, though few take the trouble to develop it. Their attention to life has changed its character, sharpened its focus: and as a result they see, some a wider landscape, some a more brilliant, more significant, more detailed world than that which is apparent to the less educated, less observant vision of common sense.

The old story of Eyes and No-Eyes is really the story of the mystical and unmystical types. "No-Eyes" has fixed his attention on the fact that he is obliged to take a walk. For him the chief factor of existence is his own movement along the road; a movement which he intends to accomplish as efficiently and comfortably as he can. He asks not to know what may be on either side of the hedges. He ignores the caress of the wind until it threatens to remove his hat. He trudges along, steadily, diligently; avoiding the muddy pools, but oblivious of the light which they reflect. "Eyes" takes the walk too: and for him it is a perpetual revelation of beauty and wonder. The sunlight inebriates him, the winds delight him, the very effort of the journey is a joy. Magic presences throng the road-side, or cry salutations to him from the hidden fields. The rich world through which he moves lies in the fore-ground of his consciousness; and it gives up new secrets to him at every step. "No-Eyes," when told of his adventures, usually refuses to believe that both have gone by the same road. He fancies that his companion has been floating about in the air, or beset by agreeable hallucinations. We shall never persuade him to the contrary unless we persuade him to look for himself.

Therefore it is to a practical mysticism that the practical man is here invited: to a training of his latent faculties, a bracing and brightening of his languid consciousness, an emancipation from the fetters of appearance, a turning of his attention to new levels of the world. Thus he may become aware of the universe which the spiritual artist is always trying to disclose to the race. This amount of mystical perception—this "ordinary contemplation," as the specialists call it— is possible to all men: without it, they are not wholly conscious, nor wholly alive. It is a natural human activity, no more involving the great powers and sublime experiences of the mystical saints and philosophers than the ordinary enjoyment of music involves the special creative powers of the great musician.

As the beautiful does not exist for the artist and poet alone—though these can find in it more poignant depths of meaning than other men—so the world of Reality exists for all; and all may participate in it, unite with it, according to their measure and to the strength and purity of their desire. "For heaven ghostly," says *The Cloud of Unknowing*, "is as nigh down as up, and up as down; behind as before, before as behind, on one side as other. Inasmuch, that whoso had a true desire for to be at heaven, then that same time he were in heaven ghostly. For the high and the next way thither is run by desires, and not by paces of feet." None therefore is condemned, save by his own pride, sloth, or perversity, to the horrors of that which Blake called "single vision"—perpetual and undivided attention to the continuous cinematograph performance, which the mind has conspired with the senses to interpose between ourselves and the living world.

the tao:
the GReat way

RICHARD WILHELM, translator (1873–1930)

Taoism grew out of the teachings of the "venerable philosopher," Lao-tse, who lived in China during the sixth century
B.C. *The Secret of the Golden Flower,* a text of Chinese Yoga,
is based on the sayings of Lü-tsu, an eighth-century disciple
of Lao-tse. The *Tao* is the "Way" to the secret of the golden
flower—the mystical unity of all things, which includes the
yin and the *yang,* the polar opposites, which are female and
male, dark and light. Yoga is the practical technique leading
to the achievement of that unity.

FROM the secret of
the Golden Flower

I. Heavenly Consciousness (the Heart)

Master Lü-tsu said, That which exists through itself is called the
Way (Tao). Tao has neither name nor shape. It is the one essence,
the one primal spirit. Essence and life cannot be seen. They are
contained in the light of heaven. The light of heaven cannot be
seen. It is contained in the two eyes. To-day I will be your guide

109

110   and will first reveal to you the secret of the Golden Flower of the great One, and starting from that, I will explain the rest in detail.

The great One is the term given to that which has nothing above it. The secret of the magic of life consists in using action in order to attain non-action. One must not wish to leap over everything and penetrate directly. The maxim handed down to us is to take in hand the work on human nature (*hsing*). In doing this it is important not to take any wrong path.

The Golden Flower is the light. What colour is the light? One uses the Golden Flower as a symbol. It is the true energy of the transcendent great One. The phrase 'The lead of the water-region has but one taste' refers to it.

. . .

The work on the circulation of the light depends entirely on the backward-flowing movement, so that the thoughts (the place of heavenly consciousness, the heavenly heart) are gathered together. The heavenly heart lies between sun and moon (i.e. between the two eyes).

The *Book of the Yellow Castle* says: 'In the square inch field of the square foot house, life can be regulated.' The square foot house is the face. The square inch field in the face: what could that be other than the heavenly heart? In the middle of the square inch dwells the splendour. In the purple hall of the city of jade dwells the God of Utmost Emptiness and Life. The Confucians call it the centre of emptiness; the Buddhists, the terrace of living; the Taoists, the ancestral land, or the yellow castle, or the dark pass, or the space of former heaven. The heavenly heart is like the dwelling place, the light is the master.

Therefore when the light circulates, the energies of the whole body appear before its throne, as, when a holy king has established the capital and has laid down the fundamental rules of order, all the states approach with tribute; or as, when the master is quiet and calm, men-servants and maids obey his orders of their own accord, and each does his work.

Therefore you only have to make the light circulate: that is the deepest and most wonderful secret. The light is easy to move, but difficult to fix. If it is made to circulate long enough, then it crystallizes itself; that is the natural spirit-body. This crystallized spirit is formed beyond the nine heavens. It is the condition of which it is said in the *Book of the Seal of the Heart:* 'Silently thou fliest upward in the morning.'

In carrying out this fundamental principle you need to seek for no other methods, but must only concentrate your thoughts on it. The book *Leng Yen* says: 'By collecting the thoughts one can fly and will be born in heaven.' Heaven is not the wide blue sky but the place where corporeality is begotten in the house of the Creative. If one keeps this up for a long time there develops quite naturally, in addition to the body, yet another spirit-body.

The Golden Flower is the Elixir of Life (*Chin-tan;* literally, golden ball, golden pill). All changes of spiritual consciousness depend upon the heart. There is a secret charm which, although it works very accurately, is yet so fluid that it needs extreme intelligence and clarity, and the most complete absorption and tranquillity. People without this highest degree of intelligence and understanding do not find the way to apply the charm; people without this utmost capacity for absorption and tranquillity cannot keep fast hold of it.

. . .

2. The Primal Spirit and the Conscious Spirit

Master Lü-tsu said, In comparison with heaven and earth, man is like a mayfly. But compared to the great Way, heaven and earth, too, are like a bubble and a shadow. Only the primal spirit and the true nature overcome time and space.

The energy of the seed, like heaven and earth, is transitory, but the primal spirit is beyond the polar differences. Here is the place whence heaven and earth derive their being. When students understand how to grasp the primal spirit they overcome the polar opposites of light and darkness and tarry no longer in the three worlds.[1] But only he who has envisioned human nature's original face is able to do this.

When men are set free from the womb, the primal spirit dwells in the square inch (between the eyes), but the conscious spirit dwells below in the heart. This lower fleshly heart has the shape of a large peach: it is covered by the wings of the lungs, supported by

[1] Heaven, earth, hell.

112   the liver, and served by the bowels. This heart is dependent on the outside world. If a man does not eat for one day even, it feels extremely uncomfortable. If it hears something terrifying it throbs; if it hears something enraging it stops; if it is faced with death it becomes sad; if it sees something beautiful it is dazzled. But the heavenly heart in the head, when would it have moved in the least? Dost thou ask: Can the heavenly heart not move? Then I answer: How could the true thought in the square inch move! If it really moves, that is not good. For when ordinary men die, then it moves, but that is not good. It is best indeed if the light has already solidified into a spirit-body and its life-energy gradually penetrated the instincts and movements. But that is a secret which has not been revealed for thousands of years.

The lower heart moves like a strong, powerful commander who despises the heavenly ruler because of his wickedness, and has usurped the leadership in affairs of state. But when the primal castle can be fortified and defended, then it is as if a strong and wise ruler sat upon the throne. The eyes start the light circulating like two ministers at the right and left who support the ruler with all their might. When rule in the centre is thus in order, all those rebellious heroes will present themselves with lances reversed ready to take orders.

The way to the Elixir of Life knows as supreme magic, seed-water, spirit-fire, and thought-earth: these three. What is seed-water? It is the true, one energy of former heaven (eros). Spirit-fire is the light (logos). Thought-earth is the heavenly heart of the middle dwelling (intuition). Spirit-fire is used for effecting, thought-earth for substance, and seed-water for the foundation. Ordinary men make their bodies through thoughts. The body is not only the seven-foot-tall outer body. In the body is the anima. The anima adheres to consciousness, in order to affect it. Consciousness depends for its origin on the anima. The anima is feminine (yin), it is the substance of consciousness. As long as this consciousness is not interrupted, it continues to beget from generation to generation, and the changes of form of the anima and the transformations of substance are unceasing.

But, besides this, there is the animus in which the spirit shelters. The animus lives in the daytime in the eyes; at night it houses in the liver. When living in the eyes, it sees; when housed in the liver, it dreams. Dreams are the wanderings of the spirit through all nine heavens and all nine earths. But whoever is in a dark and with-drawn mood on waking, and chained to his bodily form, is fettered by the anima. Therefore the concentration of the animus is brought about by the circulation of the light, and in this way the spirit is maintained, the anima subjugated, and consciousness cut off. The method used by the ancients for escaping from the world consisted in melting out completely the slag of darkness in order to return to the purely creative. This is nothing more than a reduction of the anima and a completion of the animus. And the circulation of the light is the magical means of reducing the dark, and gaining mastery over the anima. Even if the work is not directed towards bringing back the Creative, but confines itself to the magical means of the circulation of the light, it is just the light that is the Creative. By means of its circulation, one returns to the Creative. If this method is followed, plenty of seed-water will be present of itself; the spirit-fire will be ignited, and the thought-earth will solidify and crystallize. And thus the holy fruit matures. The scarabaeus rolls his ball and in the ball there develops life as the result of the undivided effort of his spiritual concentration. If now an embryo can grow in manure, and shed its shells, why should not the dwelling place of our heavenly heart also be able to create a body if we concentrate the spirit upon it?

The one effective, true human nature (logos united with vitality), when it descends into the house of the Creative, divides into animus and anima. The animus is in the heavenly heart. It is of the nature of light; it is the power of lightness and purity. It is that which we have received from the great emptiness, that which is identical in form with the primordial beginning. The anima partakes of the nature of the dark. It is the energy of the heavy and the turbid; it is bound to the bodily fleshly heart. The animus loves life. The anima seeks death. All sensuous desires and impulses of anger are effects of the anima; it is the conscious spirit which after death is nourished on blood, but which, during life, is in greatest distress. The dark returns to darkness and like things attract each other according to their kind. But the pupil understands how to distil the dark anima completely so that it transforms itself into pure light (*yang*).[2]

---

[2] Light is meant here as a world principle, the positive pole, not as light that shines.

eastern mysticism and modern western man

ALAN WATTS (1915–   )

Zen Buddhism combines many of the qualities of Taoism and
Buddhism. Lao-tse and the Buddha were, in fact, contempo-
raries. Zen is a Japanese word derived from the Chinese
(Ch'an, or Ch'an-na) and, originally, from the Sanskrit
(Dhyānā) terms meaning, roughly, "enlightenment." The Zen
Buddhist, unlike many mystics, is marked by his relative lack
of other-worldliness. This is because in Zen, the primary aim
is to reach a state of mind that remains unchanged, even
while performing life's most menial chores. *Nirvana* (spiritual
freedom achieved through unity with the Buddha nature)
exists in *samsara* (the cycle of birth, life, and death). The
mystical state of *satori* (the sudden realization of the truth of
Zen) is the Zen Buddhist's goal. In this essay, Alan Watts,
one of the leading revolutionaries of the spirit, considers Zen
and the contemporary Western world.

Beat Zen, square Zen, Zen

It is as difficult for Anglo-Saxons as for the Japanese to absorb anything quite so Chinese as Zen. For though the word "Zen" is Japanese and though Japan is now its home, Zen Buddhism is the
creation of T'ang dynasty China. I do not say this as a prelude to

114

harping upon the incommunicable subtleties of alien cultures. The $\quad$
point is simply that people who feel a profound need to justify
themselves have difficulty in understanding the viewpoints of those
who do not, and the Chinese who created Zen were the same kind
of people as Lao-tzu, who, centuries before, had said, "Those who
justify themselves do not convince." For the urge to make or prove
oneself right has always jiggled the Chinese sense of the ludicrous,
since as both Confucians and Taoists—however different these philosophies in other ways—they have invariably appreciated the man
who can "come off it." To Confucius it seemed much better to be
human-hearted than righteous, and to the great Taoists, Lao-tzu
and Chuang-tzu, it was obvious that one could not be right without also being wrong, because the two were as inseparable as back
and front. As Chuang-tzu said, "Those who would have good government without its correlative misrule, and right without its correlative wrong, do not understand the principles of the universe."

To Western ears such words may sound cynical, and the Con-
fucian admiration of "reasonableness" and compromise may appear
to be a weak-kneed lack of commitment to principle. Actually they
reflect a marvellous understanding and respect for what we call the
balance of nature, human and otherwise—a universal vision of life
as the Tao or way of nature in which the good and the evil, the
creative and the destructive, the wise and the foolish are the inseparable polarities of existence. "Tao," said the *Chung-yung*, "is that
from which one cannot depart. That from which one can depart is
not the Tao." Therefore wisdom did not consist in trying to wrest
the good from the evil but in learning to "ride" them as a cork
adapts itself to the crests and troughs of the waves. At the roots
of Chinese life there is a trust in the good-and-evil of one's own
nature which is peculiarly foreign to those brought up with the
chronic uneasy conscience of the Hebrew-Christian cultures. Yet
it was always obvious to the Chinese that a man who mistrusts
himself cannot even trust his mistrust, and must therefore be hope-
lessly confused.

For rather different reasons, Japanese people tend to be as uneasy in themselves as Westerners, having a sense of social shame
quite as acute as our more metaphysical sense of sin. This was
especially true of the class most attracted to Zen, the *samurai*. Ruth
Benedict, in that very uneven work *Chrysanthemum and Sword*,

was, I think, perfectly correct in saying that the attraction of Zen to the *samurai* class was its power to get rid of an extremely awkward self-consciousness induced in the education of the young. Part and parcel of this self-consciousness is the Japanese compulsion to compete with oneself—a compulsion which turns every craft and skill into a marathon of self-discipline. Although the attraction of Zen lay in the possibility of liberation from self-consciousness, the Japanese version of Zen fought fire with fire, overcoming the "self observing the self" by bringing it to an intensity in which it exploded. How remote from the regimen of the Japanese Zen monastery are the words of the great T'ang master Lin-chi:

> In Buddhism there is no place for using effort. Just be ordinary and nothing special. Eat your food, move your bowels, pass water, and when you're tired go and lie down. The ignorant will laugh at me, but the wise will understand.

Yet the spirit of these words is just as remote from a kind of Western Zen which would employ this philosophy to justify a very self-defensive Bohemianism.

There is no single reason for the extraordinary growth of Western interest in Zen during the last twenty years. The appeal of Zen arts to the "modern" spirit in the West, the work of Suzuki, the war with Japan, the itchy fascination of "Zen stories," and attraction of a nonconceptual, experiential philosophy in the climate of scientific relativism—all these are involved. One might mention, too, the affinities between Zen and such purely Western trends as the philosophy of Wittgenstein, Existentialism, General Semantics, the metalinguistics of B. L. Whorf, and certain movements in the philosophy of science and in psychotherapy. Always in the background there is our vague disquiet with the artificiality or "antinaturalness" of both Christianity, with its politically ordered cosmology, and technology, with its imperialistic mechanization of a natural world from which man himself feels strangely alien. For both reflect a psychology in which man is identified with a conscious intelligence and will standing apart from nature to control it, like the architect-God in whose image this version of man is conceived. The disquiet arises from the suspicion that our attempt to master the world from outside is a vicious circle in which we shall be condemned to the perpetual insomnia of controlling controls and supervising supervision ad infinitum.

To the Westerner in search of the reintegration of man and nature there is an appeal far beyond the merely sentimental in the naturalism of Zen—in the landscapes of Ma-yuan and Sesshu, in an art which is simultaneously spiritual and secular, which conveys the mystical in terms of the natural, and which, indeed, never even imagined a break between them. Here is a view of the world imparting a profoundly refreshing sense of wholeness to a culture in which the spiritual and the material, the conscious and the unconscious, have been cataclysmically split. For this reason the Chinese humanism and naturalism of Zen intrigue us much more strongly than Indian Buddhism or Vedanta. These, too, have their students in the West, but their followers seem for the most part to be displaced Christians—people in search of a more plausible philosophy than Christian supernaturalism to carry on the essentially Christian search for the miraculous. The ideal man of Indian Buddhism is clearly a superman, a yogi with absolute mastery of his own nature, according perfectly with the science-fiction ideal of "men beyond mankind." But the Buddha or awakened man of Chinese Zen is "ordinary and nothing special"; he is humorously human like the Zen tramps portrayed by Mu-ch'i and Liang-k'ai. We like this because here, for the first time, is a conception of the holy man and sage who is not impossibly remote, not superhuman but fully human, and, above all, not a solemn and sexless ascetic. Furthermore, in Zen the *satori* experience of awakening to our "original inseparability" with the universe seems, however elusive, always just around the corner. One has even met people to whom it has happened, and they are no longer mysterious occultists in the Himalayas or skinny yogis in cloistered ashrams. They are just like us, and yet much more at home in the world, floating much more easily upon the ocean of transience and insecurity.

Above all, I believe that Zen appeals to many in the post-Christian West because it does not preach, moralize, and scold in the style of Hebrew-Christian prophetism. Buddhism does not deny that there is a relatively limited sphere in which human life may be improved by art and science, reason and good will. However, it regards this sphere of activity as important but nonetheless subordinate to the comparatively limitless sphere in which things are as they are, always have been, and always will be—a sphere entirely beyond the categories of good and evil, success and failure, and individual health and sickness. On the one hand, this is the sphere of the great universe. Looking out into it at night, we make no comparisons between right and wrong stars, nor between well and badly arranged constellations. Stars are by nature big and little, bright and dim. Yet the whole thing is a splendor and a marvel which sometimes makes our flesh creep with awe. On the other hand, this is also the sphere of human, everyday life which we might call existential.

For there is a standpoint from which human affairs are as much beyond right and wrong as the stars, and from which our deeds, experiences, and feelings can no more be judged than the ups and downs of a range of mountains. Though beyond moral and social valuation, this level of human life may also be seen to be just as marvellous and uncanny as the great universe itself. This feeling may become particularly acute when the individual ego tries to fathom its own nature, to plumb the inner sources of its own actions and consciousness. For here it discovers a part of itself—the inmost and greatest part—which is strange to itself and beyond its understanding and control. Odd as it may sound, the ego finds that its own center and nature is beyond itself. The more deeply I go into myself, the more I am not myself, and yet this is the very heart of me. Here I find my own inner workings functioning of themselves, spontaneously, like the rotation of the heavenly bodies and the drifting of the clouds. Strange and foreign as this aspect of myself at first seems to be, I soon realize that it *is* me, and much more me than my superficial ego. This is not fatalism or determinism, because there is no longer anyone being pushed around or determined; there is nothing that this deep "I" is not doing. The configuration of my nervous system, like the configuration of the stars, happens of itself, and this "itself" is the real "myself."

From this standpoint—and here language reveals its limitations with a vengeance—I find that I cannot help doing and experiencing, quite freely, what is always "right," in the sense that the stars are always in their "right" places. As Hsiang-yen put it,

> There's no use for artificial discipline,
> For, move as I will, I manifest the ancient Tao.

At this level, human life is beyond anxiety, for it can never make a mistake. If we live, we live; if we die, we die; if we suffer, we suffer; if we are terrified, we are terrified. There is no problem about it. A Zen master was once asked, "It is terribly hot, and how shall we escape the heat?" "Why not," he answered, "go to the place where it is neither hot nor cold?" "Where is that place?" "In summer we sweat; in winter we shiver." In Zen one does not feel guilty about dying, or being afraid, or disliking the heat. At the same time, Zen does not insist upon this point of view as something which one *ought* to adopt; it does not preach it as an ideal. For if you don't understand it, your very not understanding is also IT. There would be no bright stars without dim stars, and, without the surrounding darkness, no stars at all.

The Hebrew-Christian universe is one in which moral urgency, the anxiety to be right, embraces and penetrates everything. God, the Absolute itself, is good as against bad, and thus to be immoral or in the wrong is to feel oneself an outcast not merely from human society but also from existence itself, from the root and ground of life. To be in the wrong therefore arouses a metaphysical anxiety and sense of guilt—a state of eternal damnation—utterly disproportionate to the crime. This metaphysical guilt is so insupportable that it must eventually issue in the rejection of God and of his laws —which is just what has happened in the whole movement of modern secularism, materialism, and naturalism. Absolute morality is profoundly destructive of morality, for the sanctions which it invokes against evil are far, far too heavy. One does not cure the headache by cutting off the head. The appeal of Zen, as of other forms of Eastern philosophy, is that it unveils behind the urgent realm of good and evil a vast region of oneself about which there need be no guilt or recrimination, where at last the self is indistinguishable from God.

But the Westerner who is attracted by Zen and who would understand it deeply must have one indispensable qualification: he must understand his own culture so thoroughly that he is no longer swayed by its premises unconsciously. He must really have come to terms with the Lord God Jehovah and with his Hebrew-Christian conscience so that he can take it or leave it without fear or rebellion. He must be free of the itch to justify himself. Lacking this, his Zen will be either "beat" or "square," either a revolt from the

120 culture and social order or a new form of stuffiness and respecta-
bility. For Zen is above all the liberation of the mind from conventional thought, and this is something utterly different from rebellion
against convention, on the one hand, or adapting foreign conventions, on the other.

Conventional thought is, in brief, the confusion of the concrete
universe of nature with the conceptual things, events, and values
of linguistic and cultural symbolism. For in Taoism and Zen the
world is seen as an inseparably interrelated field or continuum, no
part of which can actually be separated from the rest or valued
above or below the rest. It was in this sense that Hui-neng, the
Sixth Patriarch, meant that "fundamentally not one thing exists,"
for he realized that things are *terms*, not entities. They exist in the
abstract world of thought, but not in the concrete world of nature.
Thus one who actually perceives or feels this to be so no longer
feels that he is an ego, except by definition. He sees that his ego
is his *persona* or social role, a somewhat arbitrary selection of experiences with which he has been taught to identify himself. (Why,
for example, do we say "I think" but not "I am beating my heart"?)
Having seen this, he continues to play his social role without being
taken in by it. He does not precipitately adopt a new role or play
the role of having no role at all. He plays it cool.

The "beat" mentality as I am thinking of it is something much
more extensive and vague than the hipster life of New York and
San Francisco. It is a younger generation's nonparticipation in "the
American Way of Life," a revolt which does not seek to change
the existing order but simply turns away from it to find the significance of life in subjective experience rather than objective achievement. It contrasts with "square" and other-directed mentality of
beguilement by social convention, unaware of the correlativity of
right and wrong, of the mutual necessity of capitalism and com-
munism to each other's existence, of the inner identity of puritanism
and lechery, or of, say, the alliance of church lobbies and organized
crime to maintain laws against gambling.

Beat Zen is a complex phenomenon. It ranges from a use of Zen
for justifying sheer caprice in art, literature, and life to a very
forceful social criticism and "digging of the universe" such as one
may find in the poetry of Ginsberg, Whalen, and Snyder, and,
rather unevenly, in Kerouac, who is always a shade too self-

conscious, too subjective, and too strident to have the flavor of Zen.

When Kerouac gives his philosophical final statement, "I don't know. I don't care. And it doesn't make any difference"—the cat is out of the bag, for there is a hostility in these words which clangs with self-defense. But just because Zen truly surpasses convention and its values, it has no need to say "To hell with it," nor to under-line with violence the fact that anything goes.

It is indeed the basic intuition of Zen that there is an ultimate standpoint from which "anything goes." In the celebrated words of the master Yun-men, "Every day is a good day." Or as is said in the *Hsin-hsin Ming:*

> If you want to get the plain truth,
> Be not concerned with right and wrong.
> The conflict between right and wrong
> Is the sickness of the mind.

But this standpoint does not exclude and is not hostile toward the distinction between right and wrong at other levels and in more limited frames of reference. The world is seen to be beyond right and wrong when it is not framed: that is to say, when we are not looking at a particular situation by itself—out of relation to the rest of the universe. Within this room there is a clear difference between up and down; out in interstellar space there is not. Within the conventional limits of a human community there are clear dis-tinctions between good and evil. But these disappear when human affairs are seen as part and parcel of the whole realm of nature. Every framework sets up a restricted field of relationships, and restriction is law or rule.

Now a skilled photographer can point his camera at almost any scene or object and create a marvellous composition by the way in which he frames and lights it. An unskilled photographer attempting the same thing creates only messes, for he does not know how to place the frame, the border of the picture, where it will be in relation to the contents. How eloquently this demonstrates that as soon as we introduce a frame anything does *not* go. But every work of art involves a frame. A frame of some kind is precisely what distinguishes a painting, a poem, a musical composition, a play, a dance, or a piece of sculpture from the rest of the world. Some artists may argue that they do not want their works to be distinguishable from the total universe, but if this be so they should not frame them in galleries and concert halls. Above all they should not sign them nor sell them. This is as immoral as selling the moon or signing one's name to a mountain. (Such an artist may perhaps be forgiven if he knows what he is doing, and prides himself inwardly, not on being a poet or painter, but a competent crook.) Only destructive little boys and vulgar excursionists go around initialling the trees.

Today there are Western artists avowedly using Zen to justify the indiscriminate framing of simply anything—blank canvases, totally silent music, torn-up bits of paper dropped on a board and stuck where they fall, or dense masses of mangled wire. The work of the composer John Cage is rather typical of this tendency. In the name of Zen, he has forsaken his earlier and promising work with the "prepared piano," to confront audiences with eight Ampex tape recorders simultaneously bellowing forth random noises. Or he has presented silent piano recitals where the performer has a score consisting of nothing but rests, plus an assistant to turn the pages, to jolt the audience into becoming aware of the multiplicity of sounds that fill the musical void—the shifting of feet and rustling of programs, the titters of embarrassment, the coughing, and the rumble of traffic outside.

There is, indeed, a considerable therapeutic value in allowing onself to be deeply aware of any sight or sound that may arise. For one thing, it brings to mind the marvel of seeing and hearing as such. For another, the profound willingness to listen to or gaze upon anything at all frees the mind from fixed preconceptions of beauty, creating, as it were, a free space in which altogether new forms and relationships may emerge. But this is therapy; it is not yet art. It is on the level of the random ramblings of a patient on the analyst's couch: very important indeed as therapy, though it is by no means the aim of psychoanalysis to substitute such ramblings for conversation and literature. Cage's work would be redeemed if he framed and presented it as a kind of group session in audiotherapy, but as a concert it is simply absurd. One may hope, however, that *after* Cage has, by such listening, set his own mind free from the composer's almost inevitable plagiarism of the forms of the past, he will present us with the new musical patterns and relationships which he has not yet uttered.

Just as the skilled photographer often amazes us with his lighting and framing of the most unlikely subjects, so there are painters and writers in the West, as well as in modern Japan, who have mastered the authentically Zen art of controlling accidents. Historically this first arose in the Far East in the appreciation of the rough texture of brush-strokes in calligraphy and painting, and in the accidental running of the glaze on bowls made for the tea ceremony. One of the classical instances of this kind of thing came about through the shattering of a fine ceramic tea caddy, belonging to one of the old Japanese tea masters. The fragments were cemented together with gold, and its owner was amazed at the way in which the random network of thin gold lines enhanced its beauty. It must be remembered, however, that this was an *objet trouvé*—an accidental effect *selected* by a man of exquisite taste, and treasured as one might treasure and exhibit a marvellous rock or a piece of driftwood. For in the Zen-inspired art of *bonseki*, or rock gardening, the stones are selected with infinite care, and though the hand of man may never have changed them it is far from true that any old stone will do. Furthermore, in calligraphy, painting, and ceramics, the accidental effects of running glaze or of flying hair-lines of the brush were accepted and presented by the artist only when he felt them to be fortuitous and unexpected marvels within the context of the work as a whole.

What goverened his judgment? What gives *certain* accidental effects in painting the same beauty as the accidental outlines of clouds? According to Zen feeling there is no precise rule, no rule, that is to say, which can be formulated in words and taught systematically. On the other hand, there is in all these things a principle of order which in Chinese philosophy is termed *li*, and which Joseph Needham has translated "organic pattern." *Li* originally meant the markings in jade, the grain in wood, and the fiber in muscle. It designates a type of order which is too multidimensional, too subtly interrelated, and too squirmingly vital to be represented in words or mechanical images. The artist has to know it as he knows how to grow his hair. He can do it again and again, but can never explain how. In Taoist philosophy this power is called *te*, or "magical virtue." It is the element of the miraculous which we feel both at the stars in heaven and at our own ability to be conscious.

124   It is the possession of *te*, then, which makes all the difference between mere scrawls and the "white writing" of Mark Tobey, which admittedly derived its inspiration from Chinese calligraphy, or the multidimensional spontaneities of Gordon Onslow-Ford, who is, by the way, a considerable master of formal Chinese writing. It is by no means a purely haphazard drooling of paint or uncontrolled wandering of the brush, for the character and taste of such artists is visible in the grace (a possible equivalent of *te*) with which their strokes are formed even when they are not trying to represent anything except strokes. It is also what makes the difference between mere patches, smudges, and trails of black ink and the work of such Japanese moderns as Sabro Hasegawa and Onchi, which is after all in the *haboku* or "rough style" tradition of Sesshu. Anyone can write absolutely illegible Japanese, but who so enchantingly as Ryokwan? If it is true that "when the wrong man uses the right means, the right means work in the wrong way," it is often also true that when the right man uses the wrong means, the wrong means work in the right way.

The real genius of Chinese and Japanese Zen artists in their use of controlled accidents goes beyond the discovery of fortuitous beauty. It lies in being able to express, at the level of artistry, the realization of that ultimate standpoint from which "anything goes" and at which "all things are of one suchness." The mere selection of any random shape to stick in a frame simply confuses the metaphysical and the artistic domains; it does not express the one in terms of the other. Set in a frame, any old mess is at once cut off from the totality of its natural context, and for this very reason its manifestation of the Tao is concealed. The formless murmur of night noises in a great city has an enchantment which immediately disappears when formally presented as music in a concert hall. A frame outlines a universe, a microcosm, and if the contents of the frame are to rank as art they must have the same quality of relationship to the whole and to each other as events in the great universe, the macrocosm of nature. In nature the accidental is always recognized in relation to what is ordered and controlled. The dark *yin* is never without the bright *yang*. Thus the painting of Sesshu, the calligraphy of Ryokwan, and the ceramic bowls of the Hagi and Karatsu schools reveal the wonder of accidents in nature through accidents in a context of highly disciplined art.

The realization of the unswerving "rightness" of whatever happens is no more manifested by utter lawlessness in social conduct than by sheer caprice in art. As Zen has been used as a pretext for the latter in our times, its use as a pretext for the former is ancient history. Many a rogue has justified himself with the Buddhist formula, "Birth-and-death (samsara) is Nirvana; worldly passions are Enlightenment." This danger is implicit in Zen because it is implicit in freedom. Power and freedom can never be safe. They are dangerous in the same way that fire and electricity are dangerous. But it is quite pitiful to see Zen used as a pretext for license when the Zen in question is no more than an idea in the head, a simple rationalization. To some extent "Zen" is so used in the underworld which often attaches itself to artistic and intellectual communities. After all, the Bohemian way of life is primarily the natural consequence of artists and writers being so absorbed in their work that they have no interest in keeping up with the Joneses. It is also a symptom of creative changes in manners and morals which at first seem as reprehensible to conservatives as new forms in art. But every such community attracts a number of weak imitators and hangers-on, especially in the great cities, and it is mostly in this class that one now finds the stereotype of the "beatnik" with his phony Zen. Yet if Zen were not the pretext for this shiftless existence, it would be something else.

Is it, then, this underworld which is described in Kerouac's *Dharma Bums?* It is generally known that *The Dharma Bums* is not a novel but a flimsily fictionized account of the author's experiences in California in 1956. To anyone who knows the milieu described, the identity of each character is plain and it is no secret that Japhy Ryder, the hero of the story, is Gary Snyder.[1] Whatever may be said of Kerouac himself and of a few other characters in the story, it would be difficult indeed to fit Snyder into any stereotype of the Bohemian underworld. He has spent a year of Zen study in Kyoto, and has recently (1959) returned for another session, perhaps for two years, this time. He is also a serious student of

---

[1] The names were changed at the last minute, and at one point "Gary" remains instead of "Japhy." The excerpt published in the Summer, 1958, *Chicago Review* under the title "Meditation in the Woods" keeps the original names.

126 Chinese, having studied with Shih-hsiang Chen at the University of California, and superbly translated a number of the poems of the Zen hermit Han-shan.[2] His own work, scattered through many periodicals, entitles him to be regarded as one of the finest poets of the San Francisco renaissance.

But Snyder is, in the best sense, a bum. His manner of life is a quietly individualistic deviation from everything expected of a "good consumer." His temporary home is a little shack without utilities on a hillside in Mill Valley, at the top of a steep trail. When he needs money he goes to sea, or works as a firewatcher or logger. Otherwise, he stays at home or goes mountain climbing, most of the time writing, studying, or practicing Zen meditation. Part of his shack is set aside as a formal "meditation hall," and the whole place is in the best Zen tradition of clean and uncluttered simplicity. But this is not a Christian or Hinayana Buddhist style of asceticism. As *The Dharma Bums* made plain, it combines a voluntary and rather joyous poverty with a rich love-life, and for Western, and much Eastern, religiosity this is the touchstone of deviltry. This is not the place to argue the complex problem of spirituality and sexuality,[3] but one can only say, "So much the worse for such religiosity." This attitude has seldom been a part of Zen, new or old, beat or square.

In *The Dharma Bums,* however, we are seeing Snyder through Kerouac's eyes, and some distortions arise because Kerouac's own Buddhism is a true beat Zen which confuses "anything goes" at the existential level with "anything goes" on the artistic and social levels. Nevertheless, there is something endearing about Kerouac's personality as a writer, something which comes out in the warmth of his admiration for Gary, and in the lusty, generous enthusiasm for life which wells up at every point in his colorful and undisciplined prose. This exuberant warmth makes it impossible to put Kerouac in the class of the beat mentality described by John Clelland-Holmes—the cool, fake-intellectual hipster searching for kicks, name-dropping bits of Zen and jazz jargon to justify a disaffiliation from society which is in fact just ordinary, callous exploitation of other people. In the North Beach, Greenwich Village,

---

[2] "Cold Mountain Poems," *Evergreen Review,* Vol. 2, No. 6, 1958.
[3] For which see Part II of [my] *Nature, Man, and Woman.* New York, 1958.

and elsewhere such characters may occasionally be found, but no one has ever heard of any of them, and their identification with the active artists and poets of these communities is pure journalistic imagination. They are, however, the shadow of a substance, the low-level caricature which always attends spiritual and cultural movements, carrying them to extremes which their authors never intended. To this extent beat Zen is sowing confusion in idealizing as art and life what is better kept to oneself as therapy.

One of the most problematic characteristics of beat Zen, shared to some extent both by the creative artists and by their imitators, is the fascination of marijuana and peyote. That many of these people "take drugs" naturally lays them wide open to the most extreme forms of righteous indignation, despite the fact that marijuana and peyote (or its synthetic derivative, mescaline) are far less harmful and habit-forming than whiskey or tobacco. In these circles the smoking of marijuana is to some extent a sacramental point of honor, a religious defiance of square authority, equivalent to the refusal of the early Christians to burn incense to the Roman gods. Conversely, it is a matter of symbolic principle, as distinct from the enforcement of rational law, for the police to condemn marijuana, and sensational arrests of those who use it always provide a convenient diversion of public attention from serious crimes that continue to be overlooked.

The claim that these substances induce states of consciousness equivalent to *satori* or mystical experience must be treated with some reserve. They certainly do not do so automatically, and some of their effects are quite unlike anything found in genuine mysticism. However, it is certainly true that for some people, perhaps with the requisite gift or ability, peyote, mescaline, or lysergic acid induce states which are distinctly favorable to mystical experience. As to marijuana, I have my doubts, though it appears to reduce the speed of subjective time.[4]

Now the underlying protestant lawlessness of beat Zen disturbs the square Zennists very seriously. For square Zen is the Zen of

[4] As a result of experiments with lysergic acid conducted since the original version of this essay was written, I have been compelled to change the opinion then expressed as to the complete dissimilarity between some of these states of consciousness and mystical experience. The problem is discussed at length in [my] essay "The New Alchemy."

established tradition in Japan with its clearly defined hierarchy, its rigid discipline, and its specific tests of *satori*. More particularly, it is the kind of Zen adopted by Westerners studying in Japan, who will before long be bringing it back home. But there is an obvious difference between square Zen and the common or garden square-ness of the Rotary Club or the Presbyterian Church. It is infinitely more imaginative, sensitive, and interesting. But it is still square because it is a quest for the *right* spiritual experience, for a *satori* which will receive the stamp (*inka*) of approval and established authority. There will even be certificates to hang on the wall.

If square Zen falls into any serious excess it is in the direction of spiritual snobbism and artistic preciousness, though I have never known an orthodox Zen teacher who could be accused of either. These gentlemen seem to take their exalted office rather lightly, respecting its dignity without standing on it. The faults of square Zen are the faults of any spiritual in-group with an esoteric discipline and degrees of initiation. Students in the lower ranks can get unpleasantly uppity about inside knowledge which they are not at liberty to divulge—"and you wouldn't understand even if I could tell you"—and are apt to dwell rather sickeningly on the immense difficulties and iron disciplines of their task. There are times, however, when this is understandable, especially when someone who is just goofing off claims that he is following the Zen ideal of "naturalness."

The student of square Zen is also inclined at times to be niggling in his recognition of parallels to Zen in other spiritual traditions. Because the essentials of Zen can never be accurately and fully formulated, being an experience and not a set of ideas, it is always possible to be critical of anything anyone says about it, neither putting up nor shutting up. Any statement about Zen, or about spiritual experience of any kind, will always leave some aspect, some subtlety, unexpressed. No one's mouth is big enough to utter the whole thing. The Western follower of Zen should also resist the temptation to associate himself with an even worse form of snobbery, the intellectual snobbery so largely characteristic of Far Eastern studies in American universities. In this particular field the fad for making humanistic studies "scientific" has gone to such wild extremes that even Suzuki is accused of being a "popularizer" instead of a serious scholar—presumably because he is a little unsystematic about footnotes and covers a vast area instead of confining himself with rigor to a single problem, *e.g.*, "An Analysis of Some Illegible and Archaic Character-forms in the Tun-huang Manuscript of the Sutra of the Sixth Patriarch." There is a proper and honorable place in scholarship for the meticulous drudge, but when he is on top instead of on tap his dangerous envy of real intelligence drives all creative scholars from the field.[5]

In its artistic expression square Zen is often rather tediously studied and precious, a fate which all too easily befalls a venerable aesthetic tradition when its techniques are so highly developed that it takes a lifetime to master any one of them. No one has then the time to go beyond the achievements of the old masters, so that new generations are condemned to endless repetition and imitation of their refinements. The student of *sumi* painting, calligraphy, *haiku* poetry, or tea ceremony can therefore get trapped in a tiresomely repetitious affectation of styles, varied only with increasingly esoteric allusions to the work of the past. When this comes to the point of imitating the old masters' happy accidents in such a way that "primitive" and "rough" effects are produced by the utmost practice and deliberation, the whole thing becomes so painful that even the wildest excesses of beat Zen art look refreshing. Indeed, it is possible that beat Zen and square Zen will so complement and rub against one another that an amazingly pure and lively Zen will arise from the hassle.

For this reason I see no really serious quarrel with either extreme. There was never a spiritual movement without its excesses and distortions. The experience of awakening which truly constitutes Zen is too timeless and universal to be injured. The extremes of beat Zen need alarm no one since, as Blake said, "the fool who persists in his folly will become wise." As for square Zen, "author-

---

[5] Suzuki, incidentally, is a very rare bird among contemporary Asians—an original thinker. He is no mere mouthpiece for any fixed tradition, and has come forth with some ideas about comparative religion and the psychology of religion which are of enormous importance, quite aside from what he has done to translate and interpret the literature of Zen. But it is just for this reason that people in square Zen and academic Sinology have their qualms about accepting him.

itative" spiritual experiences have always had a way of wearing thin, and thus of generating the demand for something genuine and unique which needs no stamp.

I have known followers of both extremes to come up with perfectly clear *satori* experiences, for since there is no real "way" to *satori* the way you are following makes very little difference.

But the quarrel *between* the extremes is of great philosophical interest, being a contemporary form of the ancient dispute between salvation by works and salvation by faith, or between what the Hindus called the ways of the monkey and of the cat. The cat—appropriately enough—follows the effortless way, since the mother cat carries her kittens. The monkey follows the hard way, since the baby monkey has to hang on to its mother's hair. Thus for beat Zen there must be no effort, no discipline, no artificial striving to attain *satori* or to be anything but what one is. But for square Zen there can be no true *satori* without years of meditation-practice under the stern supervision of a qualified master. In seventeenth-century Japan these two attitudes were *approximately* typified by the great masters Bankei and Hakuin, and it so happens that the followers of the latter "won out" and determined the present-day character of Rinzai Zen.[6]

Satori can lie along both roads. It is the concomitant of a "non-grasping" attitude of the senses to experience, and grasping can be exhausted by the discipline of directing its utmost intensity to a single, ever-elusive objective. But what makes the way of effort and will power suspect to many Westerners is not so much an inherent laziness as a thorough familiarity with the wisdom of our own culture. The square Western Zennists are often quite naïve when it comes to an understanding of Christian theology or of all that has been discovered in modern psychiatry, for both have long been concerned with the fallibility and unconscious ambivalence of the will. Both have posed problems as to the vicious circle of seeking self-surrender or of "free-associating on purpose" or of accepting

[6] Rinzai Zen is the form most widely known in the West. There is also Soto Zen, which differs somewhat in technique, but is still closer to Hakuin than to Bankei. However, Bankei should not exactly be identified with beat Zen as I have described it, for he was certainly no advocate of the life of undisciplined whimsy despite all that he said about the importance of the uncalculated life and the folly of seeking *satori*.

one's conflicts to escape from them, and to anyone who knows anything about either Christianity or psychotherapy these are very real problems. The interest of Chinese Zen and of people like Bankei is that they deal with these problems in a most direct and stimulating way, and begin to suggest some answers. But when Herrigel's Japanese archery master was asked, "How can I give up purpose on purpose?" he replied that no one had ever asked him that before. He had no answer except to go on trying blindly, for five years.

Foreign religions can be immensely attractive and highly overrated by those who know little of their own, and especially by those who have not worked through and grown out of their own. This is why the displaced or unconscious Christian can so easily use either beat or square Zen to justify himself. The one wants a philosophy to justify him in doing what he pleases. The other wants a more plausible authoritative salvation than the Church or the psychiatrists seem to be able to provide. Furthermore the atmosphere of Japanese Zen is free from all one's unpleasant childhood associations with God the Father and Jesus Christ—though I know many young Japanese who feel just the same way about their early training in Buddhism. But the true character of Zen remains almost incomprehensible to those who have not surpassed the immaturity of needing to be justified, whether before the Lord God or before a paternalistic society.

The old Chinese Zen masters were steeped in Taoism. They saw nature in its total interrelatedness, and saw that every creature and every experience is in accord with the Tao of nature just as it is. This enabled them to accept themselves as they were, moment by moment, without the least need to justify anything. They didn't do it to defend themselves or to find an excuse for getting away with murder. They didn't brag about it and set themselves apart as rather special. On the contrary, their Zen was *wu-shih*, which means approximately "nothing special" or "no fuss." But Zen is "fuss" when it is mixed up with Bohemian affectations, and "fuss" when it is imagined that the only proper way to find it is to run off to a monastery in Japan or to do special exercises in the lotus posture for five hours a day. And I will admit that the very hullabaloo about Zen, even in such an essay as this, is also fuss—but a little less so.

132   Having said that, I would like to say something for all Zen fussers, beat or square. Fuss is all right, too. If you are hung on Zen, there's no need to try to pretend that you are not. If you really want to spend some years in a Japanese monastery, there is no earthly reason why you shouldn't. Or if you want to spend your time hopping freight cars and digging Charlie Parker, it's a free country.

In the landscape of Spring there is neither better nor worse;
The flowering branches grow naturally, some long, some short.

The Prophet Ezekiel, Ernst Fuchs

mysticism and the visionary experience

In Jungian psychology, the concept of psychic wholeness is symbolized by the *mandala,* a symmetrical arrangement of the number four and its multiples, usually in the form of a circle. *Mandala* is a Sanskrit term meaning "magic circle." Ezekiel's vision presented here is a distinctly "mandalaic" one: it is dominated by the number four and by circles in the form of wheels within wheels. In mystical terms, his vision is symbolic of the wholeness that is achieved through union with God.

FROM the old testament

Ezekiel's Wheel

[1] Now it came to pass in the thirtieth year, in the fourth *month,* in the fifth *day* of the month, as I *was* among the captives by the river of Chebar, *that* the heavens were opened, and I saw visions of God. [2] In the fifth *day* of the month, which *was* the fifth year of king Jehoi'achin's captivity,[3] the word of the LORD came expressly unto Ezekiel the priest, the son of Buzi, in the land of the Chalde'ans by the river Chebar; and the hand of the LORD was there upon him.

[4] And I looked, and, behold, a whirlwind came out of the north,

a great cloud, and a fire infolding itself, and a brightness *was* about it, and out of the midst thereof as the color of amber, out of the midst of the fire. ⁵ Also out of the midst thereof *came* the likeness of four living creatures. And this *was* their appearance; they had the likeness of a man. ⁶ And every one had four faces, and every one had four wings. ⁷ And their feet *were* straight feet; and the sole of their feet *was* like the sole of a calf's foot: and they sparkled like the color of burnished brass. ⁸ And *they had* the hands of a man under their wings on their four sides; and they four had their faces and their wings. ⁹ Their wings *were* joined one to another, they turned not when they went; they went every one straight forward. ¹⁰ As for the likeness of their faces, they four had the face of a man, and the face of a lion, on the right side: and they four had the face of an ox on the left side; they four also had the face of an eagle. ¹¹ Thus *were* their faces: and their wings *were* stretched upward; two *wings* of every one *were* joined one to another, and two covered their bodies. ¹² And they went every one straight forward: whither the spirit was to go, they went; *and* they turned not when they went. ¹³ As for the likeness of the living creatures, their appearance *was* like burning coals of fire, *and* like the appearance of lamps: it went up and down among the living creatures; and the fire was bright, and out of the fire went forth lightning. ¹⁴ And the living creatures ran and returned as the appearance of a flash of lightning.

¹⁵ Now as I beheld the living creatures, behold one wheel upon the earth by the living creatures, with his four faces. ¹⁶ The appearance of the wheels and their work *was* like unto the color of a beryl: and they four had one likeness: and their appearance and their work *was* as it were a wheel in the middle of a wheel. ¹⁷ When they went, they went upon their four sides: *and* they turned not when they went. ¹⁸ As for their rings, they were so high that they were dreadful; and their rings *were* full of eyes round about them four. ¹⁹ And when the living creatures went, the wheels went by them: and when the living creatures were lifted up from the earth, the wheels were lifted up. ²⁰ Whithersoever the spirit was to go, they went, thither *was their* spirit to go; and the wheels were lifted up over against them: for the spirit of the living creature *was* in the wheels. ²¹ When those went, *these* went; and when those stood, *these* stood; and when those were lifted up from the earth, the

136 wheels were lifted up over against them: for the spirit of the living creature *was* in the wheels.

²² And the likeness of the firmament upon the heads of the living creature *was* as the color of the terrible crystal, stretched forth over their heads above. ²³ And under the firmament *were* their wings straight, the one toward the other: every one had two, which covered on this side, and every one had two, which covered on that side, their bodies. ²⁴ And when they went, I heard the noise of their wings, like the noise of great waters, as the voice of the Almighty, the voice of speech, as the noise of a host: when they stood, they let down their wings. ²⁵ And there was a voice from the firmament that *was* over their heads, when they stood, *and* had let down their wings.

²⁶ And above the firmament that *was* over their heads *was* the likeness of a throne, as the appearance of a sapphire stone: and upon the likeness of the throne *was* the likeness as the appearance of a man above upon it. ²⁷ And I saw as the color of amber, as the appearance of fire round about within it, from the appearance of his loins even upward, and from the appearance of his loins even downward, I saw as it were the appearance of fire, and it had brightness round about. ²⁸ As the appearance of the bow that is in the cloud in the day of rain, so *was* the appearance of the brightness round about.

This *was* the appearance of the likeness of the glory of the LORD. And when I saw *it,* I fell upon my face, and I heard a voice of one that spake.

Ancient of Days, William Blake

mysticism and the poetic experience

The four poets represented in this section were avowedly mystics. William Blake's poetry grew out of his own visionary experiences. Walt Whitman found the mystical reality discussed by Evelyn Underhill in the activities of a patient spider. Francis Thompson, a Catholic mystic, in his now-famous poem, conveys the sense of passionate identification with the reality that is God. In the 1950's, Thomas Merton, a Trappist monk, wrote to a friend that the burning of the barn, described in the poem included here, reminded him of a similar incident during his childhood, the mystical result of which was that "burning barns are for me great mysteries that are important. They turn out to be the whole world, and it is the Last Judgement." Merton was much concerned with Zen Buddhism and, in a sense, describes here a state of *satori*.

WILLIAM BLAKE (1757–1827)

the mental traveller

1.
I travelled through a land of men,
   A land of men and women too;
And heard and saw such dreadful things
   As cold earth-wanderers never knew.

2.

For there the babe is born in joy   5
    That was begotten in dire woe;
Just as we reap in joy the fruit
    Which we in bitter tears did sow.

3.

And if the babe is born a boy,
    He's given to a woman old,   10
Who nails him down upon a rock,
    Catches his shrieks in cups of gold.

4.

She binds strong thorns around his head,
    She pierces both his hands and feet,
She cuts his heart out at his side,   15
    To make it feel both cold and heat.

5.

Her fingers number every nerve
    Just as a miser counts his gold;
She lives upon his shrieks and cries,
    And she grows young as he grows old.   20

6.

Till he becomes a bleeding youth,
    And she becomes a virgin bright;
Then he rends up his manacles
    And binds her down for his delight.

7.

He plants himself in all her nerves   25
    Just as a husbandman his mould,
And she becomes his dwelling-place
    And garden fruitful seventyfold.

8.

An aged shadow soon he fades,
    Wandering round an earthly cot,   30
Full fillèd all with gems and gold
    Which he by industry had got.

140

9.

And these are the gems of the human soul,
  The rubies and pearls of a lovesick eye,
The countless gold of the aching heart,   35
  The martyr's groan and the lover's sigh.

10.

They are his meat, they are his drink;
  He feeds the beggar and the poor;
To the wayfaring traveller
  For ever open is his door.   40

11.

His grief is their eternal joy,
  They make the roofs and walls to ring;
Till from the fire upon the hearth
  A little female babe doth spring.

12.

And she is all of solid fire   45
  And gems and gold, that none his hand
Dares stretch to touch her baby form
  Or wrap her in his swaddling band.

13.

But she comes to the man she loves,
  If young or old or rich or poor;   50
They soon drive out the aged host,
  A beggar at another's door.

14.

He wanders weeping far away,
  Until some other take him in;
Oft blind and age-bent, sore distress'd,   55
  Until he can a maiden win.

15.

And to allay his freezing age,
  The poor man takes her in his arms;
The cottage fades before his sight,
  The garden and its lovely charms.   60

16.
The guests are scattered through the land;
   For the eye altering alters all;
The senses roll themselves in fear,
   And the flat earth becomes a ball.

17.
The stars, sun, moon, all shrink away,   65
   A desert vast without a bound,
And nothing left to eat or drink,
   And a dark desert all around:

18.
The honey of her infant lips,
   The bread and wine of her sweet smile,   70
The wild game of her roving eye,
   Do him to infancy beguile.

19.
For as he eats and drinks he grows
   Younger and younger every day,
And on the desert wild they both   75
   Wander in terror and dismay.

20.
Like the wild stag she flees away;
   Her fear plants many a thicket wild,
While he pursues her night and day,
   By various arts of love beguiled.   80

21.
By various arts of love and hate,
   Till the wild desert's planted o'er
With labyrinths of wayward love,
   Where roam the lion, wolf, and boar.

22.
Till he becomes a wayward babe,   85
   And she a weeping woman old;
Then many a lover wanders here,
   The sun and stars are nearer rolled;

142

23.
The trees bring forth sweet ecstasy
  To all who in the desert roam;   90
Till many a city there is built,
  And many a pleasant shepherd's home.

24.
But when they find the frowning babe,
  Terror strikes through the region wide:
They cry—'the babe—the babe is born!'   95
  And flee away on every side.

25.
For who dare touch the frowning form,
  His arm is withered to its root:
Bears, lions, wolves, all howling flee,
  And every tree doth shed its fruit.   100

26.
And none can touch that frowning form
  Except it be a woman old;
She nails it down upon the rock,
  And all is done as I have told.

WALT WHITMAN (1819–1892)

a noiseless patient spider

A noiseless patient spider,
I mark'd where on a little promontory it stood isolated,
Mark'd how to explore the vacant vast surrounding,
It launch'd forth filament, filament, filament, out of itself,
Ever unreeling them, ever tirelessly speeding them.   5

And you O my soul where you stand,
Surrounded, detached, in measureless oceans of space,

Ceaselessly musing, venturing, throwing, seeking the spheres to **143**
    connect them,
Till the bridge you will need be form'd, till the ductile anchor
    hold,
Till the gossamer thread you fling catch somewhere, O my soul. 10

FRANCIS THOMPSON (1859–1907)

the hound of heaven

I fled Him, down the nights and down the days;
I fled Him down the arches of the years;
I fled Him, down the labyrinthine ways
  Of my own mind; and in the mist of tears
I hid from Him, and under running laughter.   5
        Up vistaed hopes I sped;
        And shot, precipitated,
Adown Titanic glooms of chasmèd fears,
  From those strong Feet that followed, followed after
        But with unhurrying chase,   10
        And unperturbèd pace,
  Deliberate speed, majestic instancy,
        They beat—and a Voice beat
        More instant than the Feet—
"All things betray thee, who betrayest Me."   15

        I pleaded, outlaw-wise,
By many a hearted casement, curtained red,
  Trellised with intertwining charities;
(For, though I knew His love Who followèd,
        Yet was I sore adread   20
Lest, having Him, I must have naught beside);
But, if one little casement parted wide,
  The gust of His approach would clash it to.
Fear wist not to evade, as Love wist to pursue.
Across the margent of the world I fled,

144

And troubled the gold gateways of the stars,   25
Smiting for shelter on their clangèd bars;
    Fretted to dulcet jars

And silvern chatter the pale ports o' the moon.
I said to dawn, Be sudden; to eve, Be soon;   30
    With thy young skiey blossoms heap me over
      From this tremendous Lover!
Float thy vague veil about me, lest He see!
    I tempted all His servitors, but to find   35
My own betrayal in their constancy,
In faith to Him their fickleness to me,
    Their traitorous trueness, and their loyal deceit.
To all swift things for swiftness did I sue;
    Clung to the whistling mane of every wind.
      But whether they swept, smoothly fleet,   40
     The long savannahs of the blue;
       Or whether, Thunder-driven,
      They clanged his chariot 'thwart a heaven
Plashy with flying lightnings round the spurn o' their
    feet:—
    Fear wist not to evade as Love wist to pursue.   45
      Still with unhurrying chase,
      And unperturbèd pace,
    Deliberate speed, majestic instancy,
      Came on the following Feet,
      And a Voice above their beat—
"Naught shelters thee, who wilt not shelter Me."   50

I sought no more that after which I strayed
      In face of man or maid;
But still within the little children's eyes
      Seems something, something that replies;   55
They at least are for me, surely for me!
I turned me to them very wistfully;
But, just as their young eyes grew sudden fair
      With dawning answers there,
Their angel plucked them from me by the hair.   60
"Come then, ye other children, Nature's—share

With me" (said I) "your delicate fellowship;
    Let me greet you lip to lip,
    Let me twine with you caresses,
        Wantoning   65
    With our Lady-Mother's vagrant tresses,
        Banqueting
    With her in her wind-walled palace,
    Underneath her azured daïs,
    Quaffing, as your taintless way is,   70
        From a chalice
Lucent-weeping out of the dayspring."
        So it was done:
I in their delicate fellowship was one—
Drew the bolt of Nature's secrecies.   75
I knew all the swift importings
    On the wilful face of skies;
    I knew how the clouds arise
    Spumèd of the wild sea-snortings;
        All that's born or dies   80
    Rose and drooped with—made them shapers
Of mine own moods, or wailful or divine—
    With them joyed and was bereaven.
    I was heavy with the even,
    When she lit her glimmering tapers   85
    Round the day's dead sanctities.
    I laughed in the morning's eyes.
I triumphed and I saddened with all weather,
    Heaven and I wept together,
And its sweet tears were salt with mortal mine;   90
Against the red throb of its sunset-heart
        I laid my own to beat,
        And share commingling heat;
But not by that, by that, was eased my human smart.
In vain my tears were wet on Heaven's grey cheek.   95
For ah! we know not what each other says,
    These things and I; in sound *I* speak—
Their sound is but their stir, they speak by silences.
Nature, poor stepdame, cannot slake my drouth;
    Let her, if she would owe me,   100

146   Drop yon blue bosom-veil of sky, and show me
        The breasts o' her tenderness:
Never did any milk of hers once bless
        My thirsting mouth.
        Nigh and nigh draws the chase,   105
        With unperturbèd pace,
    Deliberate speed, majestic instancy;
        And past those noisèd Feet
        A voice comes yet more fleet—
  "Lo! naught contents thee, who content'st not Me."   110

Naked I wait Thy love's uplifted stroke!
My harness piece by piece Thou hast hewn from me,
        And smitten me to my knee;
    I am defenceless utterly.
    I slept, methinks, and woke,   115
And, slowly gazing, find me stripped in sleep.
In the rash lustihead of my young powers,
    I shook the pillaring hours
And pulled my life upon me; grimed with smears,
I stand amid the dust o' the mounded years—   120
My mangled youth lies dead beneath the heap.
My days have crackled and gone up in smoke,
Have puffed and burst as sun-starts on a stream.
    Yea, faileth now even dream
The dreamer, and the lute the lutanist;   125
Even the linked fantasies, in whose blossomy twist
I swung the earth a trinket at my wrist,
Are yielding; cords of all too weak account
For earth with heavy griefs so overplussed.
    Ah! is Thy love indeed   130
A weed, albeit an amaranthine weed,
Suffering no flowers except its own to mount?
    Ah! must—
    Designer infinite!—
Ah! must Thou char the wood ere Thou canst limn
    with it?   135
My freshness spent its wavering shower i' the dust;
And now my heart is as a broken fount,

Wherein tear-drippings stagnate, split down ever
    From the dank thoughts that shiver
Upon the sighful branches of my mind.   140
    Such is; what is to be?
The pulp so bitter, how shall taste the rind?
I dimly guess what Time in mists confounds;
Yet ever and anon a trumpet sounds
From the hid battlements of Eternity;   145
Those shaken mists a space unsettle, then
Round the half-glimpsèd turrets slowly wash again.
    But not ere him who summoneth
    I first have seen, enwound
With glooming robes purpureal, cypress-crowned;   150
His name I know, and what his trumpet saith.
Whether man's heart or life it be which yields
    Thee harvest, must Thy harvest fields
    Be dunged with rotten death?

    Now of that long pursuit   155
    Comes on at hand the bruit;
That Voice is round me like a bursting sea:
    "And is thy earth so marred,
    Shattered in shard on shard?
Lo, all things fly thee, for thou fliest Me!   160
    Strange, piteous, futile thing,
Wherefore should any set thee love apart?
Seeing none but I makes much of naught" (He said),
"And human love needs human meriting:
    How hast thou merited—   165
Of all man's clotted clay the dingiest clot?
    Alack, thou knowest not
How little worthy of any love thou art!
Whom wilt thou find to love ignoble thee
    Save Me, save only Me?   170
All which I took from thee I did but take,
    Not for thy harms,
But just that thou might'st seek it in My arms.
    All which thy child's mistake
Fancies as lost, I have stored for thee at home: 175

Rise, clasp My hand, and come!"

Halts by me that footfall:
Is my gloom, after all,
Shade of His hand, outstretched caressingly?
"Ah, fondest, blindest, weakest,   180
I am He Whom thou seekest!
Thou dravest love from thee, who dravest Me."

THOMAS MERTON (1915–1968)

ELEGY FOR THE MONASTERY BARN

As though an aged person were to wear
Too gay a dress
And walk about the neighborhood
Announcing the hour of her death,

So now, one summer day's end,   5
At suppertime, when wheels are still,
The long barn suddenly puts on the traitor, beauty,
And hails us with a dangerous cry,
For: "Look!" she calls to the country,
"Look how fast I dress myself in fire!"   10

Had we half guessed how long her spacious shadows
Harbored a woman's vanity
We would be less surprised to see her now
So loved, and so attended, and so feared.

She, in whose airless heart   15
We burst our veins to fill her full of hay,
Now stands apart.

She will not have us near her. Terribly, 149
Sweet Christ, how terribly her beauty burns us now!

And yet she has another legacy, 20
More delicate, to leave us, and more rare.

Who knew her solitude?
Who heard the peace downstairs
While flames ran whispering among the rafters?
Who felt the silence, there, 25
The long, hushed gallery
Clean and resigned and waiting for the fire?

Look! They have all come back to speak their sum-
    mary:
Fifty invisible cattle, the past years
Assume their solemn places one by one. 30
This is the little minute of their destiny.
Here is their meaning found. Here is their end.

Laved in the flame as in a Sacrament
The brilliant walls are holy
In their first-last hour of joy. 35

Fly from within the barn! Fly from the silence
Of this creature sanctified by fire!
Let no man stay inside to look upon the Lord!
Let no man wait within and see the Holy
One sitting in the presence of disaster 40
Thinking upon this barn His gentle doom!

A *mandala* representing the *tetraktys* in circular movement,
drawn by one of Jung's patients

mysticism in drama

WILLIAM BUTLER YEATS (1865–1939)

In the symbolic play, *The Shadowy Waters*, William Butler Yeats, the Irish poet and playwright, expresses, through Forgael's voyages, the mystical quest. Forgael's musical powers are mystical ones, and his union with Dectora is symbolic of the mystical union of the polar opposites. At the end of the play, the lovers continue the search, which is shamanistic as well as mystical, for "a country at the end of the world/Where no child's born but to outlive the moon." Together—"knitted mesh to mesh"—they "grew immortal."

the shadowy waters

(Acting Version)

PERSONS IN THE PLAY

Forgael	Sailors
Aibric	Dectora

A mast and a great sail, a large tiller, a poop rising several feet above the stage, and from the overhanging stern a lanthorn hangs. The sea or sky is represented by

151

a semicircular cloth of which nothing can be seen except a dark abyss. The persons move but little. Some sailors are discovered crouching by the sail. Forgael is asleep and Aibric standing by the tiller on the raised poop.

FIRST SAILOR It is long enough, and too long, Forgael has been bringing us through the waste places of the great sea.

SECOND SAILOR We did not meet with a ship to make a prey of these eight weeks, or any shore or island to plunder or to harry. It is a hard thing, age to be coming on me, and I not to get the chance of doing a robbery that would enable me to live quiet and honest to the end of my lifetime.

FIRST SAILOR We are out since the new moon. What is worse again, it is the way we are in a ship, the barrels empty and my throat shrivelled with drought, and nothing to quench it but water only.

FORGAEL [*in his sleep*] Yes; there, there; that hair that is the colour of burning.

FIRST SAILOR Listen to him now, calling out in his sleep.

FORGAEL [*in his sleep*] That pale forehead, that hair the colour of burning.

FIRST SAILOR Some crazy dream he is in, and believe me it is no crazier than the thought he has waking. He is not the first that has had the wits drawn out from him through shadows and fantasies.

SECOND SAILOR That is what ails him. I have been thinking it this good while.

FIRST SAILOR Do you remember that galley we sank at the time of the full moon?

SECOND SAILOR I do. We were becalmed the same night, and he sat up there playing that old harp of his until the moon had set.

FIRST SAILOR I was sleeping up there by the bulwark, and when I woke in the sound of the harp a change came over my eyes, and I could see very strange things. The dead were floating upon the sea yet, and it seemed as if the life that went out of every one of them had turned to the shape of a man-headed bird—grey they were, and they rose up of a sudden and called out with voices like our own, and flew away singing to the west. Words like this they were singing: 'Happiness beyond measure, happiness where the sun dies.'

SECOND SAILOR   I understand well what they are doing. My mother used to be talking of birds of the sort. They are sent by the lasting watchers to lead men away from this world and its women to some place of shining women that cast no shadow, having lived before the making of the earth. But I have no mind to go following him to that place.

FIRST SAILOR   Let us creep up to him and kill him in his sleep.

SECOND SAILOR   I would have made an end of him long ago, but that I was in dread of his harp. It is said that when he plays upon it he has power over all the listeners, with or without the body, seen or unseen, and any man that listens grows to be as mad as himself.

FIRST SAILOR   What way can he play it, being in his sleep?

SECOND SAILOR   But who would be our captain then to make out a course from the Bear and the Polestar, and to bring us back home?

FIRST SAILOR   I have that thought out. We must have Aibric with us. He knows the constellations as well as Forgael. He is a good hand with the sword. Join with us; be our captain, Aibric. We are agreed to put an end to Forgael, before he wakes. There is no man but will be glad of it when it is done. Join with us, and you will have the captain's share and profit.

AIBRIC   Silence! for you have taken Forgael's pay.

FIRST SAILOR   Little pay we have had this twelvemonth. We would never have turned against him if he had brought us, as he promised, into seas that would be thick with ships. That was the bargain. What is the use of knocking about and fighting as we do unless we get the chance to drink more wine and kiss more women than lasting peaceable men through their long lifetime? You will be as good a leader as ever he was himself, if you will but join us.

AIBRIC   And do you think that I will join myself
to men like you, and murder him who has been
My master from my earliest childhood up?
No! nor to a world of men like you
When Forgael's in the other scale. Come! come!
I'll answer to more purpose when you have drawn
That sword out of its scabbard.

FIRST SAILOR   You have awaked him.

154   We had best go, for we have missed this chance. [*Sailors go out.*]

FORGAEL   Have the birds passed us? I could hear your voice,
but there were others.

AIBRIC   I have seen nothing pass.

FORGAEL   You are certain of it? I never wake from sleep
But that I am afraid they may have passed;
For they're my only pilots. I have not seen them
For many days, and yet there must be many
Dying at every moment in the world.

AIBRIC   They have all but driven you crazy, and already
The sailors have been plotting for your death;
Whatever has been cried into your ears
Has lured you on to death.

FORGAEL   No; but they promised—

AIBRIC   I know their promises. You have told me all.
They are to bring you to unheard-of passion,
To some strange love the world knows nothing of,
Some Ever-living woman as you think,
One that can cast no shadow, being unearthly.
But that's all folly. Turn the ship about,
Sail home again, be some fair woman's friend;
Be satisfied to live like other men,
And drive impossible dreams away. The world
Has beautiful women to please every man.

FORGAEL   But he that gets their love after the fashion
Loves in brief longing and deceiving hope
And bodily tenderness, and finds that even
The bed of love, that in the imagination
Had seemed to be the giver of all peace,
Is no more than a wine-cup in the tasting,
And as soon finished.

AIBRIC   All that ever loved
have loved that way—there is no other way.

FORGAEL   Yet never have two lovers kissed but they
believed there was some other near at hand,
And almost wept because they could not find it.

AIBRIC   When they have twenty years; in middle life
They take a kiss for what a kiss is worth,
And let the dream go by.

FORGAEL   It's not a dream,

But the reality that makes our passion **155**
As a lamp shadow—no—no lamp, the sun.
What the world's million lips are thirsting for
Must be substantial somewhere.
AIBRIC   I have heard the Druids
Mutter such things as they awake from trance.
It may be that the dead have lit upon it,
Or those that never lived; no mortal can.
FORGAEL   I only of all living men shall find it.
AIBRIC   Then seek it in the habitable world,
Or leap into that sea and end a journey
That has no other end.
FORGAEL   I cannot answer.
I can see nothing plain; all's mystery.
Yet sometimes there's a torch inside my head
That makes all clear, but when the light is gone
I have but images, analogies,
The mystic bread, the sacramental wine,
The red rose where the two shafts of the cross,
Body and soul, waking and sleep, death, life,
Whatever meaning ancient allegorists
Have settled on, are mixed into one joy.
For what's the rose but that? miraculous cries,
Old stories about mystic marriages,
Impossible truths? But when the torch is lit
All that is impossible is certain,
I plunge in the abyss.   [*Sailors come in.*]
FIRST SAILOR   Look there! there in the mist! A ship of spices!
SECOND SAILOR   We would not have noticed her but for the sweet
    smell through the air. Ambergris and sandalwood, and all the
    herbs the witches bring from the sunrise.
FIRST SAILOR   No; but opoponax and cinnamon.
FORGAEL [*taking the tiller from Aibric*]   The Ever-living have kept
    my bargain; they have paid you on the nail.
AIBRIC   Take up that rope to make her fast while we are plunder-
    ing her.
FIRST SAILOR   There is a king on her deck and a queen. Where
    there is one woman it is certain there will be others.
AIBRIC   Speak lower or they'll hear.
FIRST SAILOR   They cannot hear; they are too much taken up with

one another. Look! he has stooped down and kissed her on the lips.

SECOND SAILOR   When she finds out we have as good men aboard she may not be too sorry in the end.

FIRST SAILOR   She will be as dangerous as a wild cat. These queens think more of the riches and the great name they get by marriage than of a ready hand and a strong body.

SFCOND SAILOR   There is nobody is natural but a robber. That is the reason the whole world goes tottering about upon its bandy legs.

AIBRIC   Run upon them now, and overpower the crew while yet asleep.

[*Sailors and Aibric go out. The clashing of swords and confused voices are heard from the other ship, which cannot be seen because of the sail.*]

FORGAEL   [*who has remained at the tiller*] There! there! They come!

Gull, gannet, or diver,
But with a man's head, or a fair woman's.
They hover over the masthead awhile
To wait their friends, but when their friends have come
They'll fly upon that secret way of theirs,
One—and one—a couple—five together.
And now they all wheel suddenly and fly
To the other side, and higher in the air,
They've gone up thither, friend's run up by friend;
They've gone to their beloved ones in the air,
In the waste of the high air, that they may wander
Among the windy meadows of the dawn.
But why are they still waiting? Why are they
Circling and circling over the masthead?
Ah! now they all look down—they'll speak of me
What the Ever-living put into their minds,
And of that shadowless unearthly woman
At the world's end. I hear the message now,
But it's all mystery. There's one that cries,
'From love and hate.' Before the sentence ends
Another breaks upon it with a cry,
'From love and death and out of sleep and waking.'
And with the cry another cry is mixed,

'What can we do, being shadows?' All mystery,
And I am drunken with a dizzy light.
But why do they still hover overhead?
Why are you circling there? Why do you linger?
Why do you not run to your desire,
Now that you have happy winged bodies?
Being too busy in the air, and the high air,
They cannot hear my voice. But why that circling?
[*The Sailors have returned. Dectora is with them.*]
[*Turning and seeing her.*] Why are you standing with your eyes
    upon me?
You are not the world's core. O no, no, no!
That cannot be the meaning of the birds.
You are not its core. My teeth are in the world,
But have not bitten yet.

DECTORA   I am a queen,
    And ask for satisfaction upon these
    Who have slain my husband and laid hands upon me.

FORGAEL   I'd set my hopes on one that had no shadow:—
    Where do you come from? who brought you to this place?
    Why do you cast a shadow? Answer me that.

DECTORA   Would that the storm that overthrew my ships,
    And drowned the treasures of nine conquered nations,
    And blew me hither to my lasting sorrow,
    Had drowned me also. But, being yet alive,
    I ask a fitting punishment for all
    That raised their hands against him.

FORGAEL   There are some
    That weigh and measure all in these waste seas—
    They that have all the wisdom that's in life,
    And all that prophesying images
    Made of dim gold rave out in secret tombs;
    They have it that the plans of kings and queens
    Are dust on the moth's wing; that nothing matters
    But laughter and tears—laughter, laughter and tears—
    That every man should carry his own soul
    Upon his shoulders.

DECTORA   You've nothing but wild words,
    And I would know if you would give me vengeance.

FORGAEL   When she finds out that I'll not let her go—
When she knows that.

DECTORA   What is that you are muttering?
That you'll not let me go? I am a queen.

FORGAEL   Although you are more beautiful than any,
I almost long that it were possible;
But if I were to put you on that ship,
With sailors that were sworn to do your will,
And you had spread a sail for home, a wind
Would rise of a sudden, or a wave so huge
It had washed among the stars and put them out,
And beat the bulwark of your ship on mine,
Until you stood before me on the deck—
As now.

DECTORA   Has wandering in these desolate seas
And listening to the cry of wind and wave
Driven you mad?

FORGAEL   But, queen, I am not mad.

DECTORA   And yet you say the water and the wind
Would rise against me.

FORGAEL   No, I am not mad—
If it be not that hearing messages
From lasting watchers that outlive the moon
At the most quiet midnight is to be stricken.

DECTORA   And did those watchers bid you take me captive?

FORGAEL   Both you and I are taken in the net.
It was their hands that plucked the winds awake
And blew you hither; and their mouths have promised
I shall have love in their immortal fashion.
They gave me that old harp of the nine spells
That is more mighty than the sun and moon,
Or than the shivering casting-net of the stars,
That none might take you from me.

DECTORA   [first trembling back from the mast where the harp is,
     and then laughing]   For a moment
Your raving of a message and a harp
More mighty than the stars half troubled me.
But all that's raving. Who is there can compel
The daughter and granddaughter of a king
To be his bedfellow?

FORGAEL   Until your lips
  Have called me their beloved, I'll not kiss them.
DECTORA   My husband and my king died at my feet,
  And yet you talk of love.
FORGAEL   The movement of time
  Is shaken in these seas, and what one does
  One moment has no might upon the moment
  That follows after.
DECTORA   I understand you now.
  You have a Druid craft of wicked music,
  Wrung from the cold women of the sea—
  A magic that can call a demon up,
  Until my body give you kiss for kiss.
FORGAEL   Your soul shall give the kiss.
DECTORA   I am not afraid
  While there's a rope to run into a noose
  Or wave to drown. But I have done with words,
  And I would have you look into my face
  And know that it is fearless.
FORGAEL   Do what you will,
  For neither I nor you can break a mesh
  Of the great golden net that is about us.
DECTORA   There's nothing in the world that's worth a fear.
    [*She passes Forgael and stands for a moment looking into his
    face.*]
  I have good reason for that thought.
                [*She runs suddenly on to the raised part of the poop.*]
                                And now
  I can put fear away as a queen should.
            [*She mounts on the bulwark, and turns toward Forgael.*]
  Fool, fool! Although you have looked into my face
  You did not see my purpose. I shall have gone
  Before a hand can touch me.
FORGAEL [*folding his arms*]   My hands are still;
  The Ever-living hold us. Do what you will,
  You cannot leap out of the golden net.
FIRST SAILOR   There is no need for you to drown. Give us our
  pardon and we will bring you home on your own ship, and make
  an end of this man that is leading us to death.
DECTORA   I promise it.

160   AIBRIC   I stand upon his side.
I'd strike a blow for him to give him time
To cast his dreams away.

FIRST SAILOR   He has put a sudden darkness over the moon.

DECTORA   Nine swords with handles of rhinoceros horn
To him that strikes him first!

FIRST SAILOR   I will strike him first. No! for that music of his might put a beast's head upon my shoulders, or it may be two heads and they devouring one another.

DECTORA   I'll give a golden galley full of fruit
That has the heady flavour of new wine
To him that wounds him to the death.

FIRST SAILOR   I'll strike at him. His spells, when he dies, will die with him and vanish away.

SECOND SAILOR   I'll strike at him.

THE OTHERS   And I! and I! And I!

[*Forgael plays upon the harp.*]

FIRST SAILOR [*falling into a dream*]   It is what they are saying, there is some person dead in the other ship; we have to go and wake him. They did not say what way he came to his end, but it was sudden.

SECOND SAILOR   You are right, you are right. We have to go to that wake.

DECTORA   He has flung a Druid spell upon the air,
And set you dreaming.

SECOND SAILOR   What way can we raise a keen, not knowing what name to call him by?

FIRST SAILOR   Come on to his ship. His name will come to mind in a moment. All I know is he died a thousand years ago, and was never yet waked.

SECOND SAILOR   How can we wake him having no ale?

FIRST SAILOR   I saw a skin of ale aboard her—a pigskin of brown ale.

THIRD SAILOR   Come to the ale, a pigskin of brown ale, a goatskin of yellow!

FIRST SAILOR [*singing*]   Brown ale and yellow; yellow and brown ale; a goatskin of yellow!

ALL [*singing*]   Brown ale and yellow; yellow and brown ale!

[*Sailors go out.*]

DECTORA   Protect me now, gods that my people swear by!

[*Aibric has risen from the ground where he had fallen. He has begun looking for his sword as if in a dream.*]

AIBRIC   Where is my sword that fell out of my hand
When I first heard the news? Ah, there it is!
[*He goes dreamily towards the sword, but Dectora runs at it and takes it up before he can reach it.*]
[*Sleepily.*] Queen, give it me.

DECTORA   No, I have need of it.

AIBRIC   Why do you need a sword? But you may keep it.
Now that he's dead I have no need of it,
For everything is gone.

A SAILOR [*calling from the other ship*]   Come hither, Aibric,
And tell me who it is that we are waking.

AIBRIC [*half to Dectora, half to himself*]   What name had that
dead king? Arthur of Britain?
No, no—not Arthur. I remember now.
It was golden-armed Iollan, and he died
Broken-hearted, having lost his queen
Through wicked spells. That is not all the tale,
For he was killed. O! O! O! O! O! O!
For golden-armed Iollan has been killed.
[*He goes out. While he has been speaking, and through part of what follows, one hears the singing of the Sailors from the other ship. Dectora stands with the sword lifted in front of Forgael. He changes the tune.*]

DECTORA   I will end all your magic on the instant.
[*Her voice becomes dreamy, and she lowers the sword slowly, and finally lets it fall. She spreads out her hair. She takes off her crown and lays it upon the deck.*]
The sword is to lie beside him in the grave.
It was in all his battles. I will spread my hair,
And wring my hands, and wail him bitterly,
For I have heard that he was proud and laughing,
Blue-eyed, and a quick runner on bare feet,
And that he died a thousand years ago.
O! O! O! O!
[*Forgael changes the tune.*]
But no, that is not it.
I knew him well, and while I heard him laughing

162   They killed him at my feet. O! O! O! O!
For golden-armed Iollan that I loved.
But what is it that made him say I loved him?
It was that harper put it in my thoughts,
But it is true. Why did they run upon him,
And beat the golden helmet with their swords?

FORGAEL   Do you now know me, lady? I am he
That you are weeping for.

DECTORA   No, for he is dead.
O! O! O! O! for golden-armed Iollan.

FORGAEL   It was so given out, but I will prove
That the grave-diggers in a dreamy frenzy
Have buried nothing but my golden arms.
Listen to that low-laughing string of the moon
And you will recollect my face and voice,
For you have listened to me playing it
These thousand years.

    [*He starts up, listening to the birds. The harp slips from his
    hands, and remains leaning against the bulwarks behind him.*]
                        What are the birds at there?
Why are they all a-flutter of a sudden?
What are you calling out above the mast?
If railing and reproach and mockery
Because I have awakened her to love
By magic strings, I'll make this answer to it:
Being driven on by voices and by dreams
That were clear messages from the Ever-living,
I have done right. What could I but obey?
And yet you make a clamour of reproach.

DECTORA [*laughing*]   Why, it's a wonder out of reckoning
That I should keen him from the full of the moon
To the horn, and he be hale and hearty.

FORGAEL   How have I wronged her now that she is merry?
But no, no, no! your cry is not against me.
You know the councils of the Ever-living,
And all the tossing of your wings is joy,
And all that murmuring's but a marriage song;
But if it be reproach, I answer this:
There is not one among you that made love
By any other means. You call it passion,

Consideration, generosity;
But it was all deceit, and flattery
To win a woman in her own despite,
For love is war, and there is hatred in it;
And if you say that she came willingly—

DECTORA   Why do you turn away and hide your face
That I would look upon for ever?

FORGAEL   My grief!

DECTORA   Have I not loved you for a thousand years?

FORGAEL   I never have been golden-armed Iollan.

DECTORA   I do not understand. I know your face
Better than my own hands.

FORGAEL   I have deceived you
Out of all reckoning.

DECTORA   Is it not true
That you were born a thousand years ago,
In islands where the children of Aengus wind
In happy dances under a windy moon,
And that you'll bring me there?

FORGAEL   I have deceived you;
I have deceived you utterly.

DECTORA   How can that be?
Is it that though your eyes are full of love
Some other woman has a claim on you,
And I've but half?

FORGAEL   O no!

DECTORA   And if there is,
If there be half a hundred more, what matter?
I'll never give another thought to it;
No, no, nor half a thought; but do not speak.
Women are hard and proud and stubborn-hearted,
Their heads being turned with praise and flattery;
And that is why their lovers are afraid
To tell them a plain story.

FORGAEL   That's not the story;
But I have done so great a wrong against you,
There is no measure that it would not burst.
I will confess it all.

DECTORA   What do I care,
Now that my body has begun to dream,

164   And you have grown to be a burning coal
In the imagination and intellect?
If something that's most fabulous were true—
If you had taken me by magic spells,
And killed a lover or husband at my feet—
I would not let you speak, for I would know
That it was yesterday and not to-day
I loved him; I would cover up my ears,
As I am doing now. [*A pause.*] Why do you weep?

FORGAEL   I weep because I've nothing for your eyes
But desolate waters and a battered ship.

DECTORA   O, why do you not lift your eyes to mine?

FORGAEL   I weep—I weep because bare night's above,
And not a roof of ivory and gold.

DECTORA   I would grow jealous of the ivory roof,
And strike the golden pillars with my hands.
I would that there was nothing in the world
But my beloved—that night and day had perished,
And all that is and all that is to be,
And all that is not the meeting of our lips.

FORGAEL   Why do you turn your eyes upon bare night?
Am I to fear the waves, or is the moon
My enemy?

DECTORA   I looked upon the moon,
Longing to knead and pull it into shape
That I might lay it on your head as a crown.
But now it is your thoughts that wander away,
For you are looking at the sea. Do you not know
How great a wrong it is to let one's thought
Wander a moment when one is in love?

    [*He has moved away. She follows him. He is looking out over
     the sea, shading his eyes.*]

Why are you looking at the sea?

FORGAEL   Look there!
There where the cloud creeps up upon the moon.

DECTORA   What is there but a troop of ash-grey birds
That fly into the west?

    [*The scene darkens, but there is a ray of light upon the figures.*]

FORGAEL   But listen, listen!

DECTORA   What is there but the crying of the birds?

FORGAEL   If you'll but listen closely to that crying
   You'll hear them calling out to one another
   With human voices.
DECTORA   Clouds have hid the moon.
   The birds cry out, what can I do but tremble?
FORGAEL   They have been circling over our heads in the air,
   But now that they have taken to the road
   We have to follow, for they are our pilots,
   They're crying out. Can you not hear their cry?—
   'There is a country at the end of the world
   Where no child's born but to outlive the moon.'
       [*The Sailors come in with Aibric. They carry torches.*]
AIBRIC   We have lit upon a treasure that's so great
   Imagination cannot reckon it.
   The hold is full—boxes of precious spice,
   Ivory images with amethyst eyes,
   Dragons with eyes of ruby. The whole ship
   Flashes as if it were a net of herrings.
   Let us return to our own country, Forgael,
   And spend it there. Have you not found this queen?
   What more have you to look for on the seas?
FORGAEL   I cannot—I am going on to the end.
   As for this woman, I think she is coming with me.
AIBRIC   Speak to him, lady, and bid him turn the ship.
   He knows that he is taking you to death;
   He cannot contradict me.
DECTORA   Is that true?
FORGAEL   I do not know for certain.
DECTORA   Carry me
   To some sure country, some familiar place.
   Have we not everything that life can give
   In having one another?
FORGAEL   How could I rest
   If I refused the messengers and pilots
   With all those sights and all that crying out?
DECTORA   I am a woman, I die at every breath.
AIBRIC [*to the Sailors*]   To the other ship, for there's no help in
   words.
   And I will follow you and cut the rope
   When I have said farewell to this man here,

166   For neither I nor any living man
            Will look upon his face again.

> [*Sailors go out, leaving one torch perhaps in a torchholder on the bulwark.*]

FORGAEL [*to Dectora*]   Go with him,
    For he will shelter you and bring you home.

AIBRIC [*taking Forgael's hand*]   I'll do it for his sake.

DECTORA   No. Take this sword
    And cut the rope, for I go on with Forgael.

AIBRIC   Farewell! Farewell! [*He goes out. The light grows stronger.*]

DECTORA   The sword is in the rope—
    The rope's in two—it falls into the sea,
    It whirls into the foam. O ancient worm,
    Dragon that loved the world and held us to it,
    You are broken, you are broken. The world drifts away,
    And I am left alone with my beloved,
    Who cannot put me from his sight for ever.
    We are alone for ever, and I laugh,
    Forgael, because you cannot put me from you.
    The mist has covered the heavens, and you and I
    Shall be alone for ever. We two—this crown—
    I half remember. It has been in my dreams.
    Bend lower, O king, that I may crown you with it.
    O flower of the branch, O bird among the leaves,
    O silver fish that my two hands have taken
    Out of the running stream, O morning star,
    Trembling in the blue heavens like a white fawn
    Upon the misty border of the wood,
    Bend lower, that I may cover you with my hair,
    For we will gaze upon this world no longer.

> [*The harp begins to burn as with fire.*]

FORGAEL [*gathering Dectora's hair about him*]   Beloved, having
        dragged the net about us,
    And knitted mesh to mesh, we grow immortal;
    And that old harp awakens of itself
    To cry aloud to the grey birds, and dreams,
    That have had dreams for father, live in us.

THE END

mysticism in fiction

HERMANN HESSE (1877–1962)

The works of Hermann Hesse have been a major rediscovery of the youth of the 1960's and the 1970's. In *Siddhartha,* Hesse is describing the mystical quest. In the chapter reprinted here, Siddhartha experiences the *Om*—the basic Sanskirt sound symbol representing the perfect unity of all things and, more specifically, the achievement of the full mystical experience.

FROM Siddhartha

Om

The wound smarted for a long time. Siddhartha took many travellers across the river who had a son or a daughter with them, and he could not see any of them without envying them, without thinking: So many people possess this very great happiness—why not I? Even wicked people, thieves and robbers have children, love them and are loved by them, except me. So childishly and illogically did he now reason; so much had he become like the ordinary people.

He now regarded people in a different light than he had previously: not very clever, not very proud and therefore all the more warm, curious and sympathetic.

168   When he now took the usual kind of travellers across, business-
men, soldiers and women, they no longer seemed alien to him as
they once had. He did not understand or share their thoughts and
views, but he shared with them life's urges and desires. Although
he had reached a high stage of self-discipline and bore his last
wound well, he now felt as if these ordinary people were his brothers. Their vanities, desires, and trivialities no longer seemed absurd
to him; they had become understandable, lovable and even worthy
of respect. There was the blind love of a mother for her child, the
blind foolish pride of a fond father for his only son, the blind eager
strivings of a young vain woman for ornament and the admiration
of men. All these little simple, foolish, but tremendously strong,
vital, passionate urges and desires no longer seemed trivial to Siddhartha. For their sake he saw people live and do great things,
travel, conduct wars, suffer and endure immensely, and he loved
them for it. He saw life, vitality, the indestructible and Brahman
in all their desires and needs. These people were worthy of love
and admiration in their blind loyalty, in their blind strength and
tenacity. With the exception of one small thing, one tiny little
thing, they lacked nothing that the sage and thinker had, and that
was the consciousness of the unity of all life. And many a time
Siddhartha even doubted whether this knowledge, this thought,
was of such great value, whether it was not also perhaps the childish self-flattery of thinkers, who were perhaps only thinking children. The men of the world were equal to the thinkers in every
other respect and were often superior to them, just as animals in
their tenacious undeviating actions in cases of necessity may often
seem superior to human beings.

Within Siddhartha there slowly grew and ripened the knowledge
of what wisdom really was and the goal of his long seeking. It was
nothing but a preparation of the soul, a capacity, a secret art of
thinking, feeling and breathing thoughts of unity at every moment
of life. This thought matured in him slowly, and it was reflected in
Vasudeva's old childlike face: harmony, knowledge of the eternal
perfection of the world, and unity.

But the wound still smarted. Siddhartha thought yearningly and
bitterly about his son, nursed his love and feeling of tenderness for
him, let the pain gnaw at him, underwent all the follies of love.
The flame did not extinguish itself.

One day, when the wound was smarting terribly, Siddhartha rowed across the river, consumed by longing, and got out of the boat with the purpose of going to the town to seek his son. The river flowed softly and gently; it was in the dry season but its voice rang out strangely. It was laughing, it was distinctly laughing! The river was laughing clearly and merrily at the old ferryman. Siddhartha stood still; he bent over the water in order to hear better. He saw his face reflected in the quietly moving water, and there was something in this reflection that reminded him of something he had forgotten and when he reflected on it, he remembered. His face resembled that of another person, whom he had once known and loved and even feared. It resembled the face of his father, the Brahmin. He remembered how once, as a youth, he had compelled his father to let him go and join the ascetics, how he had taken leave of him, how he had gone and never returned. Had not his father also suffered the same pain that he was now suffering for his son? Had not his father died long ago, alone, without having seen his son again? Did he not expect the same fate? Was it not a comedy, a strange and stupid thing, this repetition, this course of events in a fateful circle?

The river laughed. Yes, that was how it was. Everything that was not suffered to the end and finally concluded, recurred, and the same sorrows were undergone. Siddhartha climbed into the boat again and rowed back to the hut, thinking of his father, thinking of his son, laughed at by the river, in conflict with himself, verging on despair, and no less inclined to laugh aloud at himself and the whole world. The wound still smarted; he still rebelled against his fate. There was still no serenity and conquest of his suffering. Yet he was hopeful and when he returned to the hut, he was filled with an unconquerable desire to confess to Vasudeva, to disclose everything, to tell everything to the man who knew the art of listening.

Vasudeva sat in the hut weaving a basket. He no longer worked the ferryboat; his eyes were becoming weak, also his arms and hands, but unchanged and radiant were the happiness and the serene well-being in his face.

Siddhartha sat down beside the old man and slowly began to speak. He told him now what he had never mentioned before, how he had gone to the town that time, of his smarting wound, of his

170   envy at the sight of happy fathers, of his knowledge of the folly of
such feelings, of his hopeless struggle with himself. He mentioned
everything, he could tell him everything, even the most painful
things; he could disclose everything. He displayed his wound, told
him of his flight that day, how he had rowed across the river with
the object of wandering into the town, and how the river had
laughed.

As he went on speaking and Vasudeva listened to him with a
serene face, Siddhartha was more keenly aware than ever of
Vasudeva's attentiveness. He felt his troubles, his anxieties and his
secret hopes flow across to him and then return again. Disclosing
his wound to this listener was the same as bathing it in the river,
until it became cool and one with the river. As he went on talking
and confessing, Siddhartha felt more and more that this was no
longer Vasudeva, no longer a man who was listening to him. He
felt that this motionless listener was absorbing his confession as a
tree absorbs the rain, that this motionless man was the river itself,
that he was God Himself, that he was eternity itself. As Siddhartha
stopped thinking about himself and his wound, this recognition of
the change in Vasudeva possessed him, and the more he realized
it, the less strange did he find it; the more did he realize that
everything was natural and in order, that Vasudeva had long ago,
almost always been like that, only he did not quite recognize it;
indeed he himself was hardly different from him. He felt that he
now regarded Vasudeva as the people regarded the gods and that
this could not last. Inwardly, he began to take leave of Vasudeva.
In the meantime he went on talking.

When he had finished talking, Vasudeva directed his somewhat
weakened glance at him. He did not speak, but his face silently
radiated love and serenity, understanding and knowledge. He took
Siddhartha's hand, led him to the seat on the river bank, sat down
beside him and smiled at the river.

"You have heard it laugh," he said, "but you have not heard
everything. Let us listen; you will hear more."

They listened. The many-voiced song of the river echoed softly.
Siddhartha looked into the river and saw many pictures in the
flowing water. He saw his father, lonely, mourning for his son; he
saw himself, lonely, also with the bonds of longing for his faraway
son; he saw his son, also lonely, the boy eagerly advancing along

the burning path of life's desires; each one concentrating on his goal, each one obsessed by his goal, each one suffering. The river's voice was sorrowful. It sang with yearning and sadness, flowing towards its goal.

"Do you hear?" asked Vasudeva's mute glance. Siddhartha nodded.

"Listen better!" whispered Vasudeva.

Siddhartha tried to listen better. The picture of his father, his own picture, and the picture of his son all flowed into each other. Kamala's picture also appeared and flowed on, and the picture of Govinda and others emerged and passed on. They all became part of the river. It was the goal of all of them, yearning, desiring, suffering; and the river's voice was full of longing, full of smarting woe, full of insatiable desire. The river flowed on towards its goal. Siddhartha saw the river hasten, made up of himself and his relatives and all the people he had ever seen. All the waves and water hastened, suffering, towards goals, many goals, to the waterfall, to the sea, to the current, to the ocean and all goals were reached and each one was succeeded by another. The water changed to vapor and rose, became rain and came down again, became spring, brook and river, changed anew, flowed anew. But the yearning voice had altered. It still echoed sorrowfully, searchingly, but other voices accompanied it, voices of pleasure and sorrow, good and evil voices, laughing and lamenting voices, hundreds of voices, thousands of voices.

Siddhartha listened. He was now listening intently, completely absorbed, quite empty, taking in everything. He felt that he had now completely learned the art of listening. He had often heard all this before, all these numerous voices in the river, but today they sounded different. He could no longer distinguish the different voices—the merry voice from the weeping voice, the childish voice from the manly voice. They all belonged to each other: the lament of those who yearn, the laughter of the wise, the cry of indignation and the groan of the dying. They were all interwoven and interlocked, entwined in a thousand ways. And all the voices, all the goals, all the yearnings, all the sorrows, all the pleasures, all the good and evil, all of them together was the world. All of them together was the stream of events, the music of life. When Siddhartha listened attentively to this river, to this song of a thousand voices;

when he did not listen to the sorrow or laughter, when he did not bind his soul to any one particular voice and absorb it in his Self, but heard them all, the whole, the unity; then the great song of a thousand voices consisted of one word: Om—perfection.

"Do you hear?" asked Vasudeva's glance once again.

Vasudeva's smile was radiant; it hovered brightly in all the wrinkles of his old face, as the Om hovered over all the voices of the river. His smile was radiant as he looked at his friend, and now the same smile appeared on Siddhartha's face. His wound was healing, his pain was dispersing; his Self had merged into unity.

From that hour Siddhartha ceased to fight against his destiny. There shone in his face the serenity of knowledge, of one who is no longer confronted with conflict of desires, who has found salvation, who is in harmony with the stream of events, with the stream of life, full of sympathy and compassion, surrendering himself to the stream, belonging to the unity of all things.

As Vasudeva rose from the seat on the river bank, when he looked into Siddhartha's eyes and saw the serenity of knowledge shining in them, he touched his shoulder gently in his kind protective way and said: "I have waited for this hour, my friend. Now that it has arrived, let me go. I have been Vasudeva, the ferryman, for a long time. Now it is over. Farewell hut, farewell river, farewell Siddhartha."

Siddhartha bowed low before the departing man.

"I knew it," he said softly. "Are you going into the woods?"

"Yes, I am going into the woods; I am going into the unity of all things," said Vasudeva, radiant.

And so he went away. Siddhartha watched him. With great joy and gravity he watched him, saw his steps full of peace, his face glowing, his form full of light.

commentary:
the world as
a mandala

Mysticism is a subject of vast proportions. As a phenomenon, it has been known since the beginning of civilization and has had no cultural, social, or geographic boundaries. It has flourished within Christianity, Judaism, and Islam, as well as in the Far Eastern religions, and there were also elements of it present in the ancient religions of the Near East. We might get a sense of how varied the forms of mysticism can be by noting some of the groups and individuals who can, in one way or another, be considered mystical. Sufis, Taoists, Buddhists, Hindus, and spiritualists; Jesus, Saint Theresa, Plotinus, John of the Cross, Walt Whitman, Thomas Merton, William Blake, Carl Jung, W. B. Yeats, Hermann Hesse, Alan Watts, Black Elk, Carlos Castaneda's Don Juan (in fact, most shamans), Teilhard de Chardin, Joan of Arc, and Bishop Pike. The problem of defining the term under which all these varied groups and people appear is complicated by a fact to which all mystics agree—that the mystical experience cannot be communicated to the nonmystic. "What is [mystical] Reality?" asks Evelyn Underhill. "Only a mystic can answer . . . and he in terms which other mystics alone will understand." And William James writes, in *The Varieties of Religious Experience:*

> This incommunicableness of the [mystical] transport is the keynote of all mysticism. Mystical truth exists for the individual who has the transport, but for no one else.[1]

[1] William James, *The Varieties of Religious Experience* (New York: Mentor, 1968), p. 311.

174   Yet, mystics still do try, through poetry (Whitman, Blake, Merton, Thompson, John of the Cross), philosophy (Watts, Plotinus, de Chardin), or other means, to express those experiences and to convey to others the great importance that mysticism can have. Without at least some element of it, says Evelyn Underhill, men are not "wholly alive." The revolutionaries of the spirit also speak of the importance of mysticism as one of the ways in which we can move beyond the illusory technocratic life to higher states of reality.

How, then, do we define an indefinable phenomenon? An obvious place to begin is within the self. Most of us have had some mystical experience in our lives, whether in the presence of a great painting, in the course of listening to a Bach organ prelude, or during a religious ceremony. Such personal experiences are moments during which we literally "lose ourselves" in the unknown. They provide us with sufficient insight into the mystical experience to make it possible for us to understand what mystical writers are trying to convey. If, from the works collected in this section, we can determine a few of mysticism's distinguishing characteristics, we will have done well with a subject that is so much more intuitive than conceptual.

We can begin by studying the relation of the shaman to the mystic. Both shamans and mystics make flights. While the shaman's flight is to the other world, the mystic finds the other world in a flight to a higher level of consciousness within himself. Thus, what the shaman achieves is very much related to what the mystic, ostensibly through contemplation and/or certain physical disciplines, achieves. In addition, shamans themselves may be, and most probably are, mystics. Although the mystical experience can take place within a group, as in the case of the Sufis and other mystical cults, as a general rule, it is fair to say that shamanism is involved with public concerns, whereas mysticism is involved with private ones. Ezekiel's vision can serve as a symbol for what may well be the major point of agreement between all mystics. His vision was of a *mandala*, and, to mystics, all existence is a *mandala*—a magic circle that is real only as a totally integrated whole. In the course of a mystical experience, says Evelyn Underhill, we are aware "of the difference between the neat collection of discrete objects and experiences which we call the world, and the height, the depth, the breadth of that living, growing, changing Fact, of which thought, life, and energy are parts, and in which we 'live and move and have our being.'" The mystical philosophers and poets all tell us of this great totality. In the Whitman poem included here, it is symbolized by the web of a spider; for Merton, it is the burning barn; for Siddhartha, it is *Om* and the flow of the river; for the Taoists it is the *Tao* itself and the Golden Flower. Teilhard de Chardin sees the world *mandala* in terms of the union of religion and science:

> Scientifically we can envisage an almost indefinite improvement in the human organism and human society. But as soon as we try to put our dreams into practice, we realize that the problem remains indeterminate or even insoluble unless, with some partially superrational intuition, we admit the convergent properties of the world we belong to. Hence belief is unity.[2]

Another characteristic shared by all mystics is the desire to act on the knowledge of the unity of existence. All mystics strive toward some degree of direct experience of this ultimate reality. Far Eastern mysticism makes use of Yoga to empty the mind of illusory and earthly matters so as to "make room" for the reception of the Great Reality. Various catalytic techniques are used in all forms of mysticism. Most mystics would agree, however, that no amount of preparation or techniques will bring about a mystical experience if a certain ineffable quality is not present. The word that comes closest to describing this quality is *faith,* not in the sense of belief, since belief implies an act of will and a limiting of vision through prescribed concepts, but faith in the sense of total openness to all things in the world *mandala.* "Faith," writes Alan Watts, "is, above all, open-ness—an act of trust in the unknown."[3]

One quality remains to complete our portrait of the mystic: passionate commitment. Mystical visions, such as Ezekiel's, Siddhartha's, or Saint Theresa's, are nothing, if not passionate. Mysticism, like shamanism, is a technique of ecstasy, as the four poems in this section illustrate.

[2] Teilhard de Chardin, *The Phenomenon of Man* (New York: Harper & Row, Publishers, 1965), p. 284.
[3] Alan Watts, *The Book: On the Taboo Against Knowing Who You Are* (New York: Collier Books, 1968), p. 8.

176   Some further comments on these poems will serve as a useful
final step in our attempt to understand what mysticism is. Blake's
"The Mental Traveller" is an emotional vision of man's failure to
achieve the mystic's freedom from the physical. In the poem, man
is trapped in *samsara*. The Babe "is born in joy/That was begotten
in dire woe." His birth is, thus, an expression of the tension between
the polar opposites. "He's given to a Woman Old"—to Nature—
"Who nails him down upon a rock." The Christlike or Promethean
babe or the individual spirit, which has the potential to break out
of the cycle—to return man (or the individual) to his proper place
in the unity of all things—is nailed to the firmest of material and
physical foundations, the rock. This is only the beginning of an
interpretation of the poem, but it should be a sufficient indication
of the mystical elements of the subject matter, elements that are
supported by the poem's visionary quality and its passionate tone.
Whitman's "A Noiseless Patient Spider" is a simpler poem. The
spider is a symbol of the poet's soul, which sends out filaments in
all directions in its search for union with the unknown. An overwhelming passion for the unity of all things is always Whitman's
most distinguishing mark. Both the spider web itself and the poet's
soul are *mandalas* reaching out "to explore the vacant vast surrounding." Francis Thompson's "The Hound of Heaven" is a passionate love
poem. It describes, through the metaphor of the hound, the irony
of man as he turns away from and is finally overcome by the Christian's ultimate mystical experience, the union, in love, with the
divine essence, which is God. For Thomas Merton, a burning barn
becomes a vision of holiness—the holiness of the divine presence
that exists as a spark in everything and everyone, and is waiting to
burst into flame.
        Mystical experience, say the mystics, does not come frequently
to most of us, but, the fact that it does exist, that the flame is potentially there, should leave us with the anticipation that the Great
Mystery of the totality can be seen and experienced by all individuals. Mysticism is a way to the unknown that is neither old-
fashioned nor modern. It is a way that recognizes only the eternal
Now, which is past, present, and future. As T. S. Eliot said, in
Burnt Norton: "Time present and time past / Are both perhaps present in time future, / And time future contained in time past."

part three

fantasy

Oförnuftets Lekfåglar, (*The Unreason* [*Absurdity*] *of the Playbirds*),
Max Walter Svanberg

fantasy: definitions

G. K. CHESTERTON (1874–1936)

G. K. Chesterton was a controversial English novelist, essayist, and poet. One of his major interests was fantasy. In this essay, he describes the fairy tale as a high form of art meant not for children alone, but also for those adults who would not be slaves to mere fact. By way of fantasy, he says, we can recover some of the magic and enchantment that are parts of the reality around us.

FROM the ethics of elfland

My first and last philosophy, that which I believe in with unbroken certainty, I learnt in the nursery. I generally learnt it from a nurse; that is, from the solemn and star-appointed priestess at once of democracy and tradition. The things I believed most then, the things I believe most now, are the things called fairy tales. They seem to me to be the entirely reasonable things. They are not fantasies: compared with them other things are fantastic. Compared with them religion and rationalism are both abnormal, though religion is abnormally right and rationalism abnormally wrong. Fairyland is nothing but the sunny country of common sense. It is not earth that judges heaven, but heaven that judges earth; so for me at least it was not earth that criticized elfland, but elfland that criticized the earth. I knew the magic beanstalk before I had tasted beans; I was sure of the Man in the Moon before I was certain of the moon. This was at one with all popular tradition. Modern minor poets are naturalists, and talk about the bush or the brook; but the singers of the old epics and fables were supernaturalists, and talked about the gods of brook and bush. That is what the moderns mean when they say that the ancients did not 'appreciate Nature,' because they said that Nature was divine. Old nurses do not tell children about the grass, but about the fairies that dance on the grass; and the old Greeks could not see the trees for the dryads.

But I deal here with what ethic and philosophy come from being fed on fairy tales. If I were describing them in detail I could note many noble and healthy principles that arise from them. There is the chivalrous lesson of *Jack the Giant Killer*; that giants should be killed because they are gigantic. It is a manly mutiny against pride as such. For the rebel is older than all the kingdoms, and the Jacobin has more tradition than the Jacobite. There is the lesson of *Cinderella*, which is same as that of the Magnificat—*exaltavit humiles*. There is the great lesson of *Beauty and the Beast*, that a thing must be loved before it is lovable. There is the terrible allegory of the *Sleeping Beauty*, which tells how the human creature was blessed with all birthday gifts, yet cursed with death; and how death also may perhaps be softened to a sleep. But I am not concerned with any of the separate statutes of elfland, but with the whole spirit of its law, which I learnt before I could speak, and shall retain when I cannot write. I am concerned with a certain way of looking at life, which was created in me by the fairy tales, but has since been meekly ratified by the mere facts.

It might be stated this way. There are certain sequences or developments (cases of one thing following another), which are, in the true sense of the word, necessary. Such are mathematical and merely logical sequences. We in fairyland (who are the most reasonable of all creatures) admit that reason and that necessity. For instance, if the Ugly Sisters are older than Cinderella, it is (in an iron and awful sense) necessary that Cinderella is younger than the Ugly Sisters. There is no getting out of it. Haeckel may talk as much fatalism about that fact as he pleases: it really must be. If Jack is the son of a miller, a miller is the father of Jack. Cold reason decrees it from her awful throne: and we in fairyland submit. If the three brothers all ride horses, there are six animals and eighteen legs involved: that is true rationalism, and fairyland is full of it. But as I put my head over the hedge of the elves and begin to take notice of the natural world, I observed an extraordinary thing. I observed that learned men in spectacles were talking of the actual things that happened—dawn and death and so on—as if *they* were rational and inevitable. They talked as if the fact that trees bear fruit were just as necessary as the fact that two and one trees make three. But it is not. There is an enormous difference by the test of fairyland; which is the test of the imagination. You cannot *imagine* two and one not making three. But you can easily imagine trees not growing fruit; you can imagine them growing golden candlesticks or tigers hanging on by the tail. These men in spectacles spoke much of a man named Newton, who was hit by an apple, and who discovered a law. But they could not be got to see the distinction between a true law, a law of reason, and the mere fact of apples falling. If the apple hit Newton's nose, Newton's nose hit the apple. That is a true necessity; because we cannot conceive the one occurring without the other. But we can quite well conceive the apple not falling on his nose; we can fancy it flying ardently through the air to hit some other nose, of which it had a more definite dislike. We have always in our fairy tales kept this sharp distinction between the science of mental relations, in which there really are laws, and the science of physical facts, in which there are no laws, but only weird repetitions. We believe in bodily miracles, but not in mental impossibilities. We believe that a Bean-stalk climbed up to Heaven; but that does not at all confuse our convictions on the philosophical question of how many beans make five.

Here is the peculiar perfection of tone and truth in the nursery tales. The man of science says, 'Cut the stalk, and the apple will fall'; but he says it calmly, as if the one idea really led up to the other. The witch in the fairy tale says, 'Blow the horn, and the ogre's castle will fall'; but she does not say it as if it were something in which the effect obviously arose out of the cause. Doubtless she has given the advice to many champions, and has seen many castles fall, but she does not lose either her wonder or her reason. She does not muddle her head until it imagines a necessary mental connection between a horn and a falling tower. But the scientific men do muddle their heads, until they imagine a necessary mental connection between an apple leaving the tree and an apple reaching the ground. They do really talk as if they had found not only a set of marvellous facts, but a truth connecting those facts. They do talk as if the connection of two strange things physically connected them philosophically. They feel that because one incomprehensible thing constantly follows another incomprehensible thing the two together somehow make up a comprehensible thing. Two black riddles make a white answer.

In fairyland we avoid the word 'law'; but in the land of science they are singularly fond of it. Thus they will call some interesting conjecture about how forgotten folks pronounced the alphabet, Grimm's Law. But Grimm's Law is far less intellectual than Grimm's Fairy Tales. The tales are, at any rate, certainly tales; while the law is not a law. A law implies that we know the nature of the generalization and enactment; not merely that we have noticed some of the effects. If there is a law that pick-pockets shall go to prison, it implies that there is an imaginable mental connection between the idea of prison and the idea of picking pockets. And we know what the idea is. We can say why we take liberty from a man who takes liberties. But we cannot say why an egg can turn into a chicken any more than we can say why a bear could turn into a fairy prince. As ideas, the egg and the chicken are further off from each other than the bear and the prince; for no egg in itself suggests a chicken, whereas some princes do suggest bears. Granted, then, that certain transformations do happen, it is essential that we should regard them in the philosophic manner of fairy tales, not in the unphilosophic manner of science and the 'Laws of Nature'. When we are asked why eggs turn to birds or fruits fall in autumn, we must answer exactly as the fairy godmother would answer if Cinderella asked her why mice turned to horses or her clothes fell from her at twelve o'clock. We must answer that it is *magic*. It is not a 'law', for we do not understand its general formula. It is not a necessity, for though we can count on it happening practically, we have no right to say that it must always happen. It is no argument for unalterable law (as Huxley fancied) that we count on the ordinary course of things. We do not count on it; we bet on it. We risk the remote possibility of a miracle as we do that of a poisoned pancake or a world-destroying comet. We leave it out of account, not because it is a miracle and therefore an exception. All the terms used in the science books, 'law', 'necessity', 'order', 'tendency', and so on, are really unintellectual, because they assume an inner synthesis, which we do not possess. The only words that ever satisfied me as describing Nature are the terms used in the fairy books, 'charm', 'spell', 'enchantment'. They express the arbitrariness of the fact and its mystery. A tree grows fruit because it is a *magic* tree. Water runs downhill because it is bewitched. The sun shines because it is bewitched.

I deny altogether that this is fantastic or even mystical. We may have some mysticism later on; but this fairy-tale language about things is simply rational and agnostic. It is the only way I can express in words my clear and definite perception that one thing is quite distinct from another; that there is no logical connection between flying and laying eggs. It is the man who talks about 'a law' that he has never seen who is the mystic. Nay, the ordinary scientific man is strictly a sentimentalist. He is a sentimentalist in this essential sense, that he is soaked in and swept away by mere associations. He has so often seen birds fly and lay eggs that he feels as if there must be some dreamy, tender connection between the two ideas, whereas there is none. A forlorn lover might be unable to dissociate the moon from lost love; so the materialist is unable to dissociate the moon from the tide. In both cases there is no connection, except that one has seen them together. A sentimentalist might shed tears at the smell of apple-blossom, because, by a dark association of his own, it reminded him of his boyhood. So the materialist professor (though he conceals his tears) is yet a sentimentalist, because, by a dark association of his own, apple-blossoms remind him of apples. But the cool rationalist from fairyland does not see why, in the abstract, the apple tree should not grow crimson tulips; it sometimes does in his country.

This elementary wonder, however, is not a mere fancy derived from the fairy tales; on the contrary, all the fire of the fairy tales is derived from this. Just as we all like love tales because there is an instinct of sex, we all like astonishing tales because they touch the nerve of the ancient instinct of astonishment. This is proved by the fact that when we are very young children we do not need fairy tales: we only need tales. Mere life is interesting enough. A child of seven is excited by being told that Tommy opened a door and saw a dragon. But a child of three is excited by being told that

184   Tommy opened a door. Boys like romantic tales; but babies like realistic tales—because they find them romantic. In fact, a baby is about the only person, I should think, to whom a modern realistic novel could be read without boring him. This proves that even nursery tales only echo an almost pre-natal leap of interest and amazement. These tales say that apples were golden only to refresh the forgotten moment when we found that they were green. They make rivers run with wine only to make us remember, for one wild moment, that they run with water. I have said that this is wholly reasonable and even agnostic. And, indeed, on this point I am all for the higher agnosticism; its better name is Ignorance. We have all read in scientific books, and, indeed, in all romances, the story of the man who has forgotten his name. This man walks about the streets and can see and appreciate everything; only he cannot remember who he is. Well, every man is that man in the story. Every man has forgotten who he is. One may understand the cosmos, but never the ego; the self is more distant than any star. Thou shalt love the Lord thy God; but thou shalt not know thyself. We are all under the same mental calamity; we have all forgotten our names. We have all forgotten what we really are. All that we call common sense and rationality and practicality and positivism only means that for certain dead levels of our life we forget that we have forgotten. All that we call spirit and art and ecstasy only means that for one awful instant we remember that we forget.

But though (like the man without memory in the novel) we walk the streets with a sort of half-witted admiration, still it is admiration. It is admiration in English and not only admiration in Latin. The wonder has a positive element of praise. This is the next milestone to be definitely marked on our road through fairyland. I shall speak in the next chapter about optimists and pessimists in their intellectual aspect, so far as they have one. Here I am only trying to describe the enormous emotions which cannot be described. And the strongest emotion was that life was as precious as it was puzzling. It was an ecstasy because it was an adventure; it was an adventure because it was an opportunity. The goodness of the fairy tale was not affected by the fact that there might be more dragons than princesses; it was good to be in a fairy tale. The test of all happiness is gratitude; and I felt grateful, though I hardly knew to whom. Children are grateful when Santa Claus puts in their stockings gifts of toys or sweets. Could I not be grateful to Santa Claus when he put in my stocking the gift of two miraculous legs? We thank people for birthday presents of cigars and slippers. Can I thank no one for the birthday present of birth?

There were, then, these two first feelings, indefensible and indisputable. The world was a shock, but it was not merely shocking; existence was a surprise, but it was a pleasant surprise. In fact, all my first views were exactly uttered in a riddle that stuck in my brain from boyhood. The question was, 'What did the first frog say?' And the answer was, 'Lord, how you made me jump!' That says succinctly all that I am saying. God made the frog jump; but the frog prefers jumping. But when these things are settled there enters the second great principle of the fairy philosophy.

Anyone can see it who will simply read *Grimm's Fairy Tales* or the fine collections of Mr. Andrew Lang. For the pleasure of pedantry I will call it the Doctrine of Conditional Joy. Touchstone talked of much virtue in an 'if'; according to elfin ethics, all virtue is in an 'if'. The note of the fairy utterance always is, 'You may live in a palace of gold and sapphire, *if* you do not say the word "cow"'; or 'You may live happily with the King's daughter, *if* you do not show her an onion'. The vision always hangs upon a veto. All the dizzy and colossal things conceded depend upon one small thing withheld. All the wild and whirling things that are let loose depend upon one thing that is forbidden. Mr. W. B. Yeats, in his exquisite and piercing elfin poetry, describes the elves as lawless; they plunge in innocent anarchy on the unbridled horses of the air—

> Ride on the crest of the dishevelled tide,
> And dance upon the mountains like a flame.

It is a dreadful thing to say that Mr. W. B. Yeats does not understand fairyland. But I do say it. He is an ironical Irishman, full of intellectual reactions. He is not stupid enough to understand fairyland. Fairies prefer people of the yokel type like myself; people who gape and grin and do as they are told. Mr. Yeats reads into elfland all the righteous insurrection of his own race. But the lawlessness of Ireland is a Christian lawlessness, founded on reason and justice. The Fenian is rebelling against something he understands only too well; but the true citizen of fairyland is obeying

186   something that he does not understand at all. In the fairy tale an incomprehensible happiness rests upon an incomprehensible condition. A box is opened, and all evils fly out. A word is forgotten, and cities perish. A lamp is lit, and love flies away. A flower is plucked, and human lives are forfeited. An apple is eaten, and the hope of God is gone.

the fairy tale

JACOB LUDWIG CARL GRIMM (1785–1863) and WILHELM CARL GRIMM (1786–1859)

The Brothers Grimm are the world's best known creators and collectors of fairy tale. "The Frog Prince" is one of their better-known tales and is a good example of Professor J. R. R. Tolkien's point that a true fairy tale is one that ostensibly accepts as reality the fantastic world developed within it. In the relationship of the frog and the princess, certain facts of human nature are expressed even more directly than is the case in most realistic literature.

the frog prince

In the old times, when it was still of some use to wish for the thing one wanted, there lived a King whose daughters were all handsome, but the youngest was so beautiful that the sun himself, who has seen so much, wondered each time he shone over her because of her beauty. Near the royal castle there was a great dark wood, and in the wood under an old linden-tree was a well; and when the day was hot, the King's daughter used to go forth into the wood and sit by the brink of the cool well, and if the time seemed long, she would take out a golden ball, and throw it up and catch it again, and this was her favourite pastime.

188 Now it happened one day that the golden ball, instead of falling back into the maiden's little hand which had sent it aloft, dropped to the ground near the edge of the well and rolled in. The king's daughter followed it with her eyes as it sank, but the well was deep, so deep that the bottom could not be seen. Then she began to weep, and she wept and wept as if she could never be comforted. And in the midst of her weeping she heard a voice saying to her,

"What ails thee, king's daughter? thy tears would melt a heart of stone."

And when she looked to see where the voice came from, there was nothing but a frog stretching his thick ugly head out of the water.

"Oh, is it you, old waddler?" said she; "I weep because my golden ball has fallen into the well."

"Never mind, do not weep," answered the frog; "I can help you; but what will you give me if I fetch up your ball again?"

"Whatever you like, dear frog," said she; "any of my clothes, my pearls and jewels, or even the golden crown that I wear."

"Thy clothes, thy pearls and jewels, and thy golden crown are not for me," answered the frog; "but if thou wouldst love me, and have me for thy companion and play-fellow, and let me sit by thee at table, and eat from thy plate, and drink from thy cup, and sleep in thy little bed,—if thou wouldst promise all this, then would I dive below the water and fetch thee thy golden ball again."

"Oh yes," she answered; "I will promise it all, whatever you want, if you will only get me my ball again."

But she thought to herself, "What nonsense he talks! as if he could do anything but sit in the water and croak with the other frogs, or could possibly be any one's companion."

But the frog, as soon as he heard her promise, drew his head under the water and sank down out of sight, but after a while he came to the surface again with the ball in his mouth, and he threw it on the grass.

The King's daughter was overjoyed to see her pretty plaything again, and she caught it up and ran off with it.

"Stop, stop!" cried the frog; "take me up too; I cannot run as fast as you!"

But it was of no use, for croak, croak after her as he might, she would not listen to him, but made haste home, and very soon forgot all about the poor frog, who had to betake himself to his well again.

The next day, when the King's daughter was sitting at table with the King and all the court, and eating from her golden plate, there came something pitter patter up the marble stairs, and then there came a knocking at the door, and a voice crying "Youngest King's daughter, let me in!"

And she got up and ran to see who it could be, but when she opened the door, there was the frog sitting outside. Then she shut the door hastily and went back to her seat, feeling very uneasy. The King noticed how quickly her heart was beating, and said,

"My child, what are you afraid of? is there a giant standing at the door ready to carry you away?"

"Oh no," answered she; "no giant, but a horrid frog."

"And what does the frog want?" asked the King.

"O dear father," answered she, "when I was sitting by the well yesterday, and playing with my golden ball, it fell into the water, and while I was crying for the loss of it, the frog came and got it again for me on condition I would let him be my companion, but I never thought that he could leave the water and come after me; but now there he is outside the door, and he wants to come in to me."

And then they all heard him knocking the second time and crying,

> "Youngest King's daughter,
> Open to me!
> By the well water
> What promised you me?
> Youngest King's daughter
> Now open to me!"

"That which thou hast promised must thou perform," said the King; "so go now and let him in."

So she went and opened the door, and the frog hopped in, following at her heels, till she reached her chair. Then he stopped and cried,

"Lift me up to sit by you."

But she delayed doing so until the King ordered her. When once the frog was on the chair, he wanted to get on the table, and there he sat and said,

"Now push your golden plate a little nearer, so that we may eat together."

And so she did, but everybody might see how unwilling she was, and the frog feasted heartily, but every morsel seemed to stick in her throat.

"I have had enough now," said the frog at last, "and as I am tired, you must carry me to your room, and make ready your silken bed, and we will lie down and go to sleep."

Then the King's daughter began to weep, and was afraid of the cold frog, that nothing would satisfy him but he must sleep in her pretty clean bed. Now the King grew angry with her, saying,

"That which thou hast promised in thy time of necessity, must thou now perform."

So she picked up the frog with her finger and thumb, carried him upstairs and put him in a corner, and when she had lain down to sleep, he came creeping up, saying, "I am tired and want sleep as much as you; take me up, or I will tell your father."

Then she felt beside herself with rage, and picking him up, she threw him with all her strength against the wall, crying,

"Now will you be quiet, you horrid frog!"

But as he fell, he ceased to be a frog, and became all at once a prince with beautiful kind eyes. And it came to pass that, with her father's consent, they became bride and bridegroom. And he told her how a wicked witch had bound him by her spells, and how no one but she alone could have released him, and that they two would go together to his father's kingdom. And there came to the door a carriage drawn by eight white horses, with white plumes on their heads, and with golden harness, and behind the carriage was standing faithful Henry, the servant of the young prince. Now, faithful Henry had suffered such care and pain when his master was turned into a frog, that he had been obliged to wear three iron bands over his heart, to keep it from breaking with trouble and anxiety. When the carriage started to take the prince to his kingdom, and faithful Henry had helped them both in, he got up behind, and was full of joy at his master's deliverance. And when they had gone a part of the way, the prince heard a sound at the

back of the carriage, as if something had broken, and he turned
round and cried,
  "Henry, the wheel must be breaking!" but Henry answered,

> "The wheel does not break,
> 'Tis the band round my heart
> That, to lessen its ache,
> When I grieved for your sake,
> I bound round my heart."

Again, and yet once again there was the same sound, and the
prince thought it must be the wheel breaking, but it was the breaking of the other bands from faithful Henry's heart, because it was
now so relieved and happy.

the fairy tale
in poetry

The characters of fairy tale continue to live in other art forms. Here, the Frog Prince reappears in two poems by contemporary poets. In the first, James Scully evokes a sense of magic and mystery through his portrayal of a frog who takes on the archaic and eerie qualities of a fairy-tale figure bursting into reality from the depths of time. In her poem, Stevie Smith works from within the mind of the same character in his state as frog waiting to be disenchanted. One suspects that, for the poet, disenchantment refers to more relevant magic than merely being turned from a frog into a prince.

JAMES SCULLY (1937–   )

facing up

A croak out of the marsh in the dark hollow,
drowned chord roaming.
It broke into our sleep.

                    Then
this March morning, plopped in the dooryard—
that old familiar amphibian

5

192

marooned on the crabgrass (a more rugged green)
unmoving, and bigger than life
being blurted out.

        Unbeautiful   10
who turned up, perhaps, for air.

. . . It is the Frog Prince
under a spell of wishing, just under
a cold archaic smile,

having come so far, in mottled skin   15
green and darker green
like dappled leaf, sick, bewitched,

through shades, through clammy depth
coming to be kissed.

STEVIE SMITH (1902–   )

the frog prince

I am a frog,
I live under a spell,
I live at the bottom
Of a green well.

And here I must wait   5
Until a maiden places me
on her royal pillow,
And kisses me,
In her father's palace.

The story is familiar,   10
Everybody knows it well,

194 But do other enchanted people feel as nervous
As I do? The stories do not tell,

Ask if they will be happier
When the changes come,   15
As already they are fairly happy
In a frog's doom?

I have been a frog now
For a hundred years
And in all this time   *   20
I have not shed many tears,

I am happy, I like the life,
Can swim for many a mile
(When I have hopped to the river)
And am for ever agile.   25

And the quietness,
Yes, I like to be quiet
I am habituated
To a quiet life,

But always when I think these thoughts   30
As I sit in my well
Another thought comes to me and says:
It is part of the spell

To be happy
To work up contentment   35
To make much of being a frog
To fear disenchantment

Says, It will be *heavenly*
To be set free,
Cries, *Heavenly* the girl who disenchants   40
And the royal times, *heavenly*,
And I think it will be.

Come, then, royal girl and royal times,

Come quickly,
I can be happy until you come
But I cannot be heavenly,

45

Only disenchanted people
Can be heavenly.

The King and Queen of Hearts, Sir John Tenniel

the fantasy classic

LEWIS CARROLL (1832–1898)

"Down the Rabbit-Hole" is the first chapter of *Alice's Adventures in Wonderland,* a work originally written by Lewis Carroll (C. L. Dodgson) for his young friend, Alice Liddell. It serves here as a representative, along with "The Frog Prince," of a branch of fantasy usually called Children's Literature. Now, however, the "Alice Books" are universally recognized as classics, with appeal to adult readers as well as to young ones.

FROM alice's adventures in wonderland

Down the Rabbit-Hole

Alice was beginning to get very tired of sitting by her sister on the bank, and of having nothing to do: once or twice she had peeped into the book her sister was reading, but it had no pictures or conversations in it, 'and what is the use of a book,' thought Alice, 'without pictures or conversation?'

So she was considering in her own mind (as well as she could, for the hot day made her feel very sleepy and stupid) whether the pleasure of making a daisy-chain would be worth the trouble of getting up and picking the daisies, when suddenly a White Rabbit with pink eyes ran close by her.

There was nothing so *very* remarkable in that; nor did Alice think it so *very* much out of the way to hear the Rabbit say to itself, 'Oh dear! Oh dear! I shall be too late!' (when she thought it over afterwards, it occurred to her that she ought to have wondered at this, but at the time it all seemed quite natural); but when the Rabbit actually *took a watch out of its waistcoat-pocket*, and looked at it, and then hurried on, Alice started to her feet, for it flashed across her mind that she had never before seen a rabbit with either a waistcoat-pocket, or a watch to take out of it, and burning with curiosity, she ran across the field after it, and fortunately was just in time to see it pop down a large rabbit-hole under the hedge.

In another moment down went Alice after it, never once considering how in the world she was to get out again.

The rabbit-hole went straight on like a tunnel for some way, and then dipped suddenly down, so suddenly that Alice had not a moment to think about stopping herself before she found herself falling down a very deep well.

Either the well was very deep, or she fell very slowly, for she had plenty of time as she went down to look about her, and to wonder what was going to happen next. First, she tried to look down and make out what she was coming to, but it was too dark to see anything; then she looked at the sides of the well, and noticed that they were filled with cupboards and book-shelves: here and there she saw maps and pictures hung upon pegs. She took down a jar from one of the shelves as she passed; it was labelled 'ORANGE MARMALADE,' but to her great disappointment it was empty: she did not like to drop the jar for fear of killing somebody, so managed to put it into one of the cupboards as she fell past it.

'Well!' thought Alice to herself. 'After such a fall as this, I shall think nothing of tumbling down stairs! How brave they'll all think me at home! Why, I wouldn't say anything about it, even if I fell off the top of the house!' (Which was very likely true.)

Down, down, down. Would the fall *never* come to an end? 'I wonder how many miles I've fallen by this time?' she said aloud.

'I must be getting somewhere near the centre of the earth. Let me see: that would be four thousand miles down, I think—' (for, you see, Alice had learnt several things of this sort in her lessons in the schoolroom, and though this was not a *very* good opportunity for showing off her knowledge, as there was no one to listen to her, still it was good practice to say it over) '—yes, that's about the right distance—but then I wonder what Latitude or Longitude I've got to?' (Alice had no idea what Latitude was, or Longtitude either, but thought they were nice grand words to say.)

Presently she began again. 'I wonder if I shall fall right *through* the earth! How funny it'll seem to come out among the people that walk with their heads downwards! The Antipathies, I think—' (she was rather glad there *was* no one listening, this time, as it didn't sound at all the right word) '—but I shall have to ask them what the name of the country is, you know. Please, Ma'am, is this New Zealand or Australia?' (and she tried to curtsey as she spoke—fancy *curtseying* as you're falling through the air! Do you think you could manage it?) 'And what an ignorant little girl she'll think me! No, it'll never do to ask: perhaps I shall see it written up somewhere.'

Down, down, down. There was nothing else to do, so Alice soon began talking again. 'Dinah'll miss me very much to-night, I should think!' (Dinah was the cat.) 'I hope they'll remember her saucer of milk at tea-time. Dinah, my dear, I wish you were down here with me! There are no mice in the air, I'm afraid, but you might catch a bat, and that's very like a mouse, you know. But do cats eat bats, I wonder?' And here Alice began to get rather sleepy, and went on saying to herself, in a dreamy sort of way, 'Do cats eat bats? Do cats eat bats?' and sometimes, 'Do bats eat cats?' for, you see, as she couldn't answer either question, it didn't much matter which way she put it. She felt that she was dozing off, and had just begun to dream that she was walking hand in hand with Dinah, and saying to her very earnestly, 'Now, Dinah, tell me the truth: did you ever eat a bat?' when suddenly, thump! thump! down she came upon a heap of dry leaves, and the fall was over.

Alice was not a bit hurt, and she jumepd up on to her feet in a moment: she looked up, but it was all dark overhead; before her was another long passage, and the White Rabbit was still in sight, hurrying down it. There was not a moment to be lost: away went Alice like the wind, and was just in time to hear it say, as it turned a corner, 'Oh my ears and whiskers, how late it's getting!' She was close behind it when she turned the corner, but the Rabbit was no longer to be seen: she found herself in a long, low hall, which was lit up by a row of lamps hanging from the roof.

There were doors all round the hall, but they were all locked; and when Alice had been all the way down one side and up the other, trying every door, she walked sadly down the middle, wondering how she was ever to get out again.

Suddenly she came upon a little three-legged table, all made of solid glass; there was nothing on it except a tiny golden key, and Alice's first thought was that it might belong to one of the doors of the hall; but, alas! either the locks were too large, or the key was too small, but at any rate it would not open any of them. However, the second time round, she came upon a low curtain she had not noticed before, and behind it was a little door about fifteen inches high: she tried the little golden key in the lock, and to her great delight it fitted!

Alice opened the door and found that it led into a small passage, not much larger than a rat-hole: she knelt down and looked along the passage into the loveliest garden you ever saw. How she longed to get out of that dark hall, and wander about among those beds of bright flowers and those cool fountains, but she could not even get her head through the doorway; 'and even if my head would go through,' thought poor Alice, 'it would be of very little use without my shoulders. Oh, how I wish I could shut up like a telescope! I think I could, if I only knew how to begin.' For, you see, so many out-of-the-way things had happened lately, that Alice had begun to think that very few things indeed were really impossible.

There seemed to be no use in waiting by the little door, so she went back to the table, half hoping she might find another key on it, or at any rate a book of rules for shutting people up like telescopes: this time she found a little bottle on it, ('which certainly was not here before,' said Alice,) and round its neck a paper label, with the words 'DRINK ME' beautifully printed on it in large letters.

It was all very well to say 'Drink me', but the wise little Alice was not going to do *that* in a hurry. 'No, I'll look first,' she said, 'and see whether it's marked "*poison*" or not;' for she had read several nice little histories about children who had got burnt, and eaten up by wild beasts, and many other unpleasant things, all because they *would* not remember the simple rules their friends had taught them: such as, that a red-hot poker will burn you if you hold it too long; and that, if you cut your finger *very* deeply with a knife, it usually bleeds; and she had never forgotten that, if you drink much from a bottle marked 'poison', it is almost certain to disagree with you, sooner or later.

However, this bottle was *not* marked 'poison', so Alice ventured to taste it, and finding it very nice (it had, in fact, a sort of mixed flavour of cherry-tart, custard, pineapple, roast turkey, toffee, and hot buttered toast,) she very soon finished it off.

    ❀   ❀   ❀   ❀

        ❀   ❀   ❀

    ❀   ❀   ❀   ❀

'What a curious feeling!' said Alice. 'I must be shutting up like a telescope.'

And so it was indeed: she was now only ten inches high, and her face brightened up at the thought that she was now the right size for going through the little door into that lovely garden. First, however, she waited for a few minutes to see if she was going to shrink any further: she felt a little nervous about this; 'for it might end, you know,' said Alice, 'in my going out altogether, like a candle. I wonder what I should be like then?' And she tried to fancy what the flame of a candle is like after it is blown out, for she could not remember ever having seen such a thing.

After a while, finding that nothing more happened, she decided on going into the garden at once; but, alas for poor Alice! when she got to the door, she found she had forgotten the little golden key, and when she went back to the table for it, she found she could not possibly reach it: she could see it quite plainly through the glass, and she tried her best to climb up one of the table-legs, but it was too slippery; and when she had tired herself out with trying, the poor little thing sat down and cried.

'Come, there's no use in crying like that!' said Alice to herself, rather sharply. 'I advise you to leave off this minute!' She generally gave herself very good advice (though she very seldom followed it), and sometimes she scolded herself so severely as to bring tears into her eyes; and once she remembered trying to box her own ears for having cheated herself in a game of croquet she was playing against herself, for this curious child was very fond of pretending to be two people. 'But it's no use now,' thought poor Alice, 'to pretend to be two people! Why, there's hardly enough of me left to make *one* respectable person!'

Soon her eye fell on a little glass box that was lying under the table: she opened it, and found in it a very small cake, on which the words 'EAT ME' were beautifully marked in currants. 'Well, I'll eat it,' said Alice, 'and if it makes me larger, I can reach the key; and if it makes me smaller, I can creep under the door; so either way I'll get into the garden, and I don't care which happens!'

She ate a little bit, and said anxiously to herself, 'Which way? Which way?' holding her hand on the top of her head to feel which way it was growing, and she was quite surprised to find that she remained the same size: to be sure, this generally happens when one eats cake, but Alice had got so much into the way of expecting nothing but out-of-the-way things to happen, that it seemed quite dull and stupid for life to go on in the common way.

So she set to work, and very soon finished off the cake.

the weird tale

EDGAR ALLAN POE (1809–1849)

"The Tell-Tale Heart" is a classic "weird tale" of the Gothic
tradition. In the nineteenth century, the Gothic tale was a
product of the movement against science and rationalism. A
characteristic of Poe's treatment of the genre is the use of
an almost scientifically realistic setting into which is inter-
jected something frighteningly unnatural or supernatural.

the tell-tale heart

True!—nervous—very, very dreadfully nervous I had been and am;
but why *will* you say that I am mad! The disease had sharpened
my senses—not destroyed—not dulled them. Above all was the sense
of hearing acute. I heard all things in the heaven and in the earth.
I heard many things in hell. How, then, am I mad? Hearken! and
observe how healthily—how calmly I can tell you the whole story.

It is impossible to say how first the idea entered my brain; but
once conceived, it haunted me day and night. Object there was
none. Passion there was none. I loved the old man. He had never
wronged me. He had never given me insult. For his gold I had no
desire. I think it was his eye! yes, it was this! One of his eyes resembled that of a vulture—a pale blue eye, with a film over it.
Whenever it fell upon me, my blood ran cold; and so by degrees—

The Tell-Tale Heart, Harry Clarke

very gradually—I made up my mind to take the life of the old man, and thus rid myself of the eye for ever.

Now this is the point. You fancy me mad. Madmen know nothing. But you should have seen *me*. You should have seen how wisely I proceeded—with what caution—with what foresight—with what dissimulation I went to work! I was never kinder to the old man than during the whole week before I killed him. And every night, about midnight, I turned the latch of his door and opened it —oh, so gently! And then, when I had made an opening sufficient for my head, I put in a dark lantern, all closed, closed, so that no light shone out, and then I thrust in my head. Oh, you would have laughed to see how cunningly I thrust it in! I moved it slowly—very, very slowly, so that I might not disturb the old man's sleep. It took me an hour to place my whole head within the opening so far that I could see him as he lay upon his bed. Ha!—would a madman have been so wise as this? And then, when my head was well in the room, I undid the lantern cautiously—oh, so cautiously—cautiously (for the hinges creaked)—I undid it just so much that a single thin ray fell upon the vulture eye. And this I did for seven long nights— every night just at midnight—but I found the eye always closed; and so it was impossible to do the work; for it was not the old man who vexed me, but his Evil Eye. And every morning, when the day broke, I went boldly into the chamber, and spoke courageously to him, calling him by name in a hearty tone, and inquiring how he had passed the night. So you see he would have been a very profound old man, indeed, to suspect that every night, just at twelve, I looked in upon him while he slept.

Upon the eighth night I was more than usually cautious in opening the door. A watch's minute hand moves more quickly than did mine. Never before that night, had I *felt* the extent of my own powers—of my sagacity. I could scarcely contain my feelings of triumph. To think that there I was, opening the door, little by little, and he not even to dream of my secret deeds or thoughts. I fairly chuckled at the idea; and perhaps he heard me; for he moved on the bed suddenly, as if startled. Now you may think that I drew back—but no. His room was as black as pitch with the thick darkness, (for the shutters were close fastened, through fear of robbers,) and so I knew that he could not see the opening of the door, and I kept pushing it on steadily, steadily.

I had my head in, and was about to open the lantern, when my thumb slipped upon the tin fastening, and the old man sprang up in the bed, crying out—"Who's there?"

I kept quite still and said nothing. For a whole hour I did not move a muscle, and in the mean time I did not hear him lie down. He was still sitting up in the bed, listening;—just as I have done, night after night, hearkening to the death watches in the wall.

Presently I heard a slight groan, and I knew it was the groan of mortal terror. It was not a groan of pain or of grief—oh, no!—it was the low stifled sound that arises from the bottom of the soul when overcharged with awe. I knew the sound well. Many a night, just at midnight, when all the world slept, it has welled up from my own bosom, deepening, with its dreadful echo, the terrors that distracted me. I say I knew it well. I knew what the old man felt, and pitied him, although I chuckled at heart. I knew that he had been lying awake ever since the first slight noise, when he had turned in the bed. His fears had been ever since growing upon him. He had been saying to himself—"It is nothing but the wind in the chimney—it is only a mouse crossing the floor," or "it is merely a cricket which has made a single chirp." Yes, he has been trying to comfort himself with these suppositions: but he had found all in vain. *All in vain*; because Death, in approaching him, had stalked with his black shadow before him, and enveloped the victim. And it was the mournful influence of the unperceived shadow that caused him to feel—although he neither saw nor heard—to *feel* the presence of my head within the room.

When I had waited a long time, very patiently, without hearing him lie down, I resolved to open a little—a very, very little crevice in the lantern. So I opened it—you cannot imagine how stealthily, stealthily—until, at length, a singled dim ray, like the thread of the spider, shot from out the crevice and fell upon the vulture eye.

It was open—wide, wide open—and I grew furious as I gazed upon it. I saw it with perfect distinctness—all a dull blue, with a hideous veil over it that chilled the very marrow in my bones; but I could see nothing else of the old man's face or person: for I had directed the ray as if by instinct, precisely upon the damned spot.

And now have I not told you that what you mistake for madness is but over acuteness of the senses?—now, I say, there came to my ears a low, dull, quick sound, such as a watch makes when enveloped in cotton. I knew *that* sound well, too. It was the beating of the old man's heart. It increased my fury, as the beating of a drum stimulates the soldier into courage.

But even yet I refrained and kept still. I scarcely breathed. I held the lantern motionless. I tried how steadily I could maintain the ray upon the eye. Meantime the hellish tattoo of the heart increased. It grew quicker and quicker, and louder and louder every instant. The old man's terror *must* have been extreme! It grew louder, I say, louder every moment!—do you mark me well! I have told you that I am nervous; so I am. And now at the dead hour of the night, amid the dreadful silence of that old house, so strange a noise as this excited me to uncontrollable terror. Yet, for some minutes longer I refrained and stood still. But the beating grew louder, louder! I thought the heart must burst. And now a new anxiety seized me—the sound would be heard by a neighbor! The old man's hour had come! With a loud yell, I threw open the lantern and leaped into the room. He shrieked once—once only. In an instant I dragged him to the floor, and pulled the heavy bed over him. I then smiled gaily, to find the deed so far done. But, for many minutes, the heart beat on with a muffled sound. This, however, did not vex me; it would not be heard through the wall. At length it ceased. The old man was dead. I removed the bed and examined the corpse. Yes, he was stone dead. I placed my hand upon the heart and held it there many minutes. There was no pulsation. He was stone dead. His eye would trouble me no more.

If you still think me mad, you will think so no longer when I describe the wise precautions I took for the concealment of the body. The night waned, and I worked hastily, but in silence. First of all I dismembered the corpse. I cut off the head and the arms and the legs.

I then took up three planks from the flooring of the chamber, and deposited all between the scantlings. I then replaced the boards so cleverly, so cunningly, that no human eye—not even *his*—could have detected any thing wrong. There was nothing to wash out—no stain of any kind—no blood-spot whatever. I had been too wary for that. A tub had caught all—ha! ha!

When I had made an end of these labors, it was four o'clock—still dark as midnight. As the bell sounded the hour, there came a knocking at the street door. I went down to open it with a light heart,—for what had I *now* to fear? There entered three men, who introduced themselves, with perfect suavity, as officers of the police. A shriek had been heard by a neighbor during the night; suspicion of foul play had been aroused; information had been lodged at the police office, they (the officers) had been deputed to search the premises.

I smiled,—for *what* had I to fear? I bade the gentlemen welcome. The shriek, I said, was my own in a dream. The old man, I mentioned, was absent in the country. I took my visitors all over the house. I bade them search—search *well*. I led them, at length, to *his* chamber. I showed them his treasures, secure, undisturbed. In the enthusiasm of my confidence, I brought chairs into the room, and desired them *here* to rest from their fatigues, while I myself, in the wild audacity of my perfect triumph, placed my own seat upon the very spot beneath which reposed the corpse of the victim.

The officers were satisfied. My *manner* had convinced them. I was singularly at ease. They sat, and while I answered cheerily, they chatted of familiar things. But, ere long, I felt myself getting pale and wished them gone. My head ached, and I fancied a ringing in my ears: but still they sat and still chatted. The ringing became more distinct:—it continued and became more distinct: I talked more freely to get rid of the feeling: but it continued and gained definitiveness—until, at length, I found that the noise was *not* within my ears.

No doubt I now grew *very* pale;—but I talked more fluently, and with a heightened voice. Yet the sound increased—and what could I do? It was *a low, dull, quick sound—much such a sound as a watch makes when enveloped in cotton.* I gasped for breath—and yet the officers heard it not. I talked more quickly—more vehemently; but the noise steadily increased. I arose and argued about trifles, in a high key and with violent gesticulations; but the noise steadily increased. Why *would* they not be gone? I paced the floor to and fro with heavy strides, as if excited to fury by the observations of the men—but the noise steadily increased. Oh God! what *could* I do? I foamed—I raved—I swore! I swung the chair upon which I had been sitting, and grated it upon the boards, but the noise arose over all and continually increased. It grew louder—louder—louder—*louder!* And still the men chatted pleasantly, and smiled. Was it possible they heard not? Almightly God!—no, no!

They heard!—they suspected!—they *knew!*—they were making a mockery of my horror!—this I thought, and this I think. But anything was better than this agony! Anything was more tolerable than this derision! I could bear those hypocritical smiles no longer! I felt that I must scream or die!—and now—again!—hark! louder! louder! louder! *louder!*—

"Villains!" I shrieked, "dissemble no more! I admit the deed!—tear up the planks!—here, here!—it is the beating of his hideous heart!"

science fiction

KURT VONNEGUT, JR. (1922–   )

Science fiction has become one of the most important and
popular branches of fantasy literature. It speaks, particularly,
to our age of scientific speculation and exploration. Much of
what scientists tell us about the reality of the cosmos and
about the future sounds like early science fiction: we have
already seen that the languages of science and fantasy are
not so very different. Kurt Vonnegut, Jr. is a major literary
figure of the revolution of the spirit. In this story, he uses the
device of futurity—a device familiar to most readers of
science fiction—to comment on our own civilization.

harrison bergeron

The year was 2081, and everybody was finally equal. They weren't
only equal before God and the law. They were equal every which
way. Nobody was smarter than anybody else. Nobody was better
looking than anybody else. Nobody was stronger or quicker than
anybody else. All this equality was due to the 211th, 212th, and
213th Amendments to the Constitution, and to the unceasing
vigilance of agents of the United States Handicapper General.

Some things about living still weren't quite right, though. April,
for instance, still drove people crazy by not being springtime. And

it was in that clammy month that the H-G men took George and Hazel Bergeron's fourteen-year-old son, Harrison, away.

It was tragic, all right, but George and Hazel couldn't think about it very hard. Hazel had a perfectly average intelligence, which meant she couldn't think about anything except in short bursts. And George, while his intelligence was way above normal, had a little mental handicap radio in his ear. He was required by law to wear it at all times. It was tuned to a government transmitter. Every twenty seconds or so, the transmitter would send out some sharp noise to keep people like George from taking unfair advantage of their brains.

George and Hazel were watching television. There were tears on Hazel's cheeks, but she'd forgotten for the moment what they were about.

On the television screen were ballerinas.

A buzzer sounded in George's head. His thoughts fled in panic, like bandits from a burglar alarm.

"That was a real pretty dance, that dance they just did," said Hazel.

"Huh?" said George.

"That dance—it was nice," said Hazel

"Yup," said George. He tried to think a little about the ballerinas. They weren't really very good—no better than anybody else would have been, anyway. They were burdened with sash-weights and bags of birdshot, and their faces were masked, so that no one, seeing a free and graceful gesture or a pretty face, would feel like something the cat drug in. George was toying with the vague notion that maybe dancers shouldn't be handicapped. But he didn't get very far with it before another noise in his ear radio scattered his thoughts.

George winced. So did two out of the eight ballerinas.

Hazel saw him wince. Having no mental handicap herself, she had to ask George what the latest sound had been.

"Sounded like somebody hitting a milk bottle with a ball pen hammer," said George.

"I'd think it would be real interesting, hearing all the different sounds," said Hazel, a little envious. "All the things they think up."

"Um," said George.

"Only, if I was Handicapper General, you know what I would

do?" said Hazel. Hazel, as a matter of fact, bore a strong resemblance to the Handicapper General, a woman named Diana Moon Glampers. "If I was Diana Moon Glampers," said Hazel, "I'd have chimes on Sunday—just chimes. Kind of in honor of religion."

"I could think, if it was just chimes," said George.

"Well—maybe make 'em real loud," said Hazel. "I think I'd make a good Handicapper General."

"Good as anybody else," said George.

"Who knows better'n I do what normal is?" said Hazel.

"Right," said George. He began to think glimmeringly about his abnormal son who was now in jail, about Harrison, but a twenty-one-gun salute in his head stopped that.

"Boy!" said Hazel, "that was a doozy, wasn't it?"

It was such a doozy that George was white and trembling, and tears stood on the rims of his red eyes. Two of the eight ballerinas had collapsed to the studio floor, were holding their temples.

"All of a sudden you look so tired," said Hazel. "Why don't you stretch out on the sofa, so's you can rest your handicap bag on the pillows, honeybunch." She was referring to the forty-seven pounds of birdshot in a canvas bag, which was padlocked around George's neck. "Go on and rest the bag for a little while," she said. "I don't care if you're not equal to me for a while."

George weighed the bag with his hands. "I don't mind it," he said. "I don't notice it any more. It's just a part of me."

"You been so tired lately—kind of wore out," said Hazel. "If there was just some way we could make a little hole in the bottom of the bag, and just take out a few of them lead balls. Just a few."

"Two years in prison and two thousand dollars fine for every ball I took out," said George. "I don't call that a bargain."

"If you could just take a few out when you came home from work," said Hazel. "I mean—you don't compete with anybody around here. You just set around."

"If I tried to get away with it," said George, "then other people'd get away with it—and pretty soon we'd be right back to the dark ages again, with everybody competing against everybody else. You wouldn't like that, would you?"

"I'd hate it," said Hazel.

"There you are," said George. "The minute people start cheating on laws, what do you think happens to society?"

If Hazel hadn't been able to come up with an answer to this question, George couldn't have supplied one. A siren was going off in his head.

"Reckon it'd fall all apart," said Hazel.

"What would?" said George blankly.

"Society," said Hazel uncertainly. "Wasn't that what you just said?"

"Who knows?" said George.

The television program was suddenly interrupted for a news bulletin. It wasn't clear at first as to what the bulletin was about, since the announcer, like all announcers, had a serious speech impediment. For about half a minute, and in a state of high excitement, the announcer tried to say, "Ladies and gentlemen—"

He finally gave up, handed the bulletin to a ballerina to read.

"That's all right—" Hazel said of the announcer, "he tried. That's the big thing. He tried to do the best he could with what God gave him. He should get a nice raise for trying so hard."

"Ladies and gentlemen—" said the ballerina, reading the bulletin. She must have been extraordinarily beautiful because the mask she wore was hideous. And it was easy to see that she was the strongest and most graceful of all the dancers, for her handicap bags were as big as those worn by two-hundred-pound men.

And she had to apologize at once for her voice, which was a very unfair voice for a woman to use. Her voice was a warm, luminous, timeless melody. "Excuse me—" she said, and she began again, making her voice absolutely uncompetitive.

"Harrison Bergeron, age fourteen," she said in a grackle squawk, "has just escaped from jail, where he was held on suspicion of plotting to overthrow the government. He is a genius and an athlete, is under-handicapped, and should be regarded as extremely dangerous."

A police photograph of Harrison Bergeron was flashed on the screen—upside down, then sideways, upside down again, then right side up. The picture showed the full length of Harrison against a background calibrated in feet and inches. He was exactly seven feet tall.

The rest of Harrison's appearance was Halloween and hardware. Nobody had ever borne heavier handicaps. He had outgrown hindrances faster than H-G men could think them up. Instead of a little ear radio for a mental handicap, he wore a tremendous pair of earphones, and spectacles with thick wavy lenses. The spectacles were intended to make him not only half blind, but to give him whanging headaches besides.

Scrap metal was hung all over him. Ordinarily, there was a certain symmetry, a military neatness to the handicaps issued to strong people, but Harrison looked like a walking junkyard. In the race of life, Harrison carried three hundred pounds.

And to offset his good looks, the H-G men required that he wear at all times a red rubber ball for a nose, keep his eyebrows shaved off, and cover his even white teeth with black caps at snaggle-tooth random.

"If you see this boy," said the ballerina, "do not—I repeat, do not—try to reason with him."

There was the shriek of a door being torn from its hinges.

Screams and barking cries of consternation came from the television set. The photograph of Harrison Bergeron on the screen jumped again and again, as though dancing to the tune of an earthquake.

George Bergeron correctly identified the earthquake, and well he might have—for many was the time his own home had danced to the same crashing tune. "My God—" said George, "that must be Harrison!"

The realization was blasted from his mind instantly by the sound of an automobile collision in his head.

When George could open his eyes again, the photograph of Harrison was gone. A living, breathing Harrison filled the screen.

Clanking, clownish, and huge, Harrison stood in the center of the studio. The knob of the uprooted studio door was still in his hand. Ballerinas, technicians, musicians, and announcers cowered on their knees before him, expecting to die.

"I am the Emperor!" cried Harrison. "Do you hear? I am the Emperor! Everybody must do what I say at once!" He stamped his foot and the studio shook.

"Even as I stand here—" he bellowed, "crippled, hobbled, sickened—I am a greater ruler than any man who ever lived! Now watch me become what I *can* become!"

Harrison tore the straps of his handicap harness like wet tissue paper, tore straps guaranteed to support five thousand pounds.

Harrison's scrap-iron handicaps crashed to the floor.

Harrison thrust his thumbs under the bar of the padlock that secured his head harness. The bar snapped like celery. Harrison smashed his headphones and spectacles against the wall.

He flung away his rubber-ball nose, revealed a man that would have awed Thor, the god of thunder.

"I shall now select my Empress!" he said, looking down on the cowering people. "Let the first woman who dares rise to her feet claim her mate and her throne!"

A moment passed, and then a ballerina arose, swaying like a willow.

Harrison plucked the mental handicap from her ear, snapped off her physical handicaps with marvellous delicacy. Last of all, he removed her mask.

She was blindingly beautiful.

"Now—" said Harrison, taking her hand, "shall we show the people the meaning of the word dance? Music!" he commanded.

The musicians scrambled back into their chairs, and Harrison stripped them of their handicaps, too. "Play your best," he told them, "and I'll make you barons and dukes and earls."

The music began. It was normal at first—cheap, silly, false. But Harrison snatched two musicians from their chairs, waved them like batons as he sang the music as he wanted it played. He slammed them back into their chairs.

The music began again and was much improved.

Harrison and his Empress merely listened to the music for a while—listened gravely, as though synchronizing their heartbeats with it.

They shifted their weights to their toes.

Harrison placed his big hands on the girl's tiny waist, letting her sense the weightlessness that would soon be hers.

And then, in an explosion of joy and grace, into the air they sprang!

Not only were the laws of the land abandoned, but the law of gravity and the laws of motion as well.

They reeled, whirled, swiveled, flounced, capered, gamboled, and spun.

They leaped like deer on the moon.

The studio ceiling was thirty feet high, but each leap brought the dancers nearer to it.

It became their obvious intention to kiss the ceiling.

216   They kissed it.

And then, neutralizing gravity with love and pure will, they remained suspended in air inches below the ceiling, and they kissed each other for a long, long time.

It was then that Diana Moon Glampers, the Handicapper General, came into the studio with a double-barreled ten-gauge shotgun. She fired twice, and the Emperor and the Empress were dead before they hit the floor.

Diana Moon Glampers loaded the gun again. She aimed it at the musicians and told them they had ten seconds to get their handicaps back on.

It was then that the Bergerons' television tube burned out.

Hazel turned to comment about the blackout to George. But George had gone out into the kitchen for a can of beer.

George came back in with the beer, paused while a handicap signal shook him up. And then he sat down again. "You been crying?" he said to Hazel.

"Yup," she said.

"What about?" he said.

"I forget," she said, "Something real sad on television."

"What was it?" he said.

"It's all kind of mixed up in my mind," said Hazel.

"Forget sad things," said George.

"I always do," said Hazel.

"That's my girl," said George. He winced. There was the sound of a rivetting gun in his head.

"Gee—I could tell that one was a doozy," said Hazel.

"You can say that again," said George.

"Gee—" said Hazel, "I could tell that one was a doozy."

fantasy and the
realist writer

F. SCOTT FITZGERALD (1896–1940)

F. Scott Fitzgerald is generally considered a realist. In "The
Diamond as Big as the Ritz," he makes use of his talents as
a realist writer to create an almost perfect work of fantasy.
The major task of the fantasy-maker, says J. R. R. Tolkien, is
to maintain the "inner consistency of reality." Fitzgerald
does precisely this when he sends John Unger from Saint
Midas' School near Boston to the glittering world of the
Washingtons.

the diamond as
big as the ritz

John T. Unger came from a family that had been well known in
Hades—a small town on the Mississippi River—for several generations. John's father had held the amateur golf championship through
many a heated contest; Mrs. Unger was known "from hot-box to
hot-bed," as the local phrase went, for her political addresses; and
young John T. Unger, who had just turned sixteen, had danced all
the latest dances from New York before he put on long trousers. And
now, for a certain time, he was to be away from home. That re-

spect for a New England education which is the bane of all provincial places, which drains them yearly of their most promising young men, had seized upon his parents. Nothing would suit them but that he should go to St. Midas' School near Boston—Hades was too small to hold their darling and gifted son.

Now in Hades—as you know if you ever have been there—the names of the more fashionable preparatory schools and colleges mean very little. The inhabitants have been so long out of the world that, though they make a show of keeping up to date in dress and manners and literature, they depend to a great extent on hearsay, and a function that in Hades would be considered elaborate would doubtless be hailed by a Chicago beef-princess as "perhaps a little tacky."

John T. Unger was on the eve of departure. Mrs. Unger, with maternal fatuity, packed his trunks full of linen suits and electric fans, and Mr. Unger presented his son with an asbestos pocketbook stuffed with money.

"Remember, you are always welcome here," he said. "You can be sure, boy, that we'll keep the home fires burning."

"I know," answered John huskily.

"Don't forget who you are and where you come from," continued his father proudly, "and you can do nothing to harm you. You are an Unger—from Hades."

So the old man and the young shook hands and John walked away with tears streaming from his eyes. Ten minutes later he had passed outside the city limits, and he stopped to glance back for the last time. Over the gates the old-fashioned Victorian motto seemed strangely attractive to him. His father had tried time and time again to have it changed to something with a little more push and verve about it, such as "Hades—Your Opportunity," or else a plain "Welcome" sign set over a hearty handshake pricked out in electric lights. The old motto was a little depressing, Mr. Unger had thought—but now. . . .

So John took his look and then set his face resolutely toward his destination. And, as he turned away, the lights of Hades against the sky seemed full of a warm and passionate beauty.

St. Midas' School is half an hour from Boston in a Rolls-Pierce motor-car. The actual distance will never be known, for no one, except John T. Unger, had ever arrived in a Rolls-Pierce and probably no one ever will again. St. Midas' is the most expensive and the most exclusive boys' preparatory school in the world.

John's first two years there passed pleasantly. The fathers of all the boys were money-kings and John spent his summers visiting at fashionable resorts. While he was very fond of all the boys he visited, their fathers struck him as being much of a piece, and in his boyish way he often wondered at their exceeding sameness. When he told them where his home was they would ask jovially, "Pretty hot down there?" and John would muster a faint smile and answer, "It certainly is." His response would have been heartier had they not all made this joke—at best varying it with, "Is it hot enough for you down there?" which he hated just as much.

In the middle of his second year at school, a quiet, handsome boy named Percy Washington had been put in John's form. The newcomer was pleasant in his manner and exceedingly well dressed even for St. Midas', but for some reason he kept aloof from the other boys. The only person with whom he was intimate was John T. Unger, but even to John he was entirely uncommunicative concerning his home or his family. That he was wealthy went without saying, but beyond a few such deductions John knew little of his friend, so it promised rich confectionery for his curiosity when Percy invited him to spend the summer at his home "in the West." He accepted, without hesitation.

It was only when they were in the train that Percy became, for the first time, rather communicative. One day while they were eating lunch in the dining-car and discussing the imperfect characters of several of the boys at school, Percy suddenly changed his tone and made an abrupt remark.

"My father," he said, "is by far the richest man in the world."

"Oh," said John, politely. He could think of no answer to make to this confidence. He considered "That's very nice," but it sounded hollow and was on the point of saying, "Really?" but refrained since it would seem to question Percy's statement. And such an astounding statement could scarcely be questioned.

"By far the richest," repeated Percy.

"I was reading in the *World Almanac*," began John, "that there was one man in America with an income of over five million a year and four men with incomes of over three million a year, and—"

"Oh, they're nothing," Percy's mouth was a half-moon of scorn.

"Catch-penny capitalists, financial small-fry, petty merchants and money-lenders. My father could buy them out and not know he'd done it."

"But how does he———"

"Why haven't they put down *his* income tax? Because he doesn't pay any. At least he pays a little one—but he doesn't pay any on his *real* income."

"He must be very rich," said John simply. "I'm glad. I like very rich people."

"The richer a fella is, the better I like him." There was a look of passionate frankness upon his dark face. "I visited the Schnlitzer-Murphys last Easter. Vivan Schnlitzer-Murphy had rubies as big as hen's eggs, and sapphires that were like globes with lights inside them—"

"I love jewels," agreed Percy enthusiastically. "Of course I wouldn't want any one at school to know about it, but I've got quite a collection myself. I used to collect them instead of stamps."

"And diamonds," continued John eagerly. 'The Schnlitzer-Murphys had diamonds as big as walnuts———"

"That's nothing." Percy had leaned forward and dropped his voice to a low whisper. "That's nothing at all. My father has a diamond bigger than the Ritz-Carlton Hotel."

II

The Montana sunset lay between two mountains like a gigantic bruise from which dark arteries spread themselves over a poisoned sky. An immense distance under the sky crouched the village of Fish, minute, dismal, and forgotten. There were twelve men, so it was said, in the village of Fish, twelve sombre and inexplicable souls who sucked a lean milk from the almost literally bare rock upon which a mysterious populatory force had begotten them. They had become a race apart, these twelve men of Fish, like some species developed by an early whim of nature, which on second thought had abandoned them to struggle and extermination.

Out of the blue-black bruise in the distance crept a long line of moving lights upon the desolation of the land, and the twelve men of Fish gathered like ghosts at the shanty depot to watch the passing of the seven o'clock train, the Transcontinental Express from Chicago. Six times or so a year the Transcontinental Express, through some inconceivable jurisdiction, stopped at the village of Fish, and when this occurred a figure or so would disembark, mount into a buggy that always appeared from out of the dusk, and drive off toward the bruised sunset. The observation of this pointless and preposterous phenomenon had become a sort of cult among the men of Fish. To observe, that was all; there remained in them none of the vital quality of illusion which would make them wonder or speculate, else a religion might have grown up around these mysterious visitations. But the men of Fish were beyond all religion— the barest and most savage tenets of even Christianity could gain no foothold on that barren rock—so there was no altar, no priest, no sacrifice; only each night at seven the silent concourse by the shanty depot, a congregation who lifted up a prayer of dim, anæmic wonder.

On this June night, the Great Brakeman, whom, had they deified any one, they might well have chosen as their celestial protagonist, had ordained that the seven o'clock train should leave its human (or inhuman) deposit at Fish. At two minutes after seven Percy Washington and John T. Unger disembarked, hurried past the spellbound, the agape, the fearsome eyes of the twelve men of Fish, mounted into a buggy which had obviously appeared from nowhere, and drove away.

After half an hour, when the twilight had coagulated into dark, the silent negro who was driving the buggy hailed an opaque body somewhere ahead of them in the gloom. In response to his cry, it turned upon them a luminous disk which regarded them like a malignant eye out of the unfathomable night. As they came closer, John saw that it was the tail-light of an immense automobile, larger and more magnificent than any he had ever seen. Its body was of gleaming metal richer than nickel and lighter than silver, and the hubs of the wheels were studded with irridescent geometric figures of green and yellow—John did not dare to guess whether they were glass or jewel.

Two negroes, dressed in glittering livery such as one sees in pictures of royal processions in London, were standing at attention beside the car and as the two young men dismounted from the buggy they were greeted in some language which the guest could not understand, but which seemed to be an extreme form of the Southern negro's dialect.

"Get in," said Percy to his friend, as their trunks were tossed to the ebony roof of the limousine. "Sorry we had to bring you this far in that buggy, but of course it wouldn't do for the people on the train or those Godforsaken fellas in Fish to see this automobile."

"Gosh! What a car!" This ejaculation was provoked by its interior. John saw that the upholstery consisted of a thousand minute and exquisite tapestries of silk, woven with jewels and embroideries, and set upon a background of cloth of gold. The two armchair seats in which the boys luxuriated were covered with stuff that resembled duvetyn, but seemed woven in numberless colors of the ends of ostrich feathers.

"What a car!" cried John again, in amazement.

"This thing?" Percy laughed. "Why, it's just an old junk we use for a station wagon."

By this time they were gliding along through the darkness toward the break between the two mountains.

"We'll be there in an hour and a half," said Percy, looking at the clock. "I may as well tell you it's not going to be like anything you ever saw before."

If the car was any indication of what John would see, he was prepared to be astonished indeed. The simple piety prevalent in Hades has the earnest worship of and respect for riches as the first article of its creed—had John felt otherwise than radiantly humble before them, his parents would have turned away in horror at the blasphemy.

They had now reached and were entering the break between the two mountains and almost immediately the way became much rougher.

"If the moon shone down here, you'd see that we're in a big gulch," said Percy, trying to peer out of the window. He spoke a few words into the mouthpiece and immediately the footman turned on a searchlight and swept the hillsides with an immense beam.

"Rocky, you see. An ordinary car would be knocked to pieces in half an hour. In fact, it'd take a tank to navigate it unless you knew the way. You notice we're going uphill now."

They were obviously ascending, and within a few minutes the

car was crossing a high rise, where they caught a glimpse of a pale moon newly risen in the distance. The car stopped suddenly and several figures took shape out of the dark beside it—these were negroes also. Again the two young men were saluted in the same dimly recognizable dialect; then the negroes set to work and four immense cables dangling from overhead were attached with hooks to the hubs of the great jeweled wheels. At a resounding "Hey-yah!" John felt the car being lifted slowly from the ground—up and up—clear of the tallest rocks on both sides—then higher, until he could see a wavy, moonlit valley stretched out before him in sharp contrast to the quagmire of rocks that they had just left. Only on one side was there still rock—and then suddenly there was no rock beside them or anywhere around.

It was apparent that they had surmounted some immense knife-blade of stone, projecting perpendicularly into the air. In a moment they were going down again, and finally with a soft bump they were landed upon the smooth earth.

"The worst is over," said Percy, squinting out the window. "It's only five miles from here, and our own road—tapestry brick—all the way. This belongs to us. This is where the United States ends, father says."

"Are we in Canada?"

"We are not. We're in the middle of the Montana Rockies. But you are now on the only five square miles of land in the country that's never been surveyed."

"Why hasn't it? Did they forget it?"

"No," said Percy, grinning, "they tried to do it three times. The first time my grandfather corrupted a whole department of the State survey; the second time he had the official maps of the United States tinkered with—that held them for fifteen years. The last time was harder. My father fixed it so that their compasses were in the strongest magnetic field ever artificially set up. He had a whole set of surveying instruments made with a slight defection that would allow for this territory not to appear, and he substituted them for the ones that were to be used. Then he had a river deflected and he had what looked like a village built up on its banks—so that they'd see it, and think it was a town ten miles farther up the valley. There's only one thing my father's afraid of," he concluded, "only one thing in the world that could be used to find us out."

"What's that?"

Percy sank his voice to a whisper.

"Aeroplanes," he breathed. "We've got a dozen anti-aircraft guns and we've arranged it so far—but there've been a few deaths and a great many prisoners. Not that we mind *that*, you know, father and I, but it upsets mother and the girls, and there's always the chance that some time we won't be able to arrange it."

Shreds and tatters of chinchilla, courtesy clouds in the green moon's heaven, were passing the green moon like precious Eastern stuffs paraded for the inspection of some Tartar Khan. It seemed to John that it was day, and that he was looking at some lads sailing above him in the air, showering down tracts and patent medicine circulars, with their messages of hope for despairing, rockbound hamlets. It seemed to him that he could see them look down out of the clouds and stare—and stare at whatever there was to stare at in this place whither he was bound— What then? Were they induced to land by some insidious device there to be immured far from patent medicines and from tracts until the judgment day— or, should they fail to fall into the trap, did a quick puff of smoke and the sharp round of a splitting shell bring them drooping to earth—and "upset" Percy's mother and sisters. John shook his head and the wraith of a hollow laugh issued silently from his parted lips. What desperate transaction lay hidden here? What a moral expedient of a bizarre Croesus? What terrible and golden mystery? . . .

The chinchilla clouds had drifted past now and outside the Montana night was bright as day. The tapestry brick of the road was smooth to the tread of the great tires as they rounded a still, moonlit lake; they passed into darkness for a moment, a pine grove, pungent and cool, then they came out into a broad avenue of lawn and John's exclamation of pleasure was simultaneous with Percy's taciturn "We're home."

Full in the light of the stars, an exquisite château rose from the borders of the lake, climbed in marble radiance half the height of an adjoining mountain, then melted in grace, in perfect symmetry, in translucent feminine languor, into the massed darkness of a forest of pine. The many towers, the slender tracery of the sloping parapets, the chiselled wonder of a thousand yellow windows with their oblongs and hectagons and triangles of golden light, the shattered softness of the intersecting planes of star-shine and blue shade, all trembled on John's spirit like a chord of music. On one of the towers, the tallest, the blackest at its base, an arrangement of exterior lights at the top made a sort of floating fairyland—and as John gazed up in warm enchantment the faint acciaccare sound of violins drifted down in a rococo harmony that was like nothing he had ever heard before. Then in a moment the car stopped before wide, high marble steps around which the night air was fragrant with a host of flowers. At the top of the steps two great doors swung silently open and amber light flooded out upon the darkness, silhouetting the figure of an exquisite lady with black, high-piled hair, who held out her arms toward them.

"Mother," Percy was saying, "this is my friend, John Unger, from Hades."

Afterward John remembered that first night as a daze of many colors, of quick sensory impressions, of music soft as a voice in love, and of the beauty of things, lights and shadows, and motions and faces. There was a white-haired man who stood drinking a many-hued cordial from a crystal thimble set on a golden stem. There was a girl with a flowery face, dressed like Titania with braided sapphires in her hair. There was a room where the solid, soft gold of the walls yielded to the pressure of his hand, and a room that was like a platonic conception of the ultimate prison—ceiling, floor, and all, it was lined with an unbroken mass of diamonds, diamonds of every size and shape, until, lit with tall violet lamps in the corners, it dazzled the eyes with a whiteness that could be compared only with itself, beyond human wish or dream.

Through a maze of these rooms the two boys wandered. Sometimes the floor under their feet would flame in brilliant patterns from lighting below, patterns of barbaric clashing colors, of pastel delicacy, of sheer whiteness, or of subtle and intricate mosaic, surely from some mosque on the Adriatic Sea. Sometimes beneath layers of thick crystal he would see blue or green water swirling, inhabited by vivid fish and growths of rainbow foliage. Then they would be treading on furs of every texture and color or along corridors of palest ivory, unbroken as though carved complete from the gigantic tusks of dinosaurs extinct before the age of man. . . .

Then a hazily remembered transition, and they were at dinner—where each plate was of two almost imperceptible layers of solid diamond between which was curiously worked a filigree of emerald design, a shaving sliced from green air. Music, plangent and unobtrusive, drifted down through far corridors—his chair, feathered and curved insidiously to his back, seemed to engulf and overpower him as he drank his first glass of port. He tried drowsily to answer a question that had been asked him, but the honeyed luxury that clasped his body added to the illusion of sleep—jewels, fabrics, wines, and metals blurred before his eyes into a sweet mist. . . .

"Yes," he replied with a polite effort, "it certainly is hot enough for me down there."

He managed to add a ghostly laugh; then, without movement, without resistance, he seemed to float off and away, leaving an iced dessert that was pink as a dream. . . . He fell asleep.

When he awoke he knew that several hours had passed. He was in a great quiet room with ebony walls and a dull illumination that was too faint, too subtle, to be called a light. His young host was standing over him.

"You fell asleep at dinner," Percy was saying. "I nearly did, too—it was such a treat to be comfortable again after this year of school. Servants undressed and bathed you while you were sleeping."

"Is this a bed or a cloud?" sighed John. "Percy, Percy—before you go, I want to apologize."

"For what?"

"For doubting you when you said you had a diamond as big as the Ritz-Carlton Hotel."

Percy smiled.

"I thought you didn't believe me. It's that mountain, you know."

"What mountain?"

"The mountain the château rests on. It's not very big for a mountain. But except about fifty feet of sod and gravel on top it's solid diamond. *One* diamond, one cubic mile without a flaw. Aren't you listening? Say——"

But John T. Unger had again fallen asleep.

III

Morning. As he awoke he perceived drowsily that the room had at the same moment become dense with sunlight. The ebony panels of one wall had slid aside on a sort of track, leaving his chamber half open to the day. A large negro in a white uniform stood beside his bed.

"Good-evening," muttered John, summoning his brains from the wild places.

"Good-morning, sir. Are you ready for your bath, sir? Oh, don't get up—I'll put you in, if you'll just unbutton your pajamas—there, Thank you, sir."

John lay quietly as his pajamas were removed—he was amused and delighted; he expected to be lifted like a child by this black Gargantua who was tending him, but nothing of the sort happened; instead he felt the bed tilt up slowly on its side—he began to roll, startled at first, in the direction of the wall, but when he reached the wall its drapery gave way, and sliding two yards farther down a fleecy incline he plumped gently into water the same temperature as his body.

He looked about him. The runway or rollway on which he had arrived had folded gently back into place. He had been projected into another chamber and was sitting in a sunken bath with his head above the level of the floor. All about him, lining the walls of the room and the sides and bottom of the bath itself, was a blue aquarium, and gazing through the crystal surface on which he sat, he could see fish swimming among amber lights and even gliding without curiosity past his outstretched toes, which were separated from them only by the thickness of the crystal. From overhead, sunlight came down through sea-green glass.

"I suppose, sir, that you'd like hot rosewater and soapsuds this morning, sir—and perhaps cold salt water to finish."

The negro was standing beside him.

"Yes," agreed John, smiling inanely, "as you please." Any idea of ordering this bath according to his own meagre standards of living would have been priggish and not a little wicked.

The negro pressed a button and a warm rain began to fall, apparently from overhead, but really, so John discovered after a moment, from a fountain arrangement near by. The water turned to a pale rose color and jets of liquid soap spurted into it from four miniature walrus heads at the corners of the bath. In a moment a dozen little paddle-wheels, fixed to the sides, had churned the mixture into a radiant rainbow of pink foam which enveloped him softly with its delicious lightness, and burst in shining, rosy bubbles here and there about him.

"Shall I turn on the moving-picture machine, sir?" suggested the negro deferentially. "There's a good one-reel comedy in this machine to-day, or I can put in a serious piece in a moment, if you prefer it."

"No, thanks," answered John, politely but firmly. He was enjoying his bath too much to desire any distraction. But distraction came. In a moment he was listening intently to the sound of flutes from just outside, flutes dripping a melody that was like a waterfall, cool and green as the room itself, accompanying a frothy piccolo, in play more fragile than the lace of suds that covered and charmed him.

After a cold salt-water bracer and a cold fresh finish, he stepped out into a fleecy robe, and upon a couch covered with the same material he was rubbed with oil, alcohol, and spice. Later he sat in a voluptuous chair while he was shaved and his hair was trimmed.

"Mr. Percy is waiting in your sitting-room," said the negro, when these operations were finished. "My name is Gygsum, Mr. Unger, sir. I am to see to Mr. Unger every morning."

John walked out into the brisk sunshine of his living-room, where he found breakfast waiting for him and Percy, gorgeous in white kid knickerbockers, smoking in an easy chair.

IV

This is a story of the Washington family as Percy sketched it for John during breakfast.

The father of the present Mr. Washington had been a Virginian, a direct descendant of George Washington, and Lord Baltimore. At the close of the Civil War he was a twenty-five-year-old Colonel with a played-out plantation and about a thousand dollars in gold.

Fitz-Norman Culpepper Washington, for that was the young Colonel's name, decided to present the Virginia estate to his younger brother and go West. He selected two dozen of the most faithful blacks, who, of course, worshipped him, and bought twenty-five tickets to the West, where he intended to take out land in their names and start a sheep and cattle ranch.

When he had been in Montana for less than a month and things were going very poorly indeed, he stumbled on his great discovery. He had lost his way when riding in the hills, and after a day without food he began to grow hungry. As he was without his rifle, he was forced to pursue a squirrel, and in the course of the pursuit he noticed that it was carrying something shiny in its mouth. Just before it vanished into its hole—for Providence did not intend that this squirrel should alleviate his hunger—it dropped its burden. Sitting down to consider the situation Fitz-Norman's eye was caught by a gleam in the grass beside him. In ten seconds he had completely lost his appetite and gained one hundred thousand dollars. The squirrel, which had refused with annoying persistence to become food, had made him a present of a large and perfect diamond.

Late that night he found his way to camp and twelve hours later all the males among his darkies were back by the squirrel hole digging furiously at the side of the mountain. He told them he had discovered a rhinestone mine, and, as only one or two of them had ever seen even a small diamond before, they believed him, without question. When the magnitude of his discovery became apparent to him, he found himself in a quandary. The mountain was *a* diamond —it was literally nothing else but solid diamond. He filled four saddle bags full of glittering samples and started on horseback for St. Paul. There he managed to dispose of a half dozen small stones —when he tried a larger one a storekeeper fainted and Fitz-Norman was arrested as a public disturber. He escaped from jail and caught the train for New York, where he sold a few medium-sized diamonds and received in exchange about two hundred thousand dollars in gold. But he did not dare to produce any exceptional gems—in fact, he left New York just in time. Tremendous excitement had been created in jewelry circles, not so much by the size of his diamonds as by their appearance in the city from mysterious sources. Wild rumors became current that a diamond mine had been discovered in the Catskills, on the Jersey coast, on Long Island, beneath Washington Square. Excursion trains, packed with men carrying picks and shovels began to leave New York hourly, bound for various neighboring El Dorados. But by that time young Fitz-Norman was on his way back to Montana.

By the end of a fortnight he had estimated that the diamond in the mountain was approximately equal in quantity to all the rest of the diamonds known to exist in the world. There was no valuing it by any regular computation, however, for it was *one solid diamond*—and if it were offered for sale not only would the bottom fall out of the market, but also, if the value should vary with its size in the usual arithmetical progression, there would not be enough gold in the world to buy a tenth part of it. And what could any one do with a diamond that size?

It was an amazing predicament. He was, in one sense, the richest man that ever lived—and yet was he worth anything at all? If his secret should transpire there was no telling to what measures the Government might resort in order to prevent a panic, in gold as well as in jewels. They might take over the claim immediately and institute a monopoly.

There was no alternative—he must market his mountain in secret. He sent South for his younger brother and put him in charge of his colored following—darkies who had never realized that slavery was abolished. To make sure of this, he read them a proclamation that he had composed, which announced that General Forrest had reorganized the shattered Southern armies and defeated the North in one pitched battle. The negroes believed him implicity. They passed a vote declaring it a good thing and held revival services immediately.

Fitz-Norman himself set out for foreign parts with one hundred thousand dollars and two trunks filled with rough diamonds of all sizes. He sailed for Russia in a Chinese junk and six months after his departure from Montana he was in St. Petersburg. He took obscure lodgings and called immediately upon the court jeweller, announcing that he had a diamond for the Czar. He remained in St. Petersburg for two weeks, in constant danger of being murdered, living, from lodging to lodging, and afraid to visit his trunks more than three or four times during the whole fortnight.

On his promise to return in a year with larger and finer stones, he was allowed to leave for India. Before he left, however, the Court Treasurers had deposited to his credit, in American banks, the sum of fifteen million dollars—under four different aliases.

He returned to America in 1868, having been gone a little over two years. He had visited the capitals of twenty-two countries and talked with five emperors, eleven kings, three princes, a shah, a khan, and a sultan. At that time Fitz-Norman estimated his own wealth at one billion dollars. One fact worked consistently against the disclosure of his secret. No one of his larger diamonds remained in the public eye for a week before being invested with a history of enough fatalities, amours, revolutions, and wars to have occupied it from the days of the first Babylonian Empire.

From 1870 until his death in 1900, the history of Fitz-Norman Washington was a long epic in gold. There were side issues, of course—he evaded the surveys, he married a Virginia lady, by whom he had a single son, and he was compelled, due to a series of unfortunate complications, to murder his brother, whose unfortunate habit of drinking himself into an indiscreet stupor had several times endangered their safety. But very few other murders stained these happy years of progress and expansion.

Just before he died he changed his policy, and with all but a few million dollars of his outside wealth bought up rare minerals in bulk, which he deposited in the safety vaults of banks all over the world, marked as bric-à-brac. His son, Braddock Tarleton Washington, followed this policy on an even more intensive scale. The minerals were converted into the rarest of all elements—radium—so that the equivalent of a billion dollars in gold could be placed in a receptacle no bigger than a cigar box.

When Fitz-Norman had been dead three years his son, Braddock, decided that the business had gone far enough. The amount of wealth that he and his father had taken out of the mountain was beyond all exact computation. He kept a note-book in cipher in which he set down the approximate quantity of radium in each of the thousand banks he patronized, and recorded the alias under which it was held. Then he did a very simple thing—he sealed up the mine.

He sealed up the mine. What had been taken out of it would support all the Washingtons yet to be born in unparalleled luxury for generations. His one care must be the protection of his secret, lest in the possible panic attendant on its discovery he should be reduced with all the property-holders in the world to utter poverty.

This was the family among whom John T. Unger was staying.

232   This was the story he heard in his silver-walled living-room the morning after his arrival.

V

After breakfast, John found his way out the great marble entrance, and looked curiously at the scene before him. The whole valley, from the diamond mountain to the steep granite cliff five miles away, still gave off a breath of golden haze which hovered idly above the fine sweep of lawns and lakes and gardens. Here and there clusters of elms made delicate groves of shade, contrasting strangely with the tough masses of pine forest that held the hills in a grip of dark-blue green. Even as John looked he saw three fawns in single file patter out from one clump about a half mile away and disappear with awkward gayety into the black-ribbed half-light of another. John would not have been surprised to see a goat-foot piping his way among the trees or to catch a glimpse of pink nymph-skin and flying yellow hair between the greenest of the green leaves.

In some such cool hope he descended the marble steps, disturbing faintly the sleep of two silky Russian wolfhounds at the bottom, and set off along a walk of white and blue brick that seemed to lead in no particular direction.

He was enjoying himself as much as he was able. It is youth's felicity as well as its insufficiency that it can never live in the present, but must always be measuring up the day against its own radiantly imagined future—flowers and gold, girls and stars, they are only prefigurations and prophecies of that incomparable, unattainable young dream.

John rounded a soft corner where the massed rosebushes filled the air with heavy scent, and struck off across a park toward a patch of moss under some trees. He had never lain upon moss, and he wanted to see whether it was really soft enough to justify the use of its name as an adjective. Then he saw a girl coming toward him over the grass. She was the most beautiful person he had ever seen.

She was dressed in a white gown that came just below her knees, and a wreath of mignonettes clasped with blue slices of sapphire bound up her hair. Her pink bare feet scattered the dew before them as she came. She was younger than John—not more than sixteen.

"Hello," she cried softly, "I'm Kismine."

She was much more than that to John already. He advanced toward her, scarcely moving as he drew near lest he should tread on her bare toes.

"You haven't met me," said her soft voice. Her blue eyes added, "Oh, but you've missed a great deal!" . . . "You met my sister, Jasmine, last night, I was sick with lettuce poisoning," went on her soft voice, and her eyes continued, "and when I'm sick I'm sweet— and when I'm well."

"You have made an enormous impression on me," said John's eyes, "and I'm not so slow myself"—"How do you do?" said his voice. "I hope you're better this morning."—"You darling," added his eyes tremulously.

John observed that they had been walking along the path. On her suggestion they sat down together upon the moss, the softness of which he failed to determine.

He was critical about women. A single defect—a thick ankle, a hoarse voice, a glass eye—was enough to make him utterly indifferent. And here for the first time in his life he was beside a girl who seemed to him the incarnation of physical perfection.

"Are you from the East?" asked Kismine with charming interest.

"No," answered John simply. "I'm from Hades."

Either she had never heard of Hades, or she could think of no pleasant comment to make upon it, for she did not discuss it further.

"I'm going East to school this fall," she said. "D'you think I'll make it? I'm going to New York to Miss Bulge's. It's very strict, but you see over the weekends I'm going to live at home with the family in our New York house, because father heard that the girls had to go walking two by two."

"Your father wants you to be proud," observed John.

"We are," she answered, her eyes shining with dignity. "None of us has ever been punished. Father said we never should be. Once when my sister Jasmine was a little girl she pushed him down-stairs and he just got up and limped away.

"Mother was—well, a little startled," continued Kismine, "when she heard that you were from—from where you *are* from, you know. She said that when she was a young girl—but then, you see, she's a Spaniard and old-fashioned."

"Do you spend much time out here?" asked John, to conceal the fact that he was somewhat hurt by this remark. It seemed an unkind allusion to his provincialism.

"Percy and Jasmine and I are here every summer, but next summer Jasmine is going to Newport. She's coming out in London a year from this fall. She'll be presented at court."

"Do you know," began John hesitantly, "you're much more sophisticated than I thought you were when I first saw you?"

"Oh, no, I'm not," she exclaimed hurriedly. "Oh, I wouldn't think of being. I think that sophisticated young people are *terribly* common, don't you? I'm not at all, really. If you say I am, I'm going to cry."

She was so distressed that her lip was trembling. John was impelled to protest:

"I didn't mean that; I only said it to tease you."

"Because I wouldn't mind if I *were*," she persisted, "but I'm *not*. I'm very innocent and girlish. I never smoke, or drink, or read anything except poetry. I know scarcely any mathematics or chemistry. I dress *very* simply—in fact, I scarcely dress at all. I think sophisticated is the last thing you can say about me. I believe that girls ought to enjoy their youths in a wholesome way."

"I do too," said John heartily.

Kismine was cheerful again. She smiled at him, and a still-born tear dripped from the corner of one blue eye.

"I like you," she whispered, intimately. "Are you going to spend all your time with Percy while you're here, or will you be nice to me? Just think—I'm absolutely fresh ground. I've never had a boy in love with me in all my life. I've never been allowed even to *see* boys alone—except Percy. I came all the way out here into this grove hoping to run into you, where the family wouldn't be around."

Deeply flattered, John bowed from the hips as he had been taught at dancing school in Hades.

"We'd better go now," said Kismine sweetly. "I have to be with mother at eleven. You haven't asked me to kiss you once. I thought boys always did that nowadays."

John drew himself up proudly.

"Some of them do," he answered, "but not me. Girls don't do that sort of thing—in Hades."

Side by side they walked back toward the house.

VI

John stood facing Mr. Braddock Washington in the full sunlight. The elder man was about forty with a proud, vacuous face, intelligent eyes, and a robust figure. In the mornings he smelt of horses— the best horses. He carried a plain walking-stick of gray birch with a single large opal for a grip. He and Percy were showing John around.

"The slaves' quarters are there." His walking-stick indicated a cloister of marble on their left that ran in graceful Gothic along the side of the mountain. "In my youth I was distracted for a while from the business of life by a period of absurd idealism. During that time they lived in luxury. For instance, I equipped every one of their rooms with a tile bath."

"I suppose," ventured John, with an ingratiating laugh, "that they used the bathtubs to keep coal in. Mr. Schnlitzer-Murphy told me that once he——"

"The opinions of Mr. Schnlitzer-Murphy are of little importance I should imagine," interrupted Braddock Washington, coldly. "My slaves did not keep coal in their bathtubs. They had orders to bathe every day, and they did. If they hadn't I might have ordered a sulphuric acid shampoo. I discontinued the baths for quite another reason. Several of them caught cold and died. Water is not good for certain races—except as a beverage."

John laughed, and then decided to nod his head in sober agreement. Braddock Washington made him uncomfortable.

"All these negroes are descendants of the ones my father brought North with him. There are about two hundred and fifty now. You notice that they've lived so long apart from the world that their original dialect has become an almost indistinguishable patois. We bring a few of them up to speak English—my secretary and two or three of the house servants.

"This is the golf course," he continued, as they strolled along the velvet winter grass. "It's all a green, you see—no fairway, no rough, no hazards."

He smiled pleasantly at John.

"Many men in the cage, father?" asked Percy suddenly.

Braddock Washington stumbled, and let forth an involuntary curse.

"One less than there should be," he ejaculated darkly—and then added, after a moment, "We've had difficulties."

"Mother was telling me," exclaimed Percy, "that Italian teacher——"

"A ghastly error," said Braddock Washington angrily. "But of course there's a good chance that we may have got him. Perhaps he fell somewhere in the woods or stumbled over a cliff. And then there's always the probability that if he did get away his story wouldn't be believed. Nevertheless, I've had two dozen men looking for him in different towns around here."

"And no luck?"

"Some. Fourteen of them reported to my agent that they'd each killed a man answering to that description, but of course it was probably only the reward they were after——"

He broke off. They had come to a large cavity in the earth about the circumference of a merry-go-round and covered by a strong iron grating. Braddock Washington beckoned to John, and pointed his cane down through the grating. John stepped to the edge and gazed. Immediately his ears were assailed by a wild clamor from below.

"Come on down to Hell!"

"Hello, kiddo, how's the air up there?"

"Hey! Throw us a rope!"

"Got an old doughnut, Buddy, or a couple of second-hand sandwiches?"

"Say, fella, if you'll push down that guy you're with, we'll show you a quick disappearance scene."

"Paste him one for me, will you?"

It was too dark to see clearly into the pit below, but John could tell from the coarse optimism and rugged vitality of the remarks and voices that they proceeded from middle-class Americans of the more spirited type. Then Mr. Washington put out his cane and touched a button in the grass, and the scene below sprang into light.

"These are some adventurous mariners who had the misfortune to discover El Dorado," he remarked.

Below them there had appeared a large hollow in the earth shaped like the interior of a bowl. The sides were steep and apparently of polished glass, and on its slightly concave surface stood about two dozen men clad in the half costume, half uniform, of aviators. Their upturned faces, lit with wrath, with malice, with despair, with cynical humor, were covered by long growths of beard, but with the exception of a few who had pined perceptibly away, they seemed to be a well-fed, healthy lot.

Braddock Washington drew a garden chair to the edge of the pit and sat down.

"Well, how are you, boys?" he inquired genially.

A chorus of execration in which all joined except a few too dispirited to cry out, rose up into the sunny air, but Braddock Washington heard it with unruffled composure. When its last echo had died away he spoke again.

"Have you thought up a way out of your difficulty?"

From here and there among them a remark floated up.

"We decided to stay here for love!"

"Bring us up there and we'll find us a way!"

Braddock Washington waited until they were again quiet. Then he said:

"I've told you the situation. I don't want you here. I wish to heaven I'd never seen you. Your own curiosity got you here, and any time that you can think of a way out which protects me and my interests I'll be glad to consider it. But so long as you confine your efforts to digging tunnels—yes, I know about the new one you've started—you won't get very far. This isn't as hard on you as you make it out, with all your howling for the loved ones at home. If you were the type who worried much about the loved ones at home, you'd never have taken up aviation."

A tall man moved apart from the others, and held up his hand to call his captor's attention to what he was about to say.

"Let me ask you a few questions!" he cried. "You pretend to be a fair-minded man."

"How absurd. How could a man of *my* position be fair-minded toward *you*? You might as well speak of a Spaniard being fair-minded toward a piece of steak."

At this harsh observation the faces of the two dozen steaks fell, but the tall man continued:

"All right!" he cried. "We've argued this out before. You're not a humanitarian and you're not fair-minded, but you're human—at least you say you are—and you ought to be able to put yourself in our place for long enough to think how—how—how——"

"How what?" demanded Washington, coldly.

"—how unnecessary——"

"Not to me."

"Well,—how cruel——"

"We've covered that. Cruelty doesn't exist where self-preservation is involved. You've been soldiers: you know that. Try another."

"Well, then, how stupid."

"There," admitted Washington, "I grant you that. But try to think of an alternative. I've offered to have all or any of you painlessly executed if you wish. I've offered to have your wives, sweethearts, children, and mothers kidnapped and brought out here. I'll enlarge your place down there and feed and clothe you the rest of your lives. If there was some method of producing permanent amnesia I'd have all of you operated on and released immediately, somewhere outside of my preserves. But that's as far as my ideas go."

"How about trusting us not to peach on you?" cried some one.

"You don't proffer that suggestion seriously," said Washington, with an expression of scorn. "I did take out one man to teach my daughter Italian. Last week he got away."

A wild yell of jubilation went up suddenly from two dozen throats and a pandemonium of joy ensued. The prisoners clog-danced and cheered and yodled and wrestled with one another in a sudden uprush of animal spirits. They even ran up the glass sides of the bowl as far as they could, and slid back to the bottom upon the natural cushions of their bodies. The tall man started a song in which they all joined——

"Oh, we'll hang the kaiser
On a sour apple tree——"

Braddock Washington sat in inscrutable silence until the song was over.

"You see," he remarked, when he could gain a modicum of attention. "I bear you no ill-will. I like to see you enjoying yourselves. That's why I didn't tell you the whole story at once. The man—what was his name? Critchtichiello?—was shot by some of my agents in fourteen different places."

Not guessing that the places referred to were cities, the tumult of rejoicing subsided immediately.

"Nevertheless," cried Washington with a touch of anger, "he tried to run away. Do you expect me to take chances with any of you after an experience like that?"

Again a series of ejaculations went up.

"Sure!"

"Would your daughter like to learn Chinese?"

"Hey, I can speak Italian! My mother was a wop."

"Maybe she'd like t'learna speak N'Yawk!"

"If she's the little one with the big blue eyes I can teach her a lot of things better than Italian."

"I know some Irish songs—and I could hammer brass once't."

Mr. Washington reached forward suddenly with his cane and pushed the button in the grass so that the picture below went out instantly, and there remained only that great dark mouth covered dismally with the black teeth of the grating.

"Hey!" called a single voice from below, "you ain't goin' away without givin' us your blessing?"

But Mr. Washington, followed by the two boys, was already strolling on toward the ninth hole of the golf course, as though the pit and its contents were no more than a hazard over which his facile iron had triumphed with ease.

VII

July under the lee of the diamond mountain was a month of blanket nights and of warm, glowing days. John and Kismine were in love. He did not know that the little gold football (inscribed with the legend *Pro deo et patria et St. Mida*) which he had given her rested on a platinum chain next to her bosom. But it did. And she for her part was not aware that a large sapphire which had dropped one day from her simple coiffure was stowed away tenderly in John's jewel box.

Late one afternoon when the ruby and ermine music room was quiet, they spent an hour there together. He held her hand and she gave him such a look that he whispered her name aloud. She bent toward him—then hesitated.

"Did you say 'Kismine'?" she asked softly, "or——"

She had wanted to be sure. She thought she might have misunderstood.

Neither of them had ever kissed before, but in the course of an hour it seemed to make little difference.

The afternoon drifted away. That night when a last breath of music drifted down from the highest tower, they each lay awake, happily dreaming over the separate minutes of the day. They had decided to be married as soon as possible.

VIII

Every day Mr. Washington and the two young men went hunting or fishing in the deep forests or played golf around the somnolent course—games which John diplomatically allowed his host to win——or swam in the mountain coolness of the lake. John found Mr. Washington a somewhat exacting personality—utterly uninterested in any ideas or opinions except his own. Mrs. Washington was aloof and reserved at all times. She was apparently indifferent to her two daughters, and entirely absorbed in her son Percy, with whom she held interminable conversations in rapid Spanish at dinner.

Jasmine, the elder daughter, resembled Kismine in appearance—except that she was somewhat bow-legged, and terminated in large hands and feet—but was utterly unlike her in temperament. Her favorite books had to do with poor girls who kept house for widowed fathers. John learned from Kismine that Jasmine had never recovered from the shock and disappointment caused her by the termination of the World War, just as she was about to start for Europe as a canteen expert. She had even pined away for a time, and Braddock Washington had taken steps to promote a new war in the Balkans—but she had seen a photograph of some wounded Serbian soldiers and lost interest in the whole proceedings. But Percy and Kismine seemed to have inherited the arrogant attitude in all its harsh magnificence from their father. A chaste and consistent selfishness ran like a pattern through their every idea.

John was enchanted by the wonders of the château and the valley. Braddock Washington, so Percy told him, had caused to be kidnapped a landscape gardener, an architect, a designer of stage settings, and a French decadent poet left over from the last century. He had put his entire force of negroes at their disposal, guaranteed to supply them with any materials that the world could offer, and left them to work out some ideas of their own. But one by one they had shown their uselessness. The decadent poet had at once begun bewailing his separation from the boulevards in spring—he made some vague remarks about spices, apes, and ivories, but said nothing that was of any practical value. The stage designer on his part wanted to make the whole valley a series of tricks and sensational effects—a state of things that the Washingtons would soon have grown tired of. And as for the architect and the landscape gardener, they thought only in terms of convention. They must make this like this and that like that.

But they had, at least, solved the problem of what was to be done with them—they all went mad early one morning after spending the night in a single room trying to agree upon the location of a fountain, and were now confined comfortably in an insane asylum at Westport, Connecticut.

"But," inquired John curiously, "who did plan all your wonderful reception rooms and halls, and approaches and bathrooms——?"

"Well," answered Percy, "I blush to tell you, but it was a moving-picture fella. He was the only man we found who was used to playing with an unlimited amount of money, though he did tuck his napkin in his collar and couldn't read or write."

As August drew to a close John began to regret that he must soon go back to school. He and Kismine had decided to elope the following June.

"It would be nicer to be married here," Kismine confessed, "but of course I could never get father's permission to marry you at all. Next to that I'd rather elope. It's terrible for wealthy people to be married in America at present—they always have to send out bulle-

tins to the press saying that they're going to be married in rem-
nants, when what they mean is just a peck of old second-hand
pearls and some used lace worn once by the Empress Eugénie."

"I know," agreed John fervently. "When I was visiting the Schnlitzer-Murphys, the eldest daughter, Gwendolyn, married a man
whose father owns half of West Virginia. She wrote home saying
what a tough struggle she was carrying on on his salary as a bank
clerk—and then she ended up by saying that 'Thank God, I have four
good maids anyhow, and that helps a little.'"

"It's absurd," commented Kismine. "Think of the millions and
millions of people in the world, laborers and all, who get along
with only two maids."

One afternoon late in August a chance remark of Kismine's
changed the face of the entire situation, and threw John into a state
of terror.

They were in their favorite grove, and between kisses John was
indulging in some romantic forebodings which he fancied added
poignancy to their relations.

"Sometimes I think we'll never marry," he said sadly. "You're too
wealthy, too magnificent. No one as rich as you are can be like
other girls. I should marry the daughter of some well-to-do wholesale hardware man from Omaha or Sioux City, and be content with
her half-million."

"I knew the daughter of a wholesale hardware man once," remarked Kismine. "I don't think you'd have been contented with
her. She was a friend of my sister's. She visited here."

"Oh, then you've had other guests?" exclaimed John in surprise.

Kismine seemed to regret her words.

"Oh, yes," she said hurriedly, "we've had a few."

"But aren't you—wasn't your father afraid they'd talk outside?"

"Oh, to some extent, to some extent," she answered. "Let's talk
about something pleasanter."

But John's curiosity was aroused.

"Something pleasanter!" he demanded. "What's unpleasant about
that? Weren't they nice girls?"

To his great surprise Kismine began to weep.

"Yes—th—that's the—the whole t-trouble. I grew qu-quite attached
to some of them. So did Jasmine, but she kept inv-viting them anyway. I couldn't under*stand* it."

A dark suspicion was born in John's heart.

"Do you mean that they *told,* and your father had them—removed?"

"Worse than that," she muttered brokenly. "Father took no chances —and Jasmine kept writing them to come, and they had *such* a good time!"

She was overcome by a paroxysm of grief.

Stunned with the horror of this revelation, John sat there open-mouthed, feeling the nerves of his body twitter like so many sparrows perched upon his spinal column.

"Now, I've told you, and I shouldn't have," she said, calming suddenly and drying her dark blue eyes.

"Do you mean to say that your father had them *murdered* before they left?"

She nodded.

"In August usually—or early in September. It's only natural for us to get all the pleasure out of them that we can first."

"How abominable! How—why, I must be going crazy! Did you really admit that——"

"I did," interrupted Kismine, shrugging her shoulders. "We can't very well imprison them like those aviators, where they'd be a continual reproach to us every day. And it's always been made easier for Jasmine and me, because father had it done sooner than we expected. In that way we avoided any farewell scene——"

"So you murdered them! Uh!" cried John.

"It was done very nicely. They were drugged while they were asleep—and their families were always told that they died of scarlet fever in Butte."

"But—I fail to understand why you kept on inviting them!"

"I didn't," burst out Kismine. "I never invited one. Jasmine did. And they always had a very good time. She'd give them the nicest presents toward the last. I shall probably have visitors too—I'll harden up to it. We can't let such an inevitable thing as death stand in the way of enjoying life while we have it. Think how lonesome it'd be out here if we never had *any* one. Why, father and mother have sacrificed some of their best friends just as we have."

"And so," cried John accusingly, "and so you were letting me make love to you and pretending to return it, and talking about marriage, all the time knowing perfectly well that I'd never get out of here alive——"

"No," she protested passionately. "Not any more. I did at first.

You were here. I couldn't help that, and I thought your last days might as well be pleasant for both of us. But then I fell in love with you, and—and I'm honestly sorry you're going to—going to be put away—though I'd rather you'd be put away than ever kiss another girl."

"Oh, you would, would you?" cried John ferociously.

"Much rather. Besides, I've always heard that a girl can have more fun with a man whom she knows she can never marry. Oh, why did I tell you? I've probably spoiled your whole good time now, and we were really enjoying things when you didn't know it. I knew it would make things sort of depressing for you."

"Oh, you did, did you?" John's voice trembled with anger. "I've heard about enough of this. If you haven't any more pride and decency than to have an affair with a fellow that you know isn't much better than a corpse, I don't want to have any more to do with you."

"You're not a corpse!" she protested in horror. "You're not a corpse! I won't have you saying that I kissed a corpse!"

"I said nothing of the sort!"

"You did! You said I kissed a corpse!"

"I didn't!"

Their voices had risen, but upon a sudden interruption they both subsided into immediate silence. Footsteps were coming along the path in their direction, and a moment later the rose bushes were parted displaying Braddock Washington, whose intelligent eyes set in his good-looking vacuous face were peering in at them.

"Who kissed a corpse?" he demanded in obvious disapproval.

"Nobody," answered Kismine quickly. "We were just joking."

"What are you two doing here, anyhow?" he demanded gruffly. "Kismine, you ought to be—to be reading or playing golf with your sister. Go read! Go play golf! Don't let me find you here when I come back!"

Then he bowed at John and went up the path.

"See?" said Kismine crossly, when he was out of hearing. "You've spoiled it all. We can never meet any more. He won't let me meet you. He'd have you poisoned if he thought we were in love."

"We're not, any more!" cried John fiercely, "so he can set his mind at rest upon that. Moreover, don't fool yourself that I'm going to stay around here. Inside of six hours I'll be over those mountains, if I have to gnaw a passage through them, and on my way East."

They had both got to their feet, and at this remark Kismine came close and put her arm through his.

"I'm going, too."

"You must be crazy——"

"Of course I'm going," she interrupted impatiently.

"You most certainly are not. You——"

"Very well," she said quietly, "we'll catch up with father now and talk it over with him."

Defeated, John mustered a sickly smile.

"Very well, dearest," he agreed, with pale and unconvincing affection, "we'll go together."

His love for her returned and settled placidly on his heart. She was his—she would go with him to share his dangers. He put his arms about her and kissed her fervently. After all she loved him; she had saved him, in fact.

Discussing the matter they walked slowly back toward the château. They decided that since Braddock Washington had seen them together they had best depart the next night. Nevertheless, John's lips were unusually dry at dinner, and he nervously emptied a great spoonful of peacock soup into his left lung. He had to be carried into the tourquoise and sable card-room and pounded on the back by one of the under-butlers, which Percy considered a great joke.

IX

Long after midnight John's body gave a nervous jerk, and he sat suddenly upright, staring into the veils of somnolence that draped the room. Through the squares of blue darkness that were his open windows, he had heard a faint far-away sound that died upon a bed of wind before identifying itself on his memory, clouded with uneasy dreams. But the sharp noise that had succeeded it was nearer, was just outside the room—the click of a turned knob, a footstep, a whisper, he could not tell; a hard lump gathered in the pit of his stomach, and his whole body ached in the moment that he strained agonizingly to hear. Then one of the veils seemed to dissolve, and he saw a vague figure standing by the door, a figure only faintly limned and blocked in upon the darkness, mingled so with the folds of the drapery as to seem distorted, like a reflection seen in a dirty pane of glass.

With a sudden movement of fright or resolution John pressed the button by his bedside, and the next moment he was sitting in the green sunken bath of the adjoining room, waked into alertness by the shock of the cold water which half filled it.

He sprang out, and, his wet pajamas scattering a heavy trickle of water behind him, ran for the aquamarine door which he knew led out onto the ivory landing of the second floor. The door opened noiselessly. A single crimson lamp burning in a great dome above lit the magnificent sweep of the carved stairways with a poignant beauty. For a moment John hesitated, appalled by the silent splendor massed about him, seeming to envelop in its gigantic folds and contours the solitary drenched little figure shivering upon the ivory landing. Then simultaneously two things happened. The door of his own sitting-room swung open, precipitating three naked negroes into the hall—and, as John swayed in wild terror toward the stairway, another door slid back in the wall on the other side of the corridor, and John saw Braddock Washington standing in the lighted lift, wearing a fur coat and a pair of riding boots which reached to his knees and displayed, above, the glow of his rose-colored pajamas.

On the instant the three negroes—John had never seen any of them before, and it flashed through his mind that they must be the professional executioners—paused in their movement toward John, and turned expectantly to the man in the lift, who burst out with an imperious command:

"Get in here! All three of you! Quick as hell!"

Then, within the instant, the three negroes darted into the cage, the oblong of light was blotted out as the lift door slid shut, and John was again alone in the hall. He slumped weakly down against an ivory stair.

It was apparent that something portentous had occurred, something which, for the moment at least, had postponed his own petty disaster. What was it? Had the negroes risen in revolt? Had the aviators forced aside the iron bars of the grating? Or had the men of Fish stumbled blindly through the hills and gazed with bleak, joyless eyes upon the gaudy valley? John did not know. He heard a faint whir of air as the lift whizzed up again, and then, a moment later, as it descended. It was probable that Percy was hurrying to his father's assistance, and it occurred to John that this was his opportunity to join Kismine and plan an immediate escape. He waited until the lift had been silent for several minutes; shivering a little with the night cool that whipped in through his wet pajamas, he returned to his room and dressed himself quickly. Then he mounted a long flight of stairs and turned down the corridor carpeted with Russian sable which led to Kismine's suite.

The door of her sitting-room was open and the lamps were lighted. Kismine, in an angora kimono, stood near the window of the room in a listening attitude, and as John entered noiselessly, she turned toward him.

"Oh, it's you!" she whispered, crossing the room to him. "Did you hear them?"

"I heard your father's slaves in my——"

"No," she interrupted excitedly. "Aeroplanes!"

"Aeroplanes? Perhaps that was the sound that woke me."

"There're at least a dozen. I saw one a few moments ago dead against the moon. The guard back by the cliff fired his rifle and that's what roused father. We're going to open on them right away."

"Are they here on purpose?"

"Yes, it's that Italian who got away——"

Simultaneously with her last word, a succession of sharp cracks tumbled in through the open window. Kismine uttered a little cry, took a penny with fumbling fingers from a box on her dresser, and ran to one of the electric lights. In an instant the entire château was in darkness—she had blown out the fuse.

"Come on!" she cried to him. "We'll go up to the roof garden, and watch it from there!"

Drawing a cape about her, she took his hand, and they found their way out the door. It was only a step to the tower lift, and as she pressed the button that shot them upward he put his arms around her in the darkness and kissed her mouth. Romance had come to John Unger at last. A minute later they had stepped out upon the star-white platform. Above, under the misty moon, sliding in and out of the patches of cloud that eddied below it, floated a dozen dark-winged bodies in a constant circling course. From here and there in the valley flashes of fire leaped toward them, followed by sharp detonations. Kismine clapped her hands in pleasure, which a moment later, turned to dismay as the aeroplanes at some prearranged signal, began to release their bombs and the whole of the valley became a panorama of deep reverberate sound and lurid light.

Before long the aim of the attackers became concentrated upon the points where the anti-aircraft guns were situated, and one of them was almost immediately reduced to a giant cinder to lie smouldering in a park of rose bushes.

"Kismine," begged John, "you'll be glad when I tell you that this attack came on the eve of my murder. If I hadn't heard that guard shoot off his gun back by the pass I should now be stone dead—"

"I can't hear you!" cried Kismine, intent on the scene before her. "You'll have to talk louder!"

"I simply said," shouted John, "that we'd better get out before they begin to shell the château!"

Suddenly the whole portico of the negro quarters cracked asunder, a geyser of flame shot up from under the colonnades, and great fragments of jagged marble were hurled as far as the borders of the lake.

"There go fifty thousand dollars' worth of slaves," cried Kismine, "at prewar prices. So few Americans have any respect for property."

John renewed his efforts to compel her to leave. The aim of the aeroplanes was becoming more precise minute by minute, and only two of the anti-aircraft guns were still retaliating. It was obvious that the garrison, encircled with fire, could not hold out much longer.

"Come on!" cried John, pulling Kismine's arm, "we've got to go. Do you realize that those aviators will kill you without question if they find you?"

She consented reluctantly.

"We'll have to wake Jasmine!" she said, as they hurried toward the lift. Then she added in a sort of childish delight: "We'll be poor, won't we? Like people in books. And I'll be an orphan and utterly free. Free and poor! What fun!" She stopped and raised her lips to him in a delighted kiss.

"It's impossible to be both together," said John grimly. "People have found that out. And I should choose to be free as preferable of the two. As an extra caution you'd better dump the contents of your jewel box into your pockets."

Ten mintues later the two girls met John in the dark corridor and they descended to the main floor of the château. Passing for the last time through the magnificence of the splendid halls, they stood for a moment out on the terrace, watching the burning negro quarters and the flaming embers of two planes which had fallen on the other side of the lake. A solitary gun was still keeping up a sturdy popping, and the attackers seemed timorous about descending lower, but sent their thunderous fireworks in a circle around it, until any chance shot might annihilate its Ethiopian crew.

John and the two sisters passed down the marble steps, turned sharply to the left, and began to ascend a narrow path that wound like a garter about the diamond mountain. Kismine knew a heavily wooded spot half-way up where they could lie concealed and yet be able to observe the wild night in the valley—finally to make an escape, when it should be necessary, along a secret path laid in a rocky gully.

X

It was three o'clock when they attained their destination. The obliging and phlegmatic Jasmine fell off to sleep immediately, leaning against the trunk of a large tree, while John and Kismine sat, his arm around her, and watched the desperate ebb and flow of the dying battle among the ruins of a vista that had been a garden spot that morning. Shortly after four o'clock the last remaining gun gave out a clanging sound and went out of action in a swift tongue of red smoke. Though the moon was down, they saw that the flying bodies were circling closer to the earth. When the planes had made certain that the beleaguered possessed no further resources, they would land and the dark and glittering reign of the Washingtons would be over.

With the cessation of the firing the valley grew quiet. The embers of the two aeroplanes glowed like the eyes of some monster crouching in the grass. The château stood dark and silent, beautiful without light as it had been beautiful in the sun, while the woody rattles of Nemesis filled the air above with a growing and receding complaint. Then John perceived that Kismine, like her sister, had fallen sound asleep.

It was long after four when he became aware of footsteps along the path they had lately followed, and he waited in breathless silence until the persons to whom they belonged had passed the vantagepoint he occupied. There was a faint stir in the air now that was not of human origin, and the dew was cold; he knew that the dawn would break soon. John waited until the steps had gone a safe distance up the mountain and were inaudible. Then he followed. About half-way to the steep summit the trees fell away and a hard saddle of rock spread itself over the diamond beneath. Just before he reached this point he slowed down his pace, warned by an animal sense that there was life just ahead of him. Coming to a high boulder, he lifted his head gradually above its edge. His curiosity was rewarded; this is what he saw:

Braddock Washington was standing there motionless, silhouetted against the gray sky without sound or sign of life. As the dawn came up out of the east, lending a cold green color to the earth, it brought the solitary figure into insignificant contrast with the new day.

While John watched, his host remained for a few moments absorbed in some inscrutable contemplation; then he signalled to the two negroes who crouched at his feet to lift the burden which lay between them. As they struggled upright, the first yellow beam of the sun struck through the innumerable prisms of an immense and exquisitely chiselled diamond—and a white radiance was kindled that glowed upon the air like a fragment of the morning star. The bearers staggered beneath its weight for a moment—then their rippling muscles caught and hardened under the wet shine of the skins and the three figures were again motionless in their defiant impotency before the heavens.

After a while the white man lifted his head and slowly raised his arms in a gesture of attention, as one who would call a great crowd to hear—but there was no crowd, only the vast silence of the mountain and the sky, broken by faint bird voices down among the trees. The figure on the saddle of rock began to speak ponderously and with an inextinguishable pride.

"You out there—" he cried in a trembling voice. "You—there—!" He paused, his arms still uplifted, his head held attentively as though he were expecting an answer. John strained his eyes to see whether there might be men coming down the mountain, but the mountain was bare of human life. There was only sky and a mock-

ing flute of wind along the tree-tops. Could Washington be pray-
ing? For a moment John wondered. Then the illusion passed—there
was something in the man's whole attitude antithetical to prayer.

"Oh, you above there!"

The voice was become strong and confident. This was no forlorn
supplication. If anything, there was in it a quality of monstrous
condescension.

"You there——"

Words, too quickly uttered to be understood, flowing one into
the other. . . . John listened breathlessly, catching a phrase here
and there, while the voice broke off, resumed, broke off again—now
strong and argumentative, now colored with a slow, puzzled impa-
tience. Then a conviction commenced to dawn on the single listener, and as realization crept over him a spray of quick blood
rushed through his arteries. Braddock Washington was offering a
bribe to God!

That was it—there was no doubt. The diamond in the arms of
his slaves was some advance sample, a promise of more to follow.

That, John perceived after a time, was the thread running through
his sentences. Prometheus Enriched was calling to witness forgotten
sacrifices, forgotten rituals, prayers obsolete before the birth of
Christ. For a while his discourse took the form of reminding God
of this gift or that which Divinity had deigned to accept from men
—great churches if he would rescue cities from the plague, gifts of
myrrh and gold, of human lives and beautiful women and captive
armies, of children and queens, of beasts of the forest and field,
sheep and goats, harvests and cities, whole conquered lands that
had been offered up in lust or blood for His appeasal, buying a
meed's worth of alleviation from the Divine wrath—and now he,
Braddock Washington, Emperor of Diamonds, king and priest of
the age of gold, arbiter of splendor and luxury, would offer up a
treasure such as princes before him had never dreamed of, offer it
up not in suppliance, but in pride.

He would give to God, he continued, getting down to specifications, the greatest diamond in the world. This diamond would be
cut with many more thousand facets than there were leaves on a
tree, and yet the whole diamond would be shaped with the perfection of a stone no bigger than a fly. Many men would work upon
it for many years. It would be set in a great dome of beaten gold,

wonderfully carved and equipped with gates of opal and crusted sapphire. In the middle would be hollowed out a chapel presided over by an altar of iridescent, decomposing, ever-changing radium which would burn out the eyes of any worshipper who lifted up his head from prayer—and on this altar there would be slain for the amusement of the Divine Benefactor any victim He should choose, even though it should be the greatest and most powerful man alive.

In return he asked only a simple thing, a thing that for God would be absurdly easy—only that matters should be as they were yesterday at this hour and that they should so remain. So very simple! Let but the heavens open, swallowing these men and their aeroplanes—and then close again. Let him have his slaves once more, restored to life and well.

There was no one else with whom he had ever needed to treat or bargain.

He doubted only whether he had made his bribe big enough. God had His price, of course. God was made in man's image, so it had been said: He must have His price. And the price would be rare—no cathedral whose building consumed many years, no pyramid constructed by ten thousand workmen, would be like this cathedral, this pyramid.

He paused here. That was his proposition. Everything would be up to specifications and there was nothing vulgar in his assertion that it would be cheap at the price. He implied that Providence could take it or leave it.

As he approached the end his sentences became broken, became short and uncertain, and his body seemed tense, seemed strained to catch the slightest pressure or whisper of life in the spaces around him. His hair had turned gradually white as he talked, and now he lifted his head high to the heavens like a prophet of old—magnificently mad.

Then, as John stared in giddy fascination, it seemed to him that a curious phenomenon took place somewhere around him. It was as though the sky had darkened for an instant, as though there had been a sudden murmur in a gust of wind, a sound of far-away trumpets, a sighing like the rustle of a great silken robe—for a time the whole of nature round about partook of this darkness: the birds' song ceased; the trees were still, and far over the mountain there was a mutter of dull, menacing thunder.

That was all. The wind died along the tall grasses of the valley. The dawn and the day resumed their place in a time, and the risen sun sent hot waves of yellow mist that made its path bright before it. The leaves laughed in the sun, and their laughter shook the trees until each bough was like a girl's school in fairyland. God had refused to accept the bribe.

For another moment John watched the triumph of the day. Then, turning, he saw a flutter of brown down by the lake, then another flutter, then another, like the dance of golden angels alighting from the clouds. The aeroplanes had come to earth.

John slid off the boulder and ran down the side of the mountain to the clump of trees, where the two girls were awake and waiting for him. Kismine sprang to her feet, the jewels in her pockets jingling, a question on her parted lips, but instinct told John that there was no time for words. They must get off the mountain without losing a moment. He seized a hand of each, and in silence they threaded the tree-trunks, washed with light now and with the rising mist. Behind them from the valley came no sound at all, except the complaint of the peacocks far away and the pleasant undertone of morning.

When they had gone about half a mile, they avoided the park land and entered a narrow path that led over the next rise of ground. At the highest point of this they paused and turned around. Their eyes rested upon the mountainside they had just left—oppressed by some dark sense of tragic impendency.

Clear against the sky a broken, white-haired man was slowly descending the steep slope, followed by two gigantic and emotionless negroes, who carried a burden between them which still flashed and glittered in the sun. Half-way down two other figures joined them—John could see that they were Mrs. Washington and her son, upon whose arm she leaned. The aviators had clambered from their machines to the sweeping lawn in front of the château, and with rifles in hand were starting up the diamond mountain in skirmishing formation.

But the little group of five which had formed farther up and was engrossing all the watchers' attention had stopped upon a ledge of rock. The negroes stooped and pulled up what appeared to be a trapdoor in the side of the mountain. Into this they all disappeared, the white-haired man first, then his wife and son, finally the two negroes, the glittering tips of whose jeweled head-dresses caught the sun for a moment before the trap-door descended and engulfed them all.

Kismine clutched John's arm.

"Oh," she cried wildly, "where are they going? What are they going to do?"

"It must be some underground way of escape—"

A little scream from the two girls interrupted his sentence.

"Don't you see?" sobbed Kismine hysterically. "The mountain is wired!"

Even as she spoke John put up his hands to shield his sight. Before their eyes the whole surface of the mountain had changed suddenly to a dazzling burning yellow, which showed up through the jacket of turf as light shows through a human hand. For a moment the intolerable glow continued, and then like an extinguished filament it disappeared, revealing a black waste from which blue smoke arose slowly, carrying off with it what remained of vegetation and of human flesh. Of the aviators there was left neither blood nor bone—they were consumed as completely as the five souls who had gone inside.

Simultaneously, and with an immense concussion, the château literally threw itself into the air, bursting into flaming fragments as it rose, and then tumbling back upon itself in a smoking pile that lay projecting half into the water of the lake. There was no fire— what smoke there was drifted off mingling with the sunshine, and for a few minutes longer a powdery dust of marble drifted from the great featureless pile that had once been the house of jewels. There was no more sound and the three people were alone in the valley.

XI

At sunset John and his two companions reached the high cliff which had marked the boundaries of the Washingtons' dominion, and looking back found the valley tranquil and lovely in the dusk. They sat down to finish the food which Jasmine had brought with her in a basket.

"There!" she said, as she spread the table-cloth and put the sandwiches in a neat pile upon it. "Don't they look tempting? I always think that food tastes better outdoors."

"With that remark," remarked Kismine, "Jasmine enters the middle class."

"Now," said John eagerly, "turn out your pocket and let's see what jewels you brought along. If you made a good selection we three ought to live comfortably all the rest of our lives."

Obediently Kismine put her hand in her pocket and tossed two handfuls of glittering stones before him.

"Not so bad," cried John, enthusiastically. "They aren't very big, but—Hello!" His expression changed as he held one of them up to the declining sun. "Why, these aren't diamonds! There's something the matter!"

"By golly!" exclaimed Kismine, with a startled look. "What an idiot I am!"

"Why, these are rhinestones!" cried John.

"I know." She broke into a laugh. "I opened the wrong drawer. They belonged on the dress of a girl who visited Jasmine. I got her to give them to me in exchange for diamonds. I'd never seen anything but precious stones before."

"And this is what you brought?"

"I'm afraid so." She fingered the brilliants wistfully. "I think I like these better. I'm a little tired of diamonds."

"Very well," said John gloomily. "We'll have to live in Hades. And you will grow old telling incredulous women that you got the wrong drawer. Unfortunately your father's bank-books were consumed with him."

"Well, what's the matter with Hades?"

"If I come home with a wife at my age my father is just as liable as not to cut me off with a hot coal, as they say down there."

Jasmine spoke up.

"I love washing," she said quietly. "I have always washed my own handkerchiefs. I'll take in laundry and support you both."

"Do they have washwomen in Hades?" asked Kismine innocently.

"Of course," answered John. "It's just like anywhere else."

"I thought—perhaps it was too hot to wear any clothes."

John laughed.

"Just try it!" he suggested. "They'll run you out before you're half started."

"Will father be there?" she asked.

John turned to her in astonishment.

"Your father is dead," he replied somberly. "Why should he go to

Hades? You have it confused with another place that was abolished long ago."

After supper they folded up the table-cloth and spread their blankets for the night.

"What a dream it was," Kismine sighed, gazing up at the stars. "How strange it seems to be here with one dress and a penniless fiancé!

"Under the stars," she repeated. "I never noticed the stars before. I always thought of them as great big diamonds that belonged to some one. Now they frighten me. They make me feel that it was all a dream, all my youth."

"It *was* a dream," said John quietly. "Everybody's youth is a dream, a form of chemical madness."

"How pleasant then to be insane!"

"So I'm told," said John gloomily. "I don't know any longer. At any rate, let us love for a while, for a year or so, you and me. That's a form of divine drunkenness that we can all try. There are only diamonds in the whole world, diamonds and perhaps the shabby gift of disillusion. Well, I have that last and I will make the usual nothing of it." He shivered. "Turn up your coat collar, little girl, the night's full of chill and you'll get pneumonia. His was a great sin who first invented consciousness. Let us lose it for a few hours."

So wrapping himself in his blanket he fell off to sleep.

Le Temps n'a Point de Rive (Time is a River Without Banks),
Marc Chagall, 1930-39

commentary:
fantasy and reality

Fantasy makers, like shamans, witches, and mystics make flights into the unknown. The shaman flies to the other world; the mystic flies to higher levels of consciousness; in fantasy, the imagination soars to the realms of faerie, to the scientific future, and to the "weird." And, again, like his companions in flight, the fantasy artist claims to find in the Other World something more real than that which he finds in the immediate present. "The maddest castle that ever came out of a giant's bag in a wild Gaelic story is not only much less ugly than a robot-factory, it is also (to use a very modern phrase) 'in a very real sense' a great deal more real," writes J. R. R. Tolkien.[1] G. K. Chesterton, noting the fact that the industrial world has lost touch with the enchantment and mystery of existence, suggests that "fairy land is nothing but the sunny country of common sense." C. G. Jung tells us that the psychic Spirit, which modern man has so long repressed, is freed only in fantasy, myth, and dream: "In myths and fairy tales, as in dreams, the psyche tells its own story."[2] The creator of fantasy, like the revolutionary of the spirit, warns us that we do not know our real Self and that we must work to regain our "primitive" identification with that Self. Fantasy provides one way back—a flight to the world of reality, which we have thought of for too long as the world of unreality.

[1] J. R. R. Tolkien, "On Fairy-Stories," in *The Tolkien Reader* (New York: Ballantine Books, 1966), p. 64.
[2] Carl Gustav Jung, "The Phenomenology of the Spirit in Fairytales," in Carl Gustav Jung and others, *Four Archetypes* (Princeton: Bollingen Series, 1970), p. 95.

As we all know, and, as the selections in this section indicate, fantasy can take many forms. Mere daydreaming is a form of it, as is the dreaming we do in sleep. Nursery rhymes are also fantasy. Fairy tales of the sort told by Hans Christian Andersen and the Brothers Grimm are fantasy, as is science fiction, and what might be called "pure fantasy"—the works, for instance, of Tolkien, C. S. Lewis, and Charles Williams. Much of fantasy literature is usually considered children's literature, a fact that enables us to conveniently avoid seeing the reality that our theorists claim these tales contain. This is unfortunate, since fantasy does speak, in numerous ways, to the adult human condition. Fantasy can express political or social reality. Novels such as *1984* and *Brave New World*, and stories such as "Harrison Bergeron," are, ostensibly, stories of the future, but they are also commentaries on the conditions seen by the given author to exist in the society of his day. Harrison Bergeron is a modern tragic hero, a man who is determined to be free of the mediocrity forced upon him by an overly mechanized, overly technocratic society—a society that has allowed its natural human qualities and differences to be repressed. Many commentators on the modern world, such as Carl Jung, Alan Watts, and Theodore Roszak warn us of these dangers. Vonnegut brings this warning to us directly, by way of the magical vehicle that is fiction —in this case, science fiction.

Even the simplest nursery rhymes, such as those in the Mother Goose books, can often be traced to real political and social conditions. How many of us, when we were children and read "Ring a ring o' rosies/A pocketful of posies," had any idea that the real subject of the lines might have been the great plague, that the ring referred to the rash symptomatic of the disease, that the posies were used to sweeten the air of death, and that "We all fall down" suggested the universality of death itself?[3] And how many realized that little Jack Horner was in reality a certain steward of the time of Henry VIII who managed to get his fingers, illegally, into an ecclesiastical pie in order to extract a deed to a fine manorial estate?[4]

[3] *The Annotated Mother Goose*, William and Ceil Baring-Gould, eds. (New York: Meridian Press, 1972), p. 252.
[4] *Ibid.*, p. 63.

260   Fantasy is, however, based in reality in more profound ways than this. Most important, it reminds us of our long-lost communion with the magic, mystery, and enchantment of life. Alice's descent into the rabbit-hole can symbolize our own much-needed descent to a more "primitive" reality, wherein the artificially imposed "natural laws" of the technocrat give way to what Chesterton calls "the arbitrariness of the fact and its mystery." The world of fantasy recognizes the *magic* of the happening *before* it recognizes a scientific law to explain that happening. A zoologist, biologist, or physicist can explain the phenomenon of birth or spring, but what we *feel* in experiencing these phenomena can be better expressed in the language of magic and faerie. The world of fantasy, says Chesterton, takes us back to a proper relationship to the life around us. A tree does not grow fruit as a result of scientific law, water does not run downhill because of the law of gravity: "A tree grows fruit because it is a magic tree. Water runs downhill because it is bewitched."

Professor Tolkien writes: "Other creatures are like other realms with which Man has broken relations, and sees now only from the outside from a distance, being at war with them, or on the terms of an uneasy armistice."[5] And Alan Watts believes that:

> . . . we have scrubbed the world clean of magic. We have lost even the vision of paradise, so that our artists and craftsmen can no longer discern its forms. This is the price that must be paid for attempting to control the world from the standpoint of "I" for whom everything that can be experienced is a foreign object. . . .[6]

Not only is fantasy an escape back to magic, but it is also a way to escape from the here and now. This, as illustrated, for instance, in science fiction, is perhaps its most obvious function. Escape literature, however, can have a serious intent. "The Tell-Tale Heart" and "The Diamond as Big as the Ritz," as different as they are, reflect a real human need to escape the mundane present by exercising the powers of the imagination. The mind finds such exercise

[5] Tolkien, *op. cit.*, p. 66.
[6] Alan Watts, *The Book: On the Taboo Against Knowing Who You Are* (New York: Collier Books, 1968), p. 107.

also in the thrill of horror. Both of these stories are symbolic of the ways in which we are all entrapped by the nightmare of our neuroses and material "needs." These tales, then, can serve as a kind of therapy. As we do in dreams, we safely express through them our real fears and desires.

We have come, then, to the most profound function of fantasy— the psychological one. Fantasy, like all valid literature, is one way man has of exploring his own identity. Particularly in the oldest form of the genre, the *märchen* or fairy tale, man has available to him what amounts to mirrors of his inner reality. What better way to express what we are than from behind the protective veil of fairy stories—of personalities depicted as animals or made palatable by magic castles and strange potions? Consider "The Frog Prince." On its outermost surface, it is the story of a frog and a princess. Remove one layer, and there is a parable of ugliness and beauty and of the importance of living up to promises. Remove still another layer, and a Freudian tale of sexuality involving puberty and fathers and daughters is discovered. On removing still another, the Jungian collective unconscious is revealed, and the tale becomes one of individuation. The arrival of the frog announces an inevitable rite of passage—perhaps that from childhood to womanhood. Demands are made, and certain burdens—often ugly ones—must be taken on if the road of life is to be successfully traveled. The individual must recognize the part of himself (or herself) that emerges from the depths—the shadow within—which we would rather deny. Only in this recognition can the qualities represented by the frog take their proper form and join in the total Self that is symbolized by the ritual marriage at the end of this and so many other fairy tales.

The final step in the peeling away of the layers of fantasy would take us to myth itself, where the quest of all of us for total being is expressed in the adventures of the hero. Thus, fantasy, like shamanism, witchcraft, and mysticism, is firmly based in and concerned with the world of reality, which is the unknown.

part four

myth and symbol

Anxious Journey, Giorgio de Chirico, 1913

myth and symbol:
definitions

JOSEPH CAMPBELL (1904–   )

Joseph Campbell is one of the leading mythologists in America. His major works, *The Hero with a Thousand Faces* and the four-part *The Masks of God,* are classics in their field. In this selection, Campbell compares myth to dream. Myths are, in a sense, the dreams of mankind, and they provide inroads to the great unknown of our collective Self. The adventure of the hero, whatever his identity, is the potential voyage of all of us into that unknown.

FROM the hero with a thousand faces

From Psychology to Metaphysics

It is not difficult for the modern intellectual to concede that the symbolism of mythology has a psychological significance. Particularly after the work of the psychoanalysts, there can be little doubt, either that myths are of the nature of dream, or that dreams are symptomatic of the dynamics of the psyche. Sigmund Freud, Carl G. Jung, Wilhelm Stekel, Otto Rank, Karl Abraham, Géza Róheim,

265

266   and many others have within the past few decades developed a
vastly documented modern lore of dream and myth interpretation;
and though the doctors differ among themselves, they are united
into one great modern movement by a considerable body of common principles. With their discovery that the patterns and logic of
fairy tale and myth correspond to those of dream, the long discredited chimeras of archaic man have returned dramatically to the
foreground of modern consciousness.

According to this view it appears that through the wonder tales—
which pretend to describe the lives of the legendary heroes, the
powers of the divinities of nature, the spirits of the dead, and the totem ancestors of the group—symbolic expression is given to the
unconscious desires, fears, and tensions that underlie the conscious
patterns of human behavior. Mythology, in other words, is psychology misread as biography, history, and cosmology. The modern
psychologist can translate it back to its proper denotations and thus
rescue for the contemporary world a rich and eloquent document
of the profoundest depths of human character. Exhibited here, as
in a fluoroscope, stand revealed the hidden processes of the enigma
Homo sapiens—Occidental and Oriental, primitive and civilized,
contemporary and archaic. The entire spectacle is before us. We
have only to read it, study its constant patterns, analyze its variations, and therewith come to an understanding of the deep forces
that have shaped man's destiny and must continue to determine
both our private and our public lives.

But if we are to grasp the full value of the materials, we must
note that myths are not exactly comparable to dream. Their figures
originate from the same sources—the unconscious wells of fantasy—
and their grammar is the same, but they are not the spontaneous
products of sleep. On the contrary, their patterns are consciously
controlled. And their understood function is to serve as a powerful
picture language for the communication of traditional wisdom. This
is true already of the so-called primitive folk mythologies. The
trance-susceptible shaman and the initiated antelope-priest are not
unsophisticated in the wisdom of the world, nor unskilled in the
principles of communication by analogy. The metaphors by which
they live, and through which they operate, have been brooded
upon, searched, and discussed for centuries—even millenniums; they
have served whole societies, furthermore, as the mainstays of thought
and life. The culture patterns have been shaped to them. The youth

have been educated, and the aged rendered wise, through the study, experience, and understanding of their effective initiatory forms. For they actually touch and bring into play the vital energies of the whole human psyche. They link the unconscious to the fields of practical action, not irrationally, in the manner of a neurotic projection, but in such fashion as to permit a mature and sobering, practical comprehension of the fact-world to play back, as a stern control, into the realms of infantile wish and fear. And if this be true of the comparatively simple folk mythologies (the systems of myth and ritual by which the primitive hunting and fishing tribes support themselves), what may we say of such magnificent cosmic metaphors as those reflected in the great Homeric epics, the *Divine Comedy* of Dante, the Book of Genesis, and the timeless temples of the Orient? Until the most recent decades, these were the support of all human life and the inspiration of philosophy, poetry, and the arts. Where the inherited symbols have been touched by a Lao-tse, Buddha, Zoroaster, Christ, or Mohammed—employed by a consummate master of the spirit as a vehicle of the profoundest moral and metaphysical instruction—obviously we are in the presence rather of immense consciousness than of darkness.

And so, to grasp the full value of the mythological figures that have come down to us, we must understand that they are not only symptoms of the unconscious (as indeed are all human thoughts and acts) but also controlled and intended statements of certain spiritual principles, which have remained as constant throughout the course of human history as the form and nervous structure of the human physique itself. Briefly formulated, the universal doctrine teaches that all the visible structures of the world—all things and beings—are the effects of a ubiquitous power out of which they rise, which supports and fills them during the period of their manifestation, and back into which they must ultimately dissolve. This is the power known to science as energy, to the Melanesians as *mana,* to the Sioux Indians as *wakonda,* the Hindus as *shakti,* and the Christians as the power of God. Its manifestation in the psyche is termed, by the psychoanalysts, *libido.*[1] And its manifestation in the cosmos is the structure and flux of the universe itself.

The apprehension of the *source* of this undifferentiated yet every-

---

[1] Cf. C. G. Jung, *Energetik der Seele* (Zürich—Leipzig—Stuttgart: Rascher Verlag, 1928), Ch. I.

268 where particularized substratum of being is rendered frustrate by the very organs through which the apprehension must be accomplished. The forms of sensibility and the categories of human thought,[2] which are themselves manifestations of this power,[3] so confine the mind that it is normally impossible not only to see, but even to conceive, beyond the colorful, fluid, infinitely various and bewildering phenomenal spectacle. The function of ritual and myth is to make possible, and then to facilitate, the jump—by analogy. Forms and conceptions that the mind and its senses can comprehend are presented and arranged in such a way as to suggest a truth or openness beyond. And then, the conditions for meditation having been provided, the individual is left alone. Myth is but the penultimate; the ultimate is openness—that void, or being, beyond the categories[4]—into which the mind must plunge alone and be dissolved. Therefore, God and the gods are only convenient means— themselves of the nature of the world of names and forms, though eloquent of, and ultimately conducive to, the ineffable. They are mere symbols to move and awaken the mind, and to call it past themselves.[5]

Heaven, hell, the mythological age, Olympus and all the other habitations of the gods, are interpreted by psychoanalysis as symbols of the unconscious. The key to the modern systems of psychological interpretation therefore is this: the metaphysical realm = the unconscious. Correspondingly, the key to open the door the other way is the same equation in reverse: the unconscious = the

[2] See Kant, *Critique of Pure Reason.*
[3] Sanskirt: *māyā- śakti.*
[4] Beyond the categories, and therefore not defined by either of the pair of opposites called "void" and "being." Such terms are only clues to the transcendency.
[5] This recognition of the secondary nature of the personality of whatever deity is worshiped is characteristic of most of the traditions of the world. In Christianity, Mohammedanism, and Judaism, however, the personality of the divinity is taught to be final—which makes it comparatively difficult for the members of these communions to understand how one may go beyond the limitations of their own anthropomorphic divinity. The result has been, on the one hand, a general obfuscation of the symbols, and on the other, a god-ridden bigotry such as is unmatched elsewhere in the history of religion. For a discussion of the possible origin of this aberration, see Sigmund Freud, *Moses and Monotheism* (New York: Alfred A. Knopf, Inc., 1939).

metaphysical realm. "For," as Jesus states it, "behold, the kingdom of God is within you."[6] Indeed, the lapse of superconsciousness into the state of unconsciousness is precisely the meaning of the Biblical image of the Fall. The constriction of consciousness, to which we owe the fact that we see not the source of the universal power but only the phenomenal forms reflected from that power, turns super-consciousness into unconsciousness and, at the same instant and by the same token, creates the world. Redemption consists in the return to superconsciousness and therewith the dissolution of the world. This is the great theme and formula of the cosmogonic cycle, the mythical image of the world's coming to manifestation and subsequent return into the nonmanifest condition. Equally, the birth, life, and death of the individual may be regarded as a descent into unconsciousness and return. The hero is the one who, while still alive, knows and represents the claims of the superconsciousness which throughout creation is more or less unconscious. The adventure of the hero represents the moment in his life when he achieved illumination—the nuclear moment when, while still alive, he found and opened the road to the light beyond the dark walls of our living death.

And so it is that the cosmic symbols are presented in a spirit of thought-bewildering sublime paradox. The kingdom of God is within, yet without, also; God, however, is but a convenient means to wake the sleeping princess, the soul. Life is her sleep, death the awakening. The hero, the waker of his own soul, is himself but the convenient means of his own dissolution. God, the waker of the soul, is therewith his own immediate death.

Perhaps the most eloquent possible symbol of this mystery is that of the god crucified, the god offered, "himself to himself." Read in one direction, the meaning is the passage of the phenomenal hero into superconsciousness: the body with its five senses . . . is left hanging to the cross of the knowledge of life and death, pinned in five places (the two hands, the two feet, and the head crowned with thorns). But also, God has descended voluntarily and taken upon himself this phenomenal agony. God assumes the life of man and man releases the God within himself at the mid-point of the cross-arms of the same "coincidence of opposites," the same sun door

[6] Luke, 17:21.

270   through which God descends and Man ascends—each as the other's food.

The modern student may, of course, study these symbols as he will, either as a symptom of others' ignorance, or as a sign to him of his own, either in terms of a reduction of metaphysics to psychology, or vice versa. The traditional way was to meditate on the symbols in both senses. In any case, they are telling metaphors of the destiny of man, man's hope, man's faith, and man's dark mystery.

The Shapeshifter

There is no final system for the interpretation of myths, and there will never be any such thing. Mythology is like the god Proteus, "the ancient one of the sea, whose speech is sooth." The god "will make assay, and take all manner of shapes of things that creep upon the earth, of water likewise, and of fierce fire burning."[7]

The life-voyager wishing to be taught by Proteus must "grasp him steadfastly and press him yet the more," and at length he will appear in his proper shape. But this wily god never discloses even to the skillful questioner the whole content of his wisdom. He will reply only to the question put to him, and what he discloses will be great or trivial, according to the question asked. "So often as the sun in his course stands high in mid heaven, then forth from the brine comes the ancient one of the sea, whose speech is sooth, before the breath of the West Wind he comes, and the sea's dark ripple covers him. And when he is got forth, he lies down to sleep in the hollow of the caves. And around him the seals, the brood of the fair daughter of the brine, sleep all in a flock, stolen forth from the grey sea water, and bitter is the scent they breathe of the deeps of the salt sea."[8] The Greek warrior-king Menelaus, who was guided by a helpful daughter of this old sea-father to the wild lair, and instructed by her how to wring from the god his response, desired only to ask the secret of his own personal difficulties and the whereabouts of his personal friends. And the god did not disdain to reply.

[7] *Odyssey*, IV, 401, 417–18, translation by S. H. Butcher and Andrew Lang (London, 1879).
[8] *Ibid.*, IV, 400–06.

Mythology has been interpreted by the modern intellect as a primitive, fumbling effort to explain the world of nature (Frazer); as a production of poetical fantasy from prehistoric times, misunderstood by succeeding ages (Müller); as a repository of allegorical instruction, to shape the individual to his group (Durkheim); as a group dream, symptomatic of archetypal urges within the depths of the human psyche (Jung); as the traditional vehicle of man's profoundest metaphysical insights (Coomaraswamy); and as God's Revelation to His children (the Church). Mythology is all of these. The various judgments are determined by the viewpoints of the judges. For when scrutinized in terms not of what it is but of how it functions, of how it has served mankind in the past, of how it may serve today, mythology shows itself to be as amenable as life itself to the obsessions and requirements of the individual, the race, the age.

myth, science, and modern man

THEODORE ROSZAK (1933–   )

In this selection from *The Making of a Counter Culture,*
Theodore Roszak considers various meanings of the word
myth in a modern, technocratic context. Myth, he says, ''is
that collectively created thing which crystallizes the great,
central values of a culture''—for our culture, it is the ''myth
of objective consciousness.''

FROM the making of a counter culture

From "The Myth of Objective Consciousness"

. . . to speak of "mythology" in connection with science would
seem at first glance to be a contradiction in terms. Science, after
all, purports to be precisely that enterprise of the mind which
strips life of its myths, substituting for fantasy and legend a relationship to reality based, in William James' phrase, on "irre-
ducible and stubborn facts." Is not scientific knowledge, indeed,
that residue which is left when all the myths have been filtered
away? One might in fact argue that this is exactly what dis-

tinguishes the scientific revolution of the modern West from all previous cultural transitions. In the past, when one cultural epoch has displaced another, the change frequently involved little more than a process of mythological transformation: a *re*-mythologizing of men's thinking. So the figure of Christ stepped into the place prepared long since by the savior figures of various pagan mystery cults, and in time the Christian saints inherited their status from the deities of the Greco-Roman, Teutonic, or Celtic pantheons.

But science, we are to believe, does not re-mythologize life; it *de*-mythologizes it. This is supposedly what makes the scientific revolution a radically different, if not a final, cultural episode. For, with the advent of the scientific world view, indisputable truth takes the place of make-believe.

There is no doubting the radical novelty of science in contrast to all earlier mythological world views. What all nonscientific cultural systems have had in common is the tendency to mistake their mythologies for literal statements about history and the natural world—or at least the tendency to articulate mythological insights in what a scientific mind mistakes for propositional assertions. In this way, imaginative expressions rich in moral drama or psychic perception easily degenerate into fabulous conjectures about the exotic reaches of time and space. This is how we most often use the word "mythology" in our time: to designate the telling of unverifiable, if not downright false, tales about remote ages and places. The story of the Garden of Eden is a "myth" we say, because insofar as any believing Christian or Jew has ever tried to locate the story geographically and historically, skeptics have been able to call his evidence, if any, quite cogently into question.

Mythologies which are imaginative exaggerations of our ordinary perceptions or displacements of them to other times and places—let us call them in this sense temporal-physical mythologies—have always been vulnerable to critical inquiry. The doubting Thomas in the case need not even be a scientific skeptic. A devout Christian can practice an uncompromising skepticism toward the mythologies of other faiths and cultures, in the fashion of Charlemagne striking down the Saxon idols and defying their wrath, confident that no such heathen divinities existed. But a Christian's skepticism is necessarily partisan, sparing the believer any critical examination of his own dogmas. Even liberal Christian demythologizers

274 like Rudolph Bultmann have had to stop short of extending their project to such essential teaching as the resurrection of Christ.

In contrast to such selective skepticism, the wholesale skepticism of science shows up to brilliant advantage. Science is the infidel to all gods in behalf of none. Thus there is no way around the painful dilemma in which the religious traditions of the world have found themselves trapped over the last two centuries. Every culture that has invested its convictions in a temporal-physical mythology is doomed before the onslaught of the scientific unbeliever. Any village atheist who persists in saying "show me" is in the position to hold up to ransom an entire religious culture, with little expectation that it will be able to find the price demanded. It would be difficult to say whether this situation partakes more of farce or of tragedy. Only a few generations ago, Clarence Darrow, no more than a skillful courtroom lawyer armed with a Sunday supplement knowledge of Darwin, was able to make laughingstock of a Judeo-Christian mythology that had served to inspire the finest philosophical and artistic minds of our culture over hundreds of generations. Yet, under unrelenting skeptical pressure, what choice have those who cling to temporal-physical mythologies but to undertake strategic retreat, conceding ever more ground to secular, reductionist styles of thought. The line of retreat falls back to interpretations of myth that are primarily ethical . . . or aesthetic . . . or, in some unspecified fashion, symbolic. Within the Christian tradition, this is a resort which is bound to weaken and confuse, since Christianity has had a uniquely significant commitment to the literal truth of its teachings. Indeed, the sweeping secularization of Western society that has come in the wake of scientific advance can be seen as a product of Christianity's peculiar reliance on a precarious, dogmatic literalism. Such a religious tradition need only prick its finger in order to bleed to death. And if the hard-pressed believer does turn to "symbolic" interpretations, even here the secular temperament tends to sweep the field by asserting reductionist psychological or sociological correlatives for the myth. The only other defense, that of standing fast in behalf of the literal truth, leads, as Kierkegaard recognized more than a century ago, to the crucifixion of the intellect.

The scientific world view is of course invulnerable to criticism at the same level as a temporal-physical mythology. It would be a ludicrous mistake to contend that the things and forces with which science fills time and space—electrons and galaxies, gravitational fields and natural selection, DNA and viruses—are the cultural equivalents of centaurs and Valhallas and angelic beings. What science deals in is not so poor in ordinary sensory verification—nor so rich in imaginative possibilities. Unlike the mythological traditions of the past, science is not in the first instance a body of supposed knowledge about entities and events. Science would still be science and very much in business if it encompassed no knowledge at all other than the ruins of proven ignorance and error. The scientific mind begins in the spirit of the Cartesian zero, with the doubting away of all inherited knowledge in favor of an entirely new *method* of knowing, which, whether it proceeds on rationalist or empiricist lines, purports to begin from scratch, free of all homage to authority.

What scientists know may therefore wax or wane, change in part or whole as time goes on and as evidence accumulates. If the Piltdown fossil proves to be a hoax, it can be discarded without calling the science of physical anthropology into question. If the telescopes of astronomers were to discover angels in outer space, science as a method of knowing would not be in any sense discredited; its theories would simply be reformulated in the light of new discoveries. In contrast to the way we use the phrase "world view" in other contexts, science rests itself not in the *world* the scientist beholds at any particular point in time, but in his mode of *viewing* that world. A man is a scientist not because of what he sees, but because of *how* he sees it.

At least, this is what has become the conventional way of regarding scientific knowledge. Thomas Kuhn, who has looked at the matter more carefully, has recently thrown strong and significant doubt on this "incremental" conception of the history of science. His contention comes close to suggesting that the progressive accumulation of "truth" in the scientific community is something of an illusion, created by the fact that each generation of scientists rewrites its textbooks in such a way as to select from the past what is still considered valid and to suppress the multitude of errors and false starts that are also a part of the history of science. As for the all-important principles of validation that control this natural selection of scientific truth from era to era—the so-called "scientific

276   method"—Khun is left unconvinced that they are quite as purely "rational" or "empirical" as scientists like to think.[1]

Yet the incremental conception of scientific knowledge is very much part of the mythology we are concerned with here. The capacity of science to progress stands as one of the principal validations of its objectivity. Knowledge progresses only when it is understood to survive the passing of particular minds or generations. Science, understood as the expanding application of a fixed method of knowing to ever more areas of experience, makes such a claim. A scientist, asked to explain why science progresses when other fields of thought do not, would doubtlessly refer us to the "objectivity" of his method of knowing. Objectivity, he would tell us, is what gives science its keen critical edge and its peculiarly cumulative character.

Are we using the word "mythology" illegitimately in applying it to objectivity as a state of consciousness? I think not. For the myth at its deepest level is that collectively created thing which crystallizes the great, central values of a culture. It is, so to speak, the intercommunications system of culture. If the culture of science locates its highest values not in mystic symbol or ritual or epic tales of faraway lands and times, but in a mode of consciousness, why should we hesitate to call this a myth? The myth has, after all, been identified as a universal phenomenon of human society, a constitutive factor so critical in importance that it is difficult to imagine a culture having any coherence at all if it lacked the mythological bond. Yet, in our society, myth as it is conventionally understood has become practically a synonym for falsehood. To be sure, we commonly hear discussion of various social and political myths these days (the myth of the American frontier, the myth of the Founding Fathers, etc.); the more enlightened clergy even talk freely of "the Christian myth." But myths so openly recognized as myths are precisely those that have lost much of their power. It is the myth we accept without question as truth that holds real influence over us. Is it possible that, in this sense, scientific culture is uniquely a-mythical? Or is it the case that we simply fail to look in the right place—in the deep personality structure of the ideal scientist—for the great controlling myth of our culture?

---

[1] See Thomas Kuhn, *The Structure of Scientific Revolutions* (Chicago: The University of Chicago Press, 1962).

Such, at least, is what I propose here, though it would be pointless to press any further the purely semantic question of whether or not objective consciousness meets all the requirements of a "mythology." What is essential here is the contention that objective consciousness is emphatically *not* some manner of definitive, transcultural development whose cogency derives from the fact that it is uniquely in touch with the truth. Rather, like a mythology, it is an arbitrary construct in which a given society in a given historical situation has invested its sense of meaningfulness and value. And so, like any mythology, it can be gotten round and called into question by cultural movements which find meaning and value elsewhere. In the case of the counter culture, then, we have a movement which has turned from objective consciousness as if from a place inhabited by plague—and in the moment of that turning, one can just begin to see an entire episode of our cultural history, the great age of science and technology which began with the Enlightenment, standing revealed in all its quaintly arbitrary, often absurd, and all too painfully unbalanced aspects.

Perhaps, as Michael Polanyi has argued,[2] there is no such thing as objectivity, even in the physical sciences. Certainly his critique is a formidable challenge to scientific orthodoxy. But for our purposes here, this narrowly epistemological question is a subordinate consideration. Science, under the technocracy, has become a total culture dominating the lives of millions for whom discussions of the theory of knowledge are so much foreign language. Yet objectivity, whatever its epistemological status, has become the commanding life style of our society: the one most authoritative way of regarding the self, others, and the whole of our enveloping reality. Even if it is not, indeed, possible to be objective, it *is* possible so to shape the personality that it will feel and act *as if* one were an objective observer and to treat everything that experience presents to the person in accordance with what objectivity would seem to demand.

Objectivity as a state of being fills the very air we breathe in a scientific culture; it grips us subliminally in all we say, feel, and do. The mentality of the ideal scientist becomes the very soul of the society. We seek to adapt our lives to the dictates of that mentality,

---

[2] Michael Polanyi, *Personal Knowledge: Towards a Post-Critical Philosophy* (Chicago: The University of Chicago Press, 1959).

278 or at the very least we respond to it acquiescently in the myriad images and pronouncements in which it manifests itself about us during every waking hour. The Barbarella and James Bond who keep their clinical cool while dealing out prodigious sex or sadistic violence . . . the physiologist who persuades several score of couples to undertake coitus while wired to a powerhouse of electronic apparatus so that he can achieve a statistical measure of sexual normalcy . . . the characters of *Last Year At Marienbad* who face one another as impassively as empty mirrors . . . the Secretary of Defense who tells the public without blinking an eye that our country possesses the "overkill" capacity to destroy any given enemy ten times . . . the high-rise glass and aluminum slab that deprives of visual involvement by offering us only functional linearity and massive reflecting surfaces . . . the celebrated surgeon who assures us that his heart transplant was a "success" though of course the patient died . . . the computer technician who blithely suggests that we have to wage an "all-out war on sleep" in order to take advantage of the latest breakthrough in rapid communications . . . the modish expert who seeks (with phenomenal success) to convince us that the essence of communication lies not in the truth or falsehood, wisdom or folly of the message that person transfers to person, but rather in the technical characteristics of the intervening medium . . . the political scientist who settles for being a psephological virtuoso, pretending that the statistics of meaningless elections are the veritable substance of politics . . . all these (or so I would argue) are life under the sway of objective consciousness.

In short, as science elaborates itself into the dominant cultural influence of our age, it is the psychology and not the epistemology of science that urgently requires our critical attention; for it is primarily at this level that the most consequential deficiencies and imbalances of the technocracy are revealed.[3]

[3] This is the fascinating approach to science that Abraham Maslow has opened up in his *The Psychology of Science* (New York: Harper & Row, 1966). The study gains a deal of authority from Maslow's own experience in growing painfully away from a firm commitment to behavioral psychology.

Mornings With Judd, Peter Milton

myth and literary theory

NORTHROP FRYE (1912–   )

Northrop Frye is the literary theorist who, more than any other, has demonstrated the importance of myth to literature and to literary criticism. Myth, he writes, "is the central informing power that gives archetypal significance to the ritual and archetypal narrative to the oracle." Those who persevere with this difficult selection will emerge with a new and fresh view of both myth and literature.

the archetypes of literature

Every organized body of knowledge can be learned progressively; and experience shows that there is also something progressive about the learning of literature. Our opening sentence has already got us into a semantic difficulty. Physics is an organized body of knowledge about nature, and a student of it says that he is learning physics, not that he is learning nature. Art, like nature, is the subject of a systematic study, and has to be distinguished from the study itself, which is criticism. It is therefore impossible to "learn literature": one learns about it in a certain way, but what one learns, transitively, is the criticism of literature. Similarly, the difficulty often felt in "teaching literature" arises from the fact that it cannot be done: the criticism of literature is all that can be directly taught. So while no one expects literature itself to behave like a science, there is surely no reason why criticism, as a systematic and organized study, should not be, at least partly, a science. Not a "pure" or "exact" science, perhaps, but these phrases form part of a 19th century cosmology which is no longer with us. Criticism deals with the arts and may well be something of an art itself, but it does not follow that it must be unsystematic. If it is to be related to the sciences too, it does not follow that it must be deprived of the graces of culture.

Certainly criticism as we find it in learned journals and scholarly monographs has every characteristic of a science. Evidence is examined scientifically; previous authorities are used scientifically; fields are investigated scientifically; texts are edited scientifically. Prosody is scientific in structure; so is phonetics; so is philology. And yet in studying this kind of critical science the student becomes aware of a centrifugal movement carrying him away from literature. He finds that literature is the central division of the "humanities," flanked on one side by history and on the other by philosophy. Criticism so far ranks only as a sudivision of literature; and hence, for the systematic mental organization of the subject, the student has to turn to the conceptual framework of the historian for events, and to that of the philosopher for ideas. Even the more centrally placed critical sciences, such as textual editing, seem to be part of a "background" that recedes into history or some other non-literary field. The thought suggests itself that the ancillary critical disciplines may be related to a central expanding pattern of systematic comprehension which has not yet been established, but which, if it were established, would prevent them from being centrifugal. If such a pattern exists, then criticism would be to art what philosophy is to wisdom and history to action.

Most of the central area of criticism is at present, and doubtless always will be, the area of commentary. But the commentators have little sense, unlike the researchers, of being contained within some sort of scientific discipline: they are chiefly engaged, in the words of the gospel hymn, in brightening the corner where they are. If we attempt to get a more comprehensive idea of what criticism is about, we find ourselves wandering over quaking bogs of generalities, judicious pronouncements of value, reflective comments, perorations to works of research, and other consequences of taking the large view. But this part of the critical field is so full of pseudo-propositions, sonorous nonsense that contains no truth and no falsehood, that it obviously exists only because criticism, like nature, prefers a waste space to an empty one.

The term "pseudo-proposition" may imply some sort of logical positivist attitude on my own part. But I would not confuse the significant proposition with the factual one; nor should I consider it advisable to muddle the study of literature with a schizophrenic dichotomy between subjective-emotional and objective-descriptive aspects of meaning, considering that in order to produce any literary meaning at all one has to ignore this dichotomy. I say only that the principles by which one can distinguish a significant from a meaningless statement in criticism are not clearly defined. Our first step, therefore, is to recognize and get rid of meaningless criticism: that is, talking about literature in a way that cannot help to build up a systematic structure of knowledge. Casual value-judgments belong not to criticism but to the history of taste, and reflect, at best, only the social and psychological compulsions which prompted their utterance. All judgments in which the values are not based on literary experience but are sentimental or derived from religious or political prejudice may be regarded as casual. Sentimental judgments are usually based either on non-existent categories or antitheses ("Shakespeare studied life, Milton books") or on a visceral reaction to the writer's personality. The literary chit-chat which makes the reputations of poets boom and crash in an imaginary stock exchange is pseudo-criticism. That wealthy investor Mr. Eliot, after dumping Milton on the market, is now buying him again; Donne has probably reached his peak and will begin to taper off; Tennyson may be in for a slight flutter but the Shelley stocks are still bearish. This sort of thing cannot be part of any systematic study, for a systematic study can only progress: whatever dithers or vacillates or reacts is merely leisure-class conversation.

We next meet a more serious group of critics who say: the foreground of criticism is the impact of literature on the reader. Let us, then, keep the study of literature centripetal, and base the learning

process on a structural analysis of the literary work itself. The
texture of any great work of art is complex and ambiguous, and in
unravelling the complexities we may take in as much history and
philosophy as we please, if the subject of our study remains at the
center. If it does not, we may find that in our anxiety to write about
literature we have forgotten how to read it.

The only weakness in this approach is that it is conceived primarily as the antithesis of centrifugal or "background" criticism, and
so lands us in a somewhat unreal dilemma, like the conflict of
internal and external relations in philosophy. Antitheses are usually
resolved, not by picking one side and refuting the other, or by
making eclectic choices between them, but by trying to get past
the antithetical way of stating the problem. It is right that the first
effort of critical apprehension should take the form of a rhetorical
or structural analysis of a work of art. But a purely structural approach has the same limitation in criticism that it has in biology. In
itself it is simply a discrete series of analyses based on the mere
existence of the literary structure, without developing any explanation of how the structure came to be what it was and what its
nearest relatives are. Structural analysis brings rhetoric back to
criticism, but we need a new poetics as well, and the attempt to
construct a new poetics out of rhetoric alone can hardly avoid a
mere complication of rhetorical terms into a sterile jargon. I suggest that what is at present missing from literary criticism is a co-
ordinating principle, a central hypothesis which, like the theory of
evolution in biology, will see the phenomena it deals with as parts
of a whole. Such a principle, though it would retain the centripetal
perspective of structural analysis, would try to give the same perspective to other kinds of criticism too.

The first postulate of this hypothesis is the same as that of any
science: the assumption of total coherence. The assumption refers
to the science, not to what it deals with. A belief in an order of
nature is an inference from the intelligibility of the natural sciences;
and if the natural sciences ever completely demonstrated the order
of nature they would presumably exhaust their subject. Criticism,
as a science, is totally intelligible; literature, as the subject of a
science, is, so far as we know, an inexhaustible source of new
critical discoveries, and would be even if new works of literature
ceased to be written. If so, then the search for a limiting principle

in literature in order to discourage the development of criticism is mistaken. The assertion that the critic should not look for more in a poem than the poet may safely be assumed to have been conscious of putting there is a common form of what may be called the fallacy of premature teleology. It corresponds to the assertion that a natural phenomenon is as it is because Providence in its inscrutable wisdom made it so.

Simple as the assumption appears, it takes a long time for a science to discover that it is in fact a totally intelligible body of knowledge. Until it makes this discovery it has not been born as an individual science, but remains an embryo within the body of some other subject. The birth of physics from "natural philosophy" and of sociology from "moral philosophy" will illustrate the process. It is also very approximately true that the modern sciences have developed in the order of their closeness to mathematics. Thus physics and astronomy assumed their modern form in the Renaissance, chemistry in the 18th century, biology in the 19th and the social sciences in the 20th. If systematic criticism, then, is developing only in our day, the fact is at least not an anachronism.

We are now looking for classifying principles lying in an area between two points that we have fixed. The first of these is the preliminary effort of criticism, the structural analysis of the work of art. The second is the assumption that there is such a subject as criticism, and that it makes, or could make, complete sense. We may next proceed inductively from structural analysis, associating the data we collect and trying to see larger patterns in them. Or we may proceed deductively, with the consequences that follow from postulating the unity of criticism. It is clear, of course, that neither procedure will work indefinitely without correction from the other. Pure induction will get us lost in haphazard guessing; pure deduction will lead to inflexible and over-simplified pigeonholing. Let us now attempt a few tentative steps in each direction, beginning with the inductive one.

II

The unity of a work of art, the basis of structural analysis, has not been produced solely by the unconditioned will of the artist, for the artist is only its efficient cause: it has form, and consequently a formal cause. The fact that revision is possible, that the poet makes changes not because he likes them better but because they are better, means that poems, like poets, are born and not made. The poet's task is to deliver the poem in as uninjured a state as possible, and if the poem is alive, it is equally anxious to be rid of him, and screams to be cut loose from his private memories and associations, his desire for self-expression, and all the other navel-strings and feeding tubes of his ego. The critic takes over where the poet leaves off, and criticism can hardly do without a kind of literary psychology connecting the poet with the poem. Part of this may be a psychological study of the poet, though this is useful chiefly in analysing the failures in his expression, the things in him which are still attached to his work. More important is the fact that every poet has his private mythology, his own spectroscopic band or peculiar formation of symbols, of much of which he is quite unconscious. In works with characters of their own, such as dramas and novels, the same psychological analysis may be extended to the interplay of characters, though of course literary psychology would analyse the behavior of such characters only in relation to literary convention.

There is still before us the problem of the formal cause of the poem, a problem deeply involved with the question of genres. We cannot say much about genres, for criticism does not know much about them. A good many critical efforts to grapple with such words as "novel" or "epic" are chiefly interesting as examples of the psychology of rumor. Two conceptions of the genre, however, are obviously fallacious, and as they are opposite extremes, the truth must lie somewhere between them. One is the pseudo-Platonic conception of genres as existing prior to and independently of creation, which confuses them with mere conventions of form like the sonnet. The other is that pseudo-biological conception of them as evolving species which turns up in so many surveys of the "development" of this or that form.

We next inquire for the origin of the genre, and turn first of all to the social conditions and cultural demands which produced it— in other words to the material cause of the work of art. This leads us into literary history, which differs from ordinary history in that its containing categories, "Gothic," "Baroque," "Romantic," and the like are cultural categories, of little use to the ordinary historian. Most literary history does not get as far as these categories, but even so we know more about it than about most kinds of critical scholarship. The historian treats literature and philosophy historically; the philosopher treats history and literature philosophically; and the so-called history of ideas approach marks the beginning of an attempt to treat history and philosophy from the point of view of an autonomous criticism.

But still we feel that there is something missing. We say that every poet has his own peculiar formation of images. But when so many poets use so many of the same images, surely there are much bigger critical problems involved than biographical ones. As Mr. Auden's brilliant essay *The Enchafèd Flood* shows, an important symbol like the sea cannot remain within the poetry of Shelley or Keats or Coleridge: it is bound to expand over many poets into an archetypal symbol of literature. And if the genre has a historical origin, why does the genre of drama emerge from medieval religion in a way so strikingly similar to the way it emerged from Greek religion centuries before? This is a problem of structure rather than origin, and suggests that there may be archetypes of genres as well as of images.

It is clear that criticism cannot be systematic unless there is a quality in literature which enables it to be so, an order of words corresponding to the order of nature in the natural sciences. An archetype should be not only a unifying category of criticism, but itself a part of a total form, and it leads us at once to the question of what sort of total form criticism can see in literature. Our survey of critical techniques has taken us as far as literary history. Total literary history moves from the primitive to the sophisticated, and here we glimpse the possibility of seeing literature as a complication of a relatively restricted and simple group of formulas that can be studied in primitive culture. If so, then the search for archetypes is a kind of literary anthropology, concerned with the way that literature is informed by pre-literary categories such as ritual, myth and folk tale. We realize that the relation between these categories and literature is by no means purely one of descent, as we find them reappearing in the greatest classics—in fact there seems to be a general tendency on the part of great classics to revert to them. This coincides with a feeling that we have all had: that the study of mediocre works of art, however energetic, obstinately remains a random and peripheral form of critical experience, whereas the profound masterpiece seems to draw us to a point at which we can see an enormous number of converging patterns of significance. Here we begin to wonder if we cannot see literature, not only as complicating itself in time, but as spread out in conceptual space from some unseen center.

This inductive movement towards the archetype is a process of backing up, as it were, from structural analysis, as we back up from a painting if we want to see composition instead of brush-work. In the foreground of the grave-digger scene in *Hamlet,* for instance, is an intricate verbal texture, ranging from the puns of the first clown to the *danse macabre* of the Yorick soliloquy, which we study in the printed text. One step back, and we are in the Wilson Knight and Spurgeon group of critics, listening to the steady rain of images of corruption and decay. Here too, as the sense of the place of this scene in the whole play begins to dawn on us, we are in the network of psychological relationships which were the main interest of Bradley. But after all, we say, we are forgetting the genre: *Hamlet* is a play, and an Elizabethan play. So we take another step back into the Stoll and Shaw group and see the scene conventionally as part of its dramatic context. One step more, and we can begin to glimpse the archetype of the scene, as the hero's *Liebestod* and first unequivocal declaration of his love, his struggle with Laertes and the sealing of his own fate, and the sudden sobering of his mood that marks the transition to the final scene, all take shape around a leap into and return from the grave that has so weirdly yawned open on the stage.

At each stage of understanding this scene we are dependent on a certain kind of scholarly organization. We need first an editor to clean up the text for us, then the rhetorician and philologist, then the literary psychologist. We cannot study the genre without the help of the literary social historian, the literary philosopher and the student of the "history of ideas," and for the archetype we need a literary anthropologist. But now that we have got our central pattern of criticism established, all these interests are seen as converging on literary criticism instead of receding from it into psychology and history and the rest. In particular, the literary anthropologist who chases the source of the Hamlet legend from the pre-Shakespeare play to Saxo, and from Saxo to nature-myths, is not running away from Shakespeare: he is drawing closer to the archetypal form which Shakespeare recreated. A minor result of our new perspective is that contradictions among critics, and assertions that this and not that critical approach is the right one, show a remarkable tendency to dissolve into unreality. Let us now see what we can get from the deductive end.

III

Some arts move in time, like music; others are presented in space, like painting. In both cases the organizing principle is recurrence, which is called rhythm when it is temporal and pattern when it is spatial. Thus we speak of the rhythm of music and the pattern of painting; but later, to show off our sophistication, we may begin to speak of the rhythm of painting and the pattern of music. In other words, all arts may be conceived both temporally and spatially. The score of a musical composition may be studied all at once; a picture may be seen as the track of an intricate dance of the eye. Literature seems to be intermediate between music and painting: its words form rhythms which approach a musical sequence of sounds at one of its boundaries, and form patterns which approach the hieroglyphic or pictorial image at the other. The attempts to get as near to these boundaries as possible form the main body of what is called experimental writing. We may call the rhythm of literature the narrative, and the pattern, the simultaneous mental grasp of the verbal structure, the meaning or significance. We hear or listen to a narrative, but when we grasp a writer's total pattern we "see" what he means.

The criticism of literature is much more hampered by the representational fallacy than even the criticism of painting. That is why we are apt to think of narrative as a sequential representation of events in an outside "life," and of meaning as a reflection of some external "idea." Properly used as critical terms, an author's narrative is his linear movement; his meaning is the integrity of his completed form. Similarly an image is not merely a verbal replica of an external object, but any unit of a verbal structure seen as part of a total pattern of rhythm. Even the letters an author spells his words with form part of his imagery, though only in special cases (such as alliteration) would they call for critical notice. Narrative and meaning thus become respectively, to borrow musical terms, the melodic and harmonic contexts of the imagery.

Rhythm, or recurrent movement, is deeply founded on the natural cycle, and everything in nature that we think of as having some analogy with works of art, like the flower or the bird's song, grows out of a profound synchronization between an organism and the rhythms of its environment, especially that of the solar year. With animals some expressions of synchronization, like the mating dances of birds, could almost be called rituals. But in human life a ritual seems to be something of a voluntary effort (hence the magical element in it) to recapture a lost rapport with the natural cycle. A farmer must harvest his crop at a certain time of year, but because this is involuntary, harvesting itself is not precisely a ritual. It is the deliberate expression of a will to synchronize human and natural energies at that time which produces the harvest songs, harvest sacrifices and harvest folk customs that we call rituals. In ritual, then, we may find the origin of narrative, a ritual being a temporal sequence of acts in which the conscious meaning or significance is latent: it can be seen by an observer, but is largely concealed from the participators themselves. The pull of ritual is toward pure narrative, which, if there could be such a thing, would be automatic and unconscious repetition. We should notice too the regular tendency of ritual to become encyclopedic. All the important recurrences in nature, the day, the phases of the moon, the seasons and solstices of the year, the crises of existence from birth to death, get rituals attached to them, and most of the higher religions are equipped with a definitive total body of rituals suggestive, if we may put it so, of the entire range of potentially significant actions in human life.

Patterns of imagery, on the other hand, or fragments of significance, are oracular in origin, and derive from the epiphanic moment, the flash of instantaneous comprehension with no direct reference to time, the importance of which is indicated by Cassirer in *Myth and Language*. By the time we get them, in the form of proverbs, riddles, commandments and etiological folk tales, there is already a considerable element of narrative in them. They too are encyclopedic in tendency, building up a total structure of signifi-

290   cance, or doctrine, from random and empiric fragments. And just
as pure narrative would be an unconscious act, so pure significance
would be an incommunicable state of consciousness, for communication begins by constructing narrative.

The myth is the central informing power that gives archetypal
significar.ce to the ritual and archetypal narrative to the oracle.
Hence the myth *is* the archetype, though it might be convenient
to say myth only when referring to narrative, and archetype when
speaking of significance. In the solar cycle of the day, the seasonal
cycle of the year, and the organic cycle of human life, there is a
single pattern of significance, out of which myth constructs a
central narrative around a figure who is partly the sun, partly
vegetative fertility and partly a god or archetypal human being.
The crucial importance of this myth has been forced on literary
critics by Jung and Frazer in particular, but the several books now
available on it are not always systematic in their approach, for
which reason I supply the following table of its phases:

1   The dawn, spring and birth phase. Myths of the birth of
the hero, of revival and resurrection, of creation and (because
the four phases are a cycle) of the defeat of the powers of
darkness, winter and death. Subordinate characters: the father
and the mother. The archetype of romance and of most dithy-
rambic and rhapsodic poetry.
2   The zenith, summer, and marriage or triumph phase. Myths
of apotheosis, of the sacred marriage, and of entering into Paradise. Subordinate characters: the companion and the bride.
The archetype of comedy, pastoral and idyll.
3   The sunset, autumn and death phase. Myths of fall, of the
dying god, of violent death and sacrifice and of the isolation
of the hero. Subordinate characters: the traitor and the siren.
The archetype of tragedy and elegy.
4   The darkness, winter and dissolution phase. Myths of the
triumph of these powers; myths of floods and the return of
chaos, of the defeat of the hero, and Götterdämmerung myths.
Subordinate characters: the ogre and the witch. The archetype of satire (see, for instance, the conclusion of *The
Dunciad*).

The quest of the hero also tends to assimilate the oracular and
random verbal structures, as we can see when we watch the chaos

of local legends that results from prophetic epiphanies consolidating into a narrative mythology of departmental gods. In most of the higher religions this in turn has become the same central quest-myth that emerges from ritual, as the Messiah myth became the narrative structure of the oracles of Judaism. A local flood may beget a folk tale by accident, but a comparison of flood stories will show how quickly such tales become examples of the myth of dissolution. Finally, the tendency of both ritual and epiphany to become encyclopedic is realized in the definitive body of myth which constitutes the sacred scriptures of religions. These sacred scriptures are consequently the first documents that the literary critic has to study to gain a comprehensive view of his subject. After he has understood their structure, then he can descend from archetypes to genres, and see how the drama emerges from the ritual side of myth and lyric from the epiphanic or fragmented side, while the epic carries on the central encyclopedic structure.

Some words of caution and encouragement are necessary before literary criticism has clearly staked out its boundaries in these fields. It is part of the critic's business to show how all literary genres are derived from the quest-myth, but the derivation is a logical one within the science of criticism: the quest-myth will constitute the first chapter of whatever future handbooks of criticism may be written that will be based on enough organized critical knowledge to call themselves "introductions" or "outlines" and still be able to live up to their titles. It is only when we try to expound the derivation chronologically that we find ourselves writing pseudo-prehistorical fictions and theories of mythological contract. Again, because psychology and anthropology are more highly developed sciences, the critic who deals with this kind of material is bound to appear, for some time, a dilettante of those subjects. These two phases of criticism are largely undeveloped in comparison with literary history and rhetoric, the reason being the later development of the sciences they are related to. But the fascination which *The Golden Bough* and Jung's book on libido symbols have for literary critics is not based on dilettantism, but on the fact that these books are primarily studies in literary criticism, and very important ones.

In any case the critic who is studying the principles of literary form has a quite different interest from the psychologist's concern with states of mind or the anthropologist's with social institutions. For instance: the mental response to narrative is mainly passive; to significance mainly active. From this fact Ruth Benedict's *Patterns of Culture* develops a distinction between "Apollonian" cultures based on obedience to ritual and "Dionysiac" ones based on a tense exposure of the prophetic mind to epiphany. The critic would tend rather to note how popular literature which appeals to the inertia of the untrained mind puts a heavy emphasis on narrative values, whereas a sophisticated attempt to disrupt the connection between the poet and his environment produces the Rimbaud type of *illumination*, Joyce's solitary epiphanies, and Baudelaire's conception of nature as a source of oracles. Also how literature, as it develops from the primitive to the self-conscious, shows a gradual shift of the poet's attention from narrative to significant values, this shift of attention being the basis of Schiller's distinction between naive and sentimental poetry.

The relation of criticism to religion, when they deal with the same documents, is more complicated. In criticism, as in history, the divine is always treated as a human artifact. God for the critic, whether he finds him in *Paradise Lost* or the Bible, is a character in a human story; and for the critic all epiphanies are explained, not in terms of the riddle of a possessing god or devil, but as mental phenomena closely associated in their origin with dreams. This once established, it is then necessary to say that nothing in criticism or art compels the critic to take the attitude of ordinary waking consciousness towards the dream or the god. Art deals not with the real but with the conceivable; and criticism, though it will eventually have to have some theory of conceivability, can never be justified in trying to develop, much less assume, any theory of actuality. It is necessary to understand this before our next and final point can be made.

We have identified the central myth of literature, in its narrative aspect, with the quest-myth. Now if we wish to see this central myth as a pattern of meaning also, we have to start with the workings of the subconscious where the epiphany originates, in other words in the dream. The human cycle of waking and dreaming corresponds closely to the natural cycle of light and darkness, and it is perhaps in this correspondence that all imaginative life begins.

The correspondence is largely an antithesis: it is in daylight that man is really in the power of darkness, a prey to frustration and weakness; it is in the darkness of nature that the "libido" or conquering heroic self awakes. Hence art, which Plato called a dream for awakened minds, seems to have as its final cause the resolution of the antithesis, the mingling of the sun and the hero, the realizing of a world in which the inner desire and the outward circumstance coincide. This is the same goal, of course, that the attempt to combine human and natural power in ritual has. The social function of the arts, therefore, seems to be closely connected with visualizing the goal of work in human life. So in terms of significance, the central myth of art must be the vision of the end of social effort, the innocent world of fulfilled desires, the free human society. Once this is understood, the integral place of criticism among the other social sciences, in interpreting and systematizing the vision of the artist, will be easier to see. It is at this point that we can see how religious conceptions of the final cause of human effort are as relevant as any others to criticism.

The importance of the god or hero in the myth lies in the fact that such characters, who are conceived in human likeness and yet have more power over nature, gradually build up the vision of an omnipotent personal community beyond an indifferent nature. It is this community which the hero regularly enters in his apotheosis. The world of this apotheosis thus begins to pull away from the rotary cycle of the quest in which all triumph is temporary. Hence if we look at the quest-myth as a pattern of imagery, we see the hero's quest first of all in terms of its fulfillment. This gives us our central pattern of archetypal images, the vision of innocence which sees the world in terms of total human intelligibility. It corresponds to, and is usually found in the form of, the vision of the unfallen world or heaven in religion. We may call it the comic vision of life, in contrast to the tragic vision, which sees the quest only in the form of its ordained cycle.

We conclude with a second table of contents, in which we shall attempt to set forth the central pattern of the comic and tragic visions. One essential principle of archetypal criticism is that the individual and the universal forms of an image are identical, the reasons being too complicated for just now. We proceed according to the general plan of the game of Twenty Questions, or, if we prefer, of the Great Chain of Being:

1 In the comic vision the *human* world is a community, or a hero who represents the wish-fulfillment of the reader. The archetype of images of symposium, communion, order, friendship and love. In the tragic vision the human world is a tyranny or anarchy, or an individual or isolated man, the leader with his back to his followers, the bullying giant of romance, the deserted or betrayed hero. Marriage or some equivalent consummation belongs to the comic vision; the harlot, witch and other varieties of Jung's "terrible mother" belongs to the tragic one. All divine, heroic, angelic or other superhuman communities follow the human pattern.

2 In the comic vision the *animal* world is a community of domesticated animals, usually a flock of sheep, or a lamb, or one of the gentler birds, usually a dove. The archetype of pastoral images. In the tragic vision the animal world is seen in terms of beasts and birds of prey, wolves, vultures, serpents, dragons and the like.

3 In the comic vision the *vegetable* world is a garden, grove or park, or a tree of life, or a rose or lotus. The archetype of Arcadian images, such as that of Marvell's green world or of Shakespeare's forest comedies. In the tragic vision it is a sinister forest like the one in *Comus* or at the opening of the *Inferno*, or a heath or wilderness, or tree of death.

4 In the comic vision the *mineral* world is a city, or one building or temple, or one stone, normally a glowing precious stone—in fact the whole comic series, especially the tree, can be conceived as luminous or fiery. The archetype of geometrical images: the "starlit dome" belongs here. In the tragic vision the mineral world is seen in terms of deserts, rocks and ruins, or of sinister geometrical images like the cross.

5 In the comic vision the *unformed* world is a river, traditionally fourfold, which influenced the Renaissance image of the temperate body with its four humors. In the tragic vision this world usually becomes the sea, as the narrative myth of dissolution is so often a flood myth. The combination of the sea and beast images gives us the leviathan and similar water-monsters.

Obvious as this table looks, a great variety of poetic images and forms will be found to fit it. Yeats's "Sailing to Byzantium," to take a famous example of the comic vision at random, has the city, the tree, the bird, the community of sages, the geometrical gyre and the detachment from the cyclic world. It is, of course, only the general comic or tragic context that determines the interpretation of any symbol: this is obvious with relatively neutral archetypes like the island, which may be Prospero's island or Circe's.

Our tables are, of course, not only elementary but grossly oversimplified, just as our inductive approach to the archetype was a mere hunch. The important point is not the deficiencies of either procedure, taken by itself, but the fact that, somewhere and somehow, the two are clearly going to meet in the middle. And if they do meet, the ground plan of a systematic and comprehensive development of criticism has been established.

Detail from *Bacchus and Ariadne*, Titian

myth and ancient drama

EURIPIDES   (484?–406 B.C.)

Ancient Greek drama may well have sprung from the myths
and rituals associated with the god Dionysus. Dionysus
himself is the central figure of Euripides' *The Bacchae*. One
of the latest of the Greek plays, and dedicated to the patron
of the genre, it has sometimes been called the epilogue of
Greek tragedy. Euripides was a rationalist who recognized in
this play the awesome power of the irrational and the
unknown.

the Bacchae

CHARACTERS

DIONYSUS, the god; son of Zeus and Semele
CHORUS of Asian Bacchae
TEIRESIAS, Theban prophet
CADMUS, former king of Thebes, father of Semele
PENTHEUS, king of Thebes, grandson of CADMUS
GUARD
HERDSMAN-MESSENGER
MESSENGER-SERVANT
AGAVE, daughter of CADMUS and mother of PENTHEUS

EURIPIDES

THE SCENE. *In front of the royal palace at Thebes. In the foreground is the tomb of Semele. It is still smoking as* DIONYSUS *enters. He is wearing a fawnskin and carries a* thyrsus *or wand of ivy leaves. His appearance is somewhat effeminate. He wears a smiling mask.*

DIONYSUS   I've come—the son of Zeus—to this land of Thebes—
Dionysus—whom Semele, the daughter of Cadmus, once
    produced,
dropping me from her womb when the lightning came,
and now, changed from a god into human shape,
I'm here at Dirce's streams, the water of Ismenus,
looking at the grave of my mother whom the lightning
    touched,
near the house here, and the wreck of the house itself
smoldering from the fire of Zeus that lives on and on,
a perpetual insult to my mother from Hera.
But I congratulate Cadmus, who put this sacred ground here
for his daughter's grave, which I've covered
with a vine's green cluster of grapes.
I left the very golden fields of Lydia
and Phrygia, and the sunburned flats of Persia,
and the forts of Bactria, and the land of the Medes
with its terrible winters. I passed through marvelous Arabia
and all Asia, which lies along salt waters
with Greeks and foreigners integrated
in cities packed with beautiful towers,
though this is the first Greek city I've come to,
after getting my dances started elsewhere, my dances
and ceremonies, so that I would be without doubt a god to men.
And the first in the Greek world I've excited
is Thebes, putting a fawnskin over its flesh
and a wand in its hand, a stick of ivy—
all because my mother's sisters, who should have been the last
    ones
to speak, said Dionysus was not fathered by Zeus,
and that Semele, having done it with some man,
blamed her pregnancy on Zeus, "a scheme of Cadmus,"
they snickered, and said Zeus killed her,

because she lied about him as her lover—
so for all this I've pricked them out of their homes
with a craziness, and they now live in the hills, their minds
    shot,
forced to go around in my orgy costumes—
everyone in fact who was a woman, all the female side
of Cadmus' people, I drove out of their homes,
so that they sit around now on open rocks, under pine trees,
together with the daughters of Cadmus.
For want to or not this city has got to learn
that it doesn't yet know my Bacchic program,
and that my mother's name will be cleared by me
when people see me as the god she produced with Zeus.
And Pentheus too, whom Cadmus gave the country and his
    power to,
who was born from a different daughter,
Pentheus too, who fights the god in me, who pushes me away
from drink offerings, who never mentions me in his prayers,
I'll show Pentheus and every Theban that I am god,
and when I've set up everything here
I'll head for some other place,
exposing myself there—and if Thebes becomes mad
and tries to drive my Bacchae out of the hills by force,
I'll get maenads and take command myself.
This is why I have a human form, why I changed my shape,
why I turned my nature into a man's—
but hey, you women who left Fort Tmolus in Lydia,
my gang, whom I brought from foreign towns,
my helpers my traveling companions,
lift up your native drums from Phrygia,
the ones I contrived, and Mother Rhea's,
and go around the royal house of Pentheus
banging them, so that the city of Cadmus will see it,
while I take off for the forests of Cithaeron,
where my Bacchae are, and where I will join their dancing.

[*Exit* DIONYSUS *as the* CHORUS *of Asian Bacchae enters.*]

CHORUS   We're Asians,
    we come from holy Tmolus,

300   we came as fast as we could, working
for Bromius, hard work but sweet too,
we have sweet jobs, we say:
"Bacchus, evoi!"

Who's on the street? Who's on the street? Who?
If anyone's still at home come on out,
but be quiet, and act holy,
I'm going to sing now
The Hymn to Dionysus:

1st Strophe

Oh how lucky you are, how really lucky you are,
if you know the gods from within,
if you're for clean living,
if you get the feel of Bacchus
and you do it in the hills
pure in your soul,
and to sit in on the orgies
of Great Mother Cybele,
to shake a wand in the air,
to wear ivy on your head,
to serve Dionysus, how lucky you are!
Go Bacchae! oh go Bacchae!
Bring home Bromius, the god Bromius, son of a god,
who? Dionysus! bring him from the Phrygian hills
through the highways of Greece! who? Bromius!

1st Antistrophe

He was born
when the wings of Zeus' thunder
forced his mother
to deliver, and how it hurt,
that being the end of her life
when the lightning struck,
and then the baby changed its womb
into father Zeus,

who tied him up inside his thigh
with golden pins
and hid the child from his wife,
and when the Fates were finally ready,
Zeus produced a god, bull-horned,
crowned him with a garland of snakes,
and that's why his maenads, holding their wands,
do up their hair that way.

2ND STROPHE

Come on, Thebes, you nursed Semele,
put some ivy in your hair and
teem, I said teem with green
of the beautiful smilax flower,
and do our Bacchic dance
with oak shoots and pine shoots,
and put a fringe on your spotted fawnskins,
a fringe of white-haired wool,
and be pious when you wave our lusty wands,
for every bit of this land will be dancing
when Bromius leads his gang
from hill to hill, where
his pack of females wait
crazed by Dionysus,
away from their shuttles and looms.

2ND ANTISTROPHE

O cave of the Curetes,
O sacred tenements of Crete
where Zeus was born,
where the Corybants dance
in their three-cornered hats
with the skin-stretched drum they found,
where they mixed up the Bacchic roar
with an intense sweet cry blasted
from Phrygian flutes, and with Bacchic screams
put this banging thing in Mother Rhea's hand,

302   after whom it ended up
          in the hands of crazy satyrs,
          and then our choral dance used it,
          the one we have every year
          in honor of Dionysus.

                              EPODE

          Oh how tremendous it is, when someone is in the hills
          and getting dizzy from all the fun
          and he falls on the ground and the fawnskin
          falls over him while he was chasing the goat for its blood,
          and because he likes raw meat,
          all the way to the hills of Phrygia, or Lydia,
          and Bromius is leading you, Evoi!

          The ground is flowing with milk, it's flowing with wine,
          it's flowing with the nectar of bees, and a smoke
          like Syrian incense, it's the Bacchant
          who's holding the firelike pine torch
          for a wand, and it spurts as he runs and dances
          and as he pricks the slowpokes
          screaming as if he'll throw it,
          throwing his gorgeously curly hair to the wind,
          and on top of everyone's screaming, he yells
          "Go Bacchae!
          Go Bacchae!
          You glamorous girls of gold-flowing Tmolus,
          demonstrate for Dionysus
          with a strong beat on your drums
          and enjoy your enjoyable god
          with Phrygian shouts and songs,
          when the holy flute blasts beautifully
          the holy songs held in your feet
          as you go from hill to hill." Then, thrilled,
          like a colt jumping around its mother,
          every Bacchant, one foot after the other, leaps.

          [*Enter* TEIRESIAS, *who knocks on the gates of the palace.*]

TEIRESIAS   Is there anybody here at these gates, call Cadmus out **303**
  for me,
  Agenor's son, the man who left the town of Sidon
  and put the towers on this city of Thebes,
  oh please will somebody go and tell him Teiresias wants him,
  he'll know why I'm here,
  what we agreed on, as one old man to another—
  to decorate wands and put on the skins of fawns
  and crown our heads with pieces of ivy!

[*Enter* CADMUS *from the palace.*]

CADMUS   Why my dear friend, I heard your voice in my house
  and I knew it was you, the wise voice of a wise man,
  and I'm all set, I came wearing the costume of the god,
  who is, after all, the son of my own daughter,
  this Dionysus, who's shown everybody he's a god,
  so that it's only right we honor him as much as we can, but
  where should we dance, and where should we place our feet,
  and where should we shake our grey heads, Teiresias,
  tell me, as one old-timer to another, you who are the wise one,
  and all night and all day I won't get tired
  banging my wand on the ground, for how sweetly,
  how sweetly we'll forget we're old men!
TEIRESIAS   You feel the same way I do then,
  as I feel young myself, and I'll certainly try these dances!
CADMUS   Do you want to go to the hills in our chariots?
TEIRESIAS   No, there wouldn't be much honor for the god in that.
CADMUS   Then as one old man leading the other, I'll show you
  the way.
TEIRESIAS   The god will guide us there with no trouble at all.
CADMUS   Are we going to be the only ones in town dancing for
  Bacchus?
TEIRESIAS   We're the only ones who know what we're doing, not
  those others.
CADMUS   We're taking too long. Take my hand and come on.
TEIRESIAS   Careful, hold my hand tight and lock it in yours.
CADMUS   I'm only a man, so I don't say anything against gods.
TEIRESIAS   No, we don't have much to do with theology, not we
  who've got our father's traditions, things old

304 as time itself, which no argument's going to knock down,
since no mind is sharp enough for that,
and people will say I ought to be ashamed of myself,
dancing at my age, putting ivy on my head,
but the god didn't say anything about only the young
ought to dance or only the old,
he wants everybody to honor him,
and what he doesn't want is segregation!

CADMUS Since you can't even see this torch, Teiresias,
I'll be your interpreter for you, and tell you that
Pentheus is coming this way, in a hurry for the palace,
Echion's son, the one I gave the government to,
and he looks excited. He's got something to tell.

[*Enter* PENTHEUS, *first addressing the audience.*]

PENTHEUS It just so happens that while I'm out of town
I hear about some new trouble in this city,
how our women are leaving home
pretending they're Bacchae or something, jumping in and out
of the hill trees, dancing, all for this Dionysus god,
who's the latest, whoever he is,
and right in the middle of all this ruckus are their wine jugs,
and each one sneaking off into a corner
where she takes care of some man's lust
on the excuse that they're maenad priestesses no less,
while it's really Aphrodite they take care of before Bacchus,
    so that
I've arrested some of them, and my deputies have them
    handcuffed
for safe keeping in the prison,
and those who got away I'll hunt down out of the hills,
those like Ino, and even Agave, who's my mother through
    Echion,
and Actaeon's mother too, Autonoë,
all of whom I'll fit into iron nets
and stop this Bacchic trouble-making right away,
and as for this stranger they tell me has also come to town,
this trickster magician from the land of Lydia,
this curly-haired goldilocks who perfumes his hair,

who goes around with a sexy look in his eye,
who gets together with girls, daytime and nighttime,
proposing some secret pleasures to them,
well if I ever get him inside,
I'll put a stop to his wand-banging, I'll stop his hair
from tossing, why I'll cut his head right off his neck,
he's the one who says Dionysus is a god,
he's the one who says he was sewn up in Zeus' thigh,
when actually he and his mother both burned up
in the flames of lightning, when she lied about Zeus loving
    her—
(To be so lewd, so insolent, doesn't it call for a hanging,
no matter who this stranger is?)
but isn't that Teiresias
I see in the spots of a fawnskin
and my grandfather too, laughing it up,
waving the wand of a Bacchant—Grandfather,
I can't stand seeing you without a brain in your old head,
won't you shake off that ivy stuff—
Grandfather, won't you please take that wand out of your
    hand—
it's you who got him into this, Teiresias,
you who just want to read bird omens and make more money
    on sacrifices,
so you thought you'd bring people this new god,
you who the only thing that's saving from sitting in prison
locked up with the rest of that Bacchic bunch is old age,
bringing here such sneaky rites, when in my opinion,
whenever an intoxicating beverage is served women at a party
it's the end of any good clean fun!
CHORUS   Such blasphemy! Stranger, where's your respect for gods,
    or even for Cadmus, who, after all, first propagated the race,
    you who are the son of Echion, are you speaking against your
      own family?
TEIRESIAS   When a wise man finds a good opening for a speech
    it's no great accomplishment to be eloquent,
    and you talk like a man with some sense in him, your tongue
      rolls on,
    but there's no sense in any of your words,

306   and even if you're bold, powerful, and always ready to speak,
       you're still a bad citizen if you're stupid,
       for this new god whom you go around ridiculing
       will have so much greatness in Greece that even I
       can't say it, and yet there are two prime elements in human
           affairs,
       young man, and the goddess Demeter is one of them—
       she's earth—call her by whatever name you want—
       she's what feeds people with solid food,
       and right after her came the son of Semele, Dionysus,
       who invented wine from grape juice and presented it to men,
       wine which puts a stop to the misery of a weary man
       once he fills up on what flows from the vine,
       wine that is sleep-inducing and makes you forget your daily
           worries,
       the only medicine there is for anxiety,
       pouring like the god it is in libations,
       so that through it men get good things,
       and if you are mocking him because he was sewn into Zeus'
           thigh,
       I'll show you how beautiful this really is,
       for when Zeus grabbed him out of the flame of the lightning
       and brought the fetus up to Olympus,
       Hera wanted to throw the divine little thing out of heaven,
       but Zeus, like the god he is, counteracted,
       breaking off a part of the gases which encircle the world
       and making a copy of Dionysus, *to hide him* from Hera's
           anger,
       but, in time, people twisted the expression,
       and said that Zeus *thighed him* from Hera's anger,
       and so they made a legend out of it,
       because Zeus copied the real Dionysus, *to hide him* from Hera,
       and this god is a prophet, there's a lot of prophecy
       in these Bacchic doings and in their hysteria,
       and when that god gets deep in a man's body, why
       he can make you tell the future, if you're really "gone,"
       being a little like Ares, doing a little of Ares' job,
       as when an army's all set up, all equipped and in line

and it panics even before it touches a spear, **307**
another madness that you get from Dionysus,
whom you'll see on the rocks at Delphi yet,
jumping with his torches over the double peaks up there,
and he'll be leaping and he'll be shaking his Bacchic wand
and he'll be great throughout Greece, so listen to me, Pentheus,
and don't go boasting that force is the important thing with
    men,
and don't think you're smart just because that sick mind of
    yours
tells you so, but welcome the god into your land,
pouring libations, living it up, putting a crown on your head!
And Dionysus is not going to *force* women to be chaste—
certainly not—it's always in the character of a woman
whether or not she'll be chaste,
which you'd better take into consideration, and even in Bacchic
    ceremonies
if a woman's really chaste, she won't get hurt,
and you know how happy *you* get when mobs crowd the gates
and the whole city cheers the name Pentheus—
well it's like that with Dionysus, who likes to be honored too,
which is why Cadmus and I, whom you sneer at,
will ivy our heads and dance,
two old crackpots maybe, but we have to dance,
we won't fight the god just on your say-so.
You're the one who's really sick, and there's no medicine
you can take for it, because it's the medicine that made you sick!
CHORUS   Hey, old-timer, you certainly didn't knock Apollo with
    your speech,
and you honored the great god Bromius very nicely!
CADMUS   Listen, son, Teiresias has given you good advice,
to live with our customs, not outside them,
you who fly off without knowing a thing you're talking about,
and even if this god isn't a god, as you say,
say he is anyway, for it's a beautiful lie to say he is,
and our Semele will then be a god's mother,
and think of the honor for our whole family.
You know how horribly Actaeon died,

308   how those vicious dogs he raised himself
           tore him apart savagely because he bragged
           he was better than Artemis in hunting,
           well don't you go through something like that—here,
           I'll cover your head with ivy, now honor the god with us.
PENTHEUS   Don't put your hands on me, go, play your Bacchus
           but don't try to wipe off your nonsense on *me,*
           though I'll get even with your teacher here in this foolishness—
           quick, somebody go right away
           to the place where this man does his birdwatching.
           Use crowbars to heave it and turn it all upside down,
           throw things all over the place,
           toss his ribbons into the wind and into the storm,
           that's the way to really hurt him,
           and some of you go into the city and track down
           the effeminate newcomer who's carrying this strange disease
           to our women and spoiling our beds,
           and when you catch him, bring him here
           in chains—the punishment he gets is stoning,
           so that he'll die feeling how sharply we appreciate revelry in
               Thebes!

           [*Exit* PENTHEUS.]

TEIRESIAS Why you cruel thing you, you don't really know what
               you're saying,
           you're insane now, where before you were only out of your
               mind—
           let's go, Cadmus, let's pray for this one,
           wild as he is, let's pray for the city too,
           so the god won't do anything strange,
           come on, follow me with your ivy wand,
           and try to hold my body up while I try to hold up yours,
           for it's a shame if two old men like us fall. But we must go,
           as Bacchus, the son of Zeus, must be served,
           though watch out, Cadmus, that your house doesn't echo with
               repentance
           for Pentheus! And I'm not talking prophet talk either,
           these are facts—a fool like that is asking for it!

           [*Exit* TEIRESIAS *and* CADMUS.]

1st Strophe

CHORUS   Did you hear what Pentheus said,
    did you, Holiness, did you, queen of gods, did you,
    Holiness that brings that golden wing of yours
    right down to earth,
    did you hear his outrageous stuff against Bromius,
    it wasn't very holy! against the son of Semele!
    against the top god at festivals
    where the beautiful garlands are!
    The god who does these things: who
    makes us riot in dances,
    makes us chuckle to the flute,
    makes us put an end to our worries
    when the glory of the grape comes
    to a party for the gods
    and the wine jug snuggles us asleep
    in our ivy, at feasts.

1st Antistrophe

    When a man's tongue just won't stay tied
    and his nonsense gets out of hand,
    what comes is disaster!
    And it's a life of peace and quiet,
    of common sense,
    that lasts without sagging,
    that keeps your house together, without sagging,
    and the gods up there living in that sky
    are a long way off
    but they see what's going on with people,
    and a wise-guy isn't wisdom,
    and if you won't think about human limits
    you won't live very long,
    and if you start chasing after the hardest prizes
    you won't even end up with the easy ones—
    it's crazy people do such stuff,
    if you ask me, and people who like being mean!

2ND STROPHE

I wish I could go to Cyprus,
Aphrodite's island,
where those lovely spirits live
who make men love-crazy,
and I wish I could go to Paphos
where the hundred mouths of that foreign river
saturate you with food though it never rains,
and I'd like to go to Pieria, which is just lovely,
where the Muses all sit around,
and I wish I could go to the sacred hill of Olympus,
oh take me there, Bromius, Bromius,
you're boss of Bacchae, you're our god,
take me where the Graces are and where Desire is
and where there's no law against living it up for Bacchants!

2ND ANTISTROPHE

It's our god, Zeus' son
who gets fun out of feasting,
it's he loves Peace, who brings good things,
a goddess who nurses youth,
and to the man on top
and the man on the bottom too
he brings the careless pleasure of wine,
but he hates the man who isn't interested,
who doesn't want to have the time of his life
by day and by beautiful night,
and he wisely shuns intellectualism
and he stays away from *superior* people,
and it's what the little man believes and does,
what the masses believe and do, that I'm for.

[*Enter* GUARD *with* DIONYSUS. PENTHEUS *enters from the palace.*]

GUARD We're back, Pentheus, and we didn't go in vain,
    since we've caught that animal you sent us for,
    this wild one, though, was actually tame, not darting away
      from us

trying to escape on foot, but holding out his hands of his own
   free will,
and not turning pale, his cheeks weren't even flushed,
but he laughed and told me to go ahead and tie him up
and lead him away, and he waited, making my job a snap,
though I was ashamed of myself, and I said: "I'm not taking
   you, mister,
because I want to, but because I got orders from Pentheus. He
   sent me."
And remember those women you locked up, Pentheus, the ones
   you arrested
and put in chains in prison,
well, they're gone, they got free, they're out in the hill country
   somewhere
jumping up and down calling on "Bromius" their "god,"
their chains having come off their feet all by themselves,
the doors unbolted by themselves without anyone's hand on
   them—
this one came to Thebes with a lot of miracles in him,
and you take it from there!

PENTHEUS   Untie him—now that I've got him in my net
he's not so quick that he'll get away from me—
well, stranger, you aren't unattractive looking after all,
for women anyway—which is why you're in Thebes,
and judging by your long hair, I'd say you're no wrestler,
since it hangs all the way down to your cheeks—very sexy!
And you have white skin, what care that takes,
you must keep out of sunshine—it's in darkness
you go hunting for Aphrodite with your beauty—
well, first of all, tell me what country you're from.

DIONYSUS   That's an easy one, it's nothing to brag of,
I'm sure you've heard of Tmolus, and its flowers?

PENTHEUS   Yes, I've heard of it, it circles the town of Sardis.

DIONYSUS   That's where I'm from, Lydia's my native land.

PENTHEUS   Why did you bring these ceremonies into Greece?

DIONYSUS   Dionysus, the son of Zeus, consecrated me.

PENTHEUS   You mean there's some Zeus there who's manufacturing
   new gods?

DIONYSUS   Oh no, it's the same Zeus who put the yoke of marriage
   on Semele here.

312   PENTHEUS Tell me, did he force you into this when you were
asleep, or with eyes open?

DIONYSUS Oh we saw eye to eye on the matter of orgies.

PENTHEUS What exactly are these orgies that you've got?

DIONYSUS That's a secret, and if you're not a Bacchant, you can't
find out.

PENTHEUS Well what does it do for you, to be in on this?

DIONYSUS You're not allowed to hear about it, but it would be
worth your while to know.

PENTHEUS You're trying to fake me out, just so I'll want to hear it!

DIONYSUS A man who does unholy things would loathe the god's
orgies.

PENTHEUS You mean you actually saw the god—what was he like?

DIONYSUS He was like what he wanted to be like—I didn't
compose him you know.

PENTHEUS You got around that question too without saying
anything.

DIONYSUS Say something clever to a fool and he'll always think
it's silly.

PENTHEUS Is this the first place you've come to, bringing this god?

DIONYSUS No, every foreign country is dancing to these orgies.

PENTHEUS They aren't as bright then in their thinking as Greeks
are.

DIONYSUS No, they're smarter—they do have different customs
you know.

PENTHEUS Do you go through these ceremonies in daytime or
at night?

DIONYSUS Mostly at night, since darkness makes it all the more
solemn.

PENTHEUS Yes and more effective in tricking and corrupting the
women!

DIONYSUS You can find lewdness in the daytime, too.

PENTHEUS You'll pay for your wise little answers!

DIONYSUS And you for your stupidity and your irreverence to
the god.

PENTHEUS How bold our Bacchant is, and by no means unskilled
in words.

DIONYSUS Alright, what am I going to suffer—what terrible thing
are you going to do?

PENTHEUS   First of all, I'm going to cut off your pretty little
    hairdo.
DIONYSUS   My hair is sacred property, and I grow it for the god.
PENTHEUS   Next, hand over that wand of yours!
DIONYSUS   Take it yourself. I carry Dionysus' very own!
PENTHEUS   We'll keep your body under guard in prison.
DIONYSUS   The god himself will release me whenever I want.
PENTHEUS   Sure, sure, and you'll be calling him with the Bacchants
    too!
DIONYSUS   Even now he's near, watching what I have to take
    from you.
PENTHEUS   Well where is he, he isn't registering on my eyes!
DIONYSUS   Right by me, you can't see him yourself because you're
    not holy.
PENTHEUS   Seize him, he's mocking me and Thebes too!
DIONYSUS   I'm warning you—don't chain me—I know better than
    you do.
PENTHEUS   I'm the king around here, not you—and I said chain
    him!
DIONYSUS   You don't even know your limits, or what you're doing,
    or who you are!
PENTHEUS   I'm Pentheus, Agave's my mother, Echion's my father.
DIONYSUS   Your name is quite appropriate—it sounds like
    repentance!
PENTHEUS   Get out of here—lock him up in the horse barn
    so that he can only see darkness and gloom—
    dance in *there,* and as for these ladies you've brought here,
    your co-workers in crime, I'll sell them for slaves
    or use them for laborers at my looms,
    but I'll stop their thumbs from strumming on drums!
DIONYSUS   I'm going, but since I never have to suffer, I'm not
    going to,
    and Dionysus will get even with you for these insults,
    the same Dionysus you say doesn't exist,
    it's him you lead away in chains when you think you're
    hurting me!

[GUARD *leads* DIONYSUS *away to the stables with* PENTHEUS.]

314

CHORUS   Dirce, you're the daughter of Achelous,
   blessed virgin Dirce,
   it was you who received the fetus of Zeus once
   in your streams
   when Zeus, who made him, scooped him up into his thigh
   out of that continuing fire,
   and screamed as follows:
   "Come on, Dithyrambus,
   get into this male womb of mine,
   I'm naming you 'Dithyrambus'
   and that's how I'm proclaiming you to Thebes."
   And yet you drive me away, Dirce, you blessed stream, you,
   when I come to you
   wearing garlands and living it up, oh
   why do you refuse me, why do you avoid me,
   for I swear by the grapes
   on the vines of Dionysus:
   Bromius will interest you yet!

A<small>NTISTROPHE</small>

   How outrageously
   Pentheus gives away his own very earthly origin,
   a product of the dragon
   that Echion himself produced,
   Echion the earthly, yes,
   making Pentheus a wild-eyed monster
   and not a human being,
   a sanguinary giant that stands against the gods,
   and he wants to put his ropes on me,
   one of Bromius' own,
   he already has our leader
   inside his place, hidden away,
   in the darkness of his dungeon, and oh,
   do you see all this, Dionysus, son of Zeus,
   do you see how we, your agents,
   are forced into chains—

come on down from Olympus
and shake your golden wand
and cool off his murderer's rage.

Where are you, Dionysus, are you on Mount Nysa,
the mother of animals, waving
to your friends with your wand,
or are you on the tops of Corycia
or are you in some spot on Olympus
where all those trees are
and where Orpheus playing on his lyre
draws all those trees together with his songs
and draws all those wild animals together too,
but oh what a happy place you are, Pieria,
even Evius likes you,
he will come dancing with his Bacchae
when he has crossed the quick Axius river,
bringing his maenads as they gyrate
over Lydias too the Father of Waters,
the one that gives all good things to us all,
its beautiful waves fattening a land
famed for its horses.

DIONYSUS LISTEN TO ME BACCHAE
LISTEN TO MY VOICE BACCHAE

CHORUS What was that, that noise that sounded like Evius
calling me?

DIONYSUS THIS IS THE SON OF SEMELE
THIS IS THE SON OF ZEUS CALLING YOU AGAIN

CHORUS Oh master, master
come on out here to our activities,
oh Bromius, it's Bromius!

DIONYSUS NOW BREAK, EARTH, LET THE FLOOR OF
THE EARTH BREAK OPEN!

CHORUS Suddenly the palace of Pentheus is shaking and
it's going to fall!
and Dionysus is inside the palace,
let us all adore Dionysus—
we bow before him—
look everyone, those blocks over the door

316   are slipping from their pillars
       and Bromius is shouting "Victory" in the palace!
DIONYSUS   BLAST THE LIGHTNING NOW, BLAST THE
       BRIGHT LIGHTNING!
       SPREAD THE FIRE AROUND PENTHEUS' PALACE!

[*The flame on Semele's tomb increases.*]

CHORUS   Do you see where the fire is! don't you see it
       around the sacred tomb of Semele,
       the same fire that Semele left us once before
       when she was electrocuted by lightning from Zeus!
       Throw yourselves down on the ground, maenads,
       throw your trembling bodies down on the ground,
       for here comes the one who destroyed this palace,
       our king, the son of Zeus!
DIONYSUS   Ladies of Asia, were you so scared
       that you had to fall on the ground, when you saw
       Bacchus shaking up the palace of Pentheus—stand up, please,
       and cheer up, get that trembling out of your systems!
CHORUS   Oh you are the brightest light in all our Bacchic activity,
       and how happy I am to see you, for I was so lonely, so alone.
DIONYSUS   Were you all depressed when I was taken in,
       as if I were really falling into Pentheus' dark dungeon?
CHORUS   How could we help it, for where was our protection if
       something happened to you?
       And how did you ever get away from that heathen?
DIONYSUS   I saved myself, and it was easy, no trouble at all.
CHORUS   But didn't he have you in handcuffs?
DIONYSUS   That's where I really insulted him—he thought he was
       chaining me up
       but he never touched me, never laid a finger on me, only his
       hopes feeding him,
       and in the stable he found a bull where he thought he was
       getting me,
       a bull which he tried to rope around its hooves and knees,
       all the time panting away, sweating from every pore in his body,
       biting his lips with his teeth, and I was right beside him
       watching him from where I sat very calmly, and it was at this
       time

that Bacchus came and shook the palace, and set fire to his
    mother's tomb,

which, when Pentheus saw it, thinking his palace was on fire,
he rushed back and forth yelling to his slaves: Bring water,
    bring water,
and every slave he had was on the job—a waste of energy,
but then he put this work aside, afraid I was getting away,
and grabbing his black sword he ran into the palace,
where in the courtyard Bromius had made a kind of phantom
    of me,
or at least that's my opinion, a phantom, or how it appeared
    to me,
and going right for this thing, Pentheus slashed and stabbed at it,
the blazing air! as if he were cutting me up!
in addition to which, Bacchus, humiliating him some more,
knocked down his whole palace, it's all in shambles,
and how bitter he must have felt then for locking me up,
but anyway, out of sheer exhaustion, he dropped his sword,
only a man after all, though he dared to fight it out with a god,
and I walked away quietly and came out here to you, not caring
    about Pentheus,
although I think that sound from heavy shoes in there
means he'll be out front here right away—but what will he say
    after all this?
Even if he comes out with a big snort, though, I think I can
    handle him.
A wise man keeps his temper under control.

[*Enter* PENTHEUS.]

PENTHEUS   Oh, what I've been through! and the stranger got away
    from me,
he was just a minute ago locked up as a prisoner—
but there he is—what's going on here, what are you doing
standing out front of my house here, how did you get out?
DIONYSUS   Calm down, and don't walk so heavily even if you *are*
    angry.
PENTHEUS   Tell me how you got out of my prison and got here?
DIONYSUS   Didn't I tell you, or didn't you hear me, that someone
    would set me free?

318   PENTHEUS   Who? You always say such strange things!
DIONYSUS   It was the one who grows vines for people—
you scoff at this beautiful thing Dionysus does?
PENTHEUS   I'm ordering all the towers in this area to be locked up.
DIONYSUS   What for, don't you think gods can walk over walls?
PENTHEUS   You're a wise-guy, a real wise-guy, except where you
ought to be wise.
DIONYSUS   Where I really ought to be wise I'm wise, don't worry,
but listen first to what that man there has to say,
he's come all the way from the hills just to tell you something,
and I'll wait for you, don't worry, I'm not going anywhere.

[*Enter the* HERDSMAN—MESSENGER.]

MESSENGER   Oh Pentheus, you who rule over this land of Thebes,
I have come from Mount Cithaeron, whereon never fail to fall
the bright white arrows of the snow—
PENTHEUS   Alright, what's so important, what's the message?
MESSENGER   I have seen Bacchants raging, who, stung with frenzy,
shot forth their feet of white, like darts, from this land,
and I have come to tell you and the city
what strange things they do—fantastic things!
But first I have to know if I can talk freely,
or if I have to cut my speech,
for the swiftness of your moods, O king, I fear,
and your anger that is so quick, so over-kingly.
PENTHEUS   Feel free to speak, you won't have any trouble from me,
for with honest men like you I know better than to get angry,
and the more you say about how bad these Bacchants are,
the more I'll punish *this* man,
who taught all these tricks to our women.
MESSENGER   Our cattle that were at pasture
were even now on the hillside, climbing,
where the sun sent up its rays to warm the earth,
and I see these three bands of Bacchic women
dancing, the first led by Autonoë,
the second by your mother, Agave, the third by Ino,
and all asleep they were, their bodies at rest,
and some would lean their backs on pines
and some on leaves of oak thrown careless on the ground

would lean their heads, modest—not as you might think,
stoned from drinking and wandering after desire
through the wild wood with a noising of the flute—
and then your mother, standing up, cried out
to the Bacchae: "Wake up, everybody, don't sleep!"
when she heard the mooing of our herd.
And they stood upright, thrusting soft sleep
from their eyes, and it was marvelous, so orderly,
the young women, the old women, the virgins,
and first they dropped their hair down to their shoulders,
then they hitched up their fawnskins, whose bands
had loosened, and then they tied the dappled skins
with serpents that would lick upon their cheeks,
and some, holding wild fawns or wolf cubs
in their arms, gave them their own milk to drink—
they were new mothers who had left their babies
and their breasts were bursting, and they put ivy wreaths on
and wreaths of oak and the flowery smilax,
and one took her wand and beat upon the rock,
and a splash of dewlike water washed up,
and another cast her wand on the floor of the earth
where the god shot out a spring of wine,
and for anyone wanting milk
she sliced the earth with her fingertips
and milk was released, sweet streams of honey
dripping from their wands of ivy.
If you had been there, seeing all this,
you would have approached with prayer the god you now revile.
And then we herdsmen and shepherds came together,
to get each other's view
of what terrible things they were doing, terrible and marvelous,
when a man from the city, one quick with words,
said to us all: "You hill people,
what do you say we hunt for Pentheus' mother, Agave,
get her out of all this horsing around
and get ourselves in good with the king?"
And this seemed like a good idea to us, hiding ourselves in the
    leaves
for ambush, until at their appointed time

320   the Bacchae moved their wands in revelry, calling
     "Iacchus, the son of Zeus," all together,
     calling for Bromius, and then all the hillside
     and all the beasts reveled too, and nothing was unmoved as they
         moved.
     Then quite by chance Agave leaped near me,
     and I ran out to try to grab her,
     leaving behind the leaves where I was hid,
     and she cried: "You bitches running with me:
     MEN ARE AFTER US! Follow me,
     use your wands as weapons!"
     We immediately ran away, escaping
     a Bacchic slaughter, while they, unarmed,
     swooped down on our catle grazing there,
     and then you could have seen a heifer, deep-uddered,
     mooing, cut in two by a woman's hands,
     and others chopped up the calves into pieces
     and ribs and cloven hooves
     were thrown here and there, scraps of flesh
     dabbled with blood dripping from the fir trees,
     and bulls raging, angry in their horns,
     stumbled their bodies onto the earth,
     dragged down by the hands of masses of girls,
     and they stripped the flesh
     faster than you could blink your royal eyes,
     and they went along like birds lifted soaring
     over the on-lying plains which bear rich harvests
     to the Theban people by the streams of Asopus,
     on Hysiae, on Erythrae, towns beneath the hills of Cithaeron,
     they swooped down like an enemy
     turning over everything, up and down
     they turned over everything, and they grabbed up
     babies from their homes and all these
     they put on their shoulders, and though they tied up nothing
     with bonds, nothing fell down to the black earth,
     nothing of bronze, nothing of iron, and they carried fire
     in their hair, though it did not burn them,
     till in anger people came out bearing arms against the Bacchae.
     Then this terrible thing happened, O king,
     sharp spears drew no blood from them,

but instead, the Bacchae, firing their wands from their hands
  wounded *men,* and they, *women,* drove away *men*
  in flight, some god being on their side,
  and back they went to where they first moved their feet,
  to those same founts sprung for them by the god
  where they washed off the blood, and serpents from their cheeks
  licked with their tongues the drops of gore.
  Whoever, then, this god is, my lord,
  welcome him to this city, for in addition to all this,
  they say of him, I hear,
  that he gave wine to man, an end to anxiety.
  And when man shall be no longer wined,
  there shall be no love, no further joy for humankind.
CHORUS I'm scared to speak freely to this tyrant of ours,
  but now I'll say it anyway:
  No god is better than Dionysus!
PENTHEUS What these Bacchae are stirring up is getting too hot
    for us,
  it's spreading like wildfire, it's disgracing us all over Greece,
  so we'll waste no time—you, go to the Electra Gate,
  order every soldier that's got a shield,
  every rider than can handle a fast horse,
  every man who can bend a bow with his hand,
  everyone who can carry anything,
  we're going to attack the Bacchae—this is going too far
  to put up with all we've had to take from our women!
DIONYSUS So you're still not convinced, Pentheus, after all I've said,
  but though you've made me suffer terribly
  I'll tell you again: don't lift a finger against a god
  and hold your peace, for Bromius will not stand by
  while you blast his Bacchae out of the hills they love.
PENTHEUS Don't tell *me* what to do, you who got out of prison
    once,
  do you want me to punish you again?
DIONYSUS I'd rather offer a sacrifice than get angry
  and have to kick against the pricks all the time, when it's man
    versus god!
PENTHEUS Oh I'll sacrifice alright, and what's a worthy victim?
    His women!
  There'll be a hot time in the woods of Cithaeron tonight!

EURIPIDES

322 DIONYSUS: You'll all end up running away from it, and what a disgrace then,
shields of bronze retreating from the wands of Bacchae!

PENTHEUS It's no use getting all tangled up with this stranger, for even when it hurts him he doesn't shut up.

DIONYSUS My friend, I tell you this business can still turn out well.

PENTHEUS What do I have to do, bow down to my own slaves?

DIONYSUS I'll bring the women back here, and without an army.

PENTHEUS Oh my, now you're trying to put me in a trap!

DIONYSUS Where's the trap—can't I just want to save you with my own methods?

PENTHEUS You're in cahoots with them, you just want this rabble-rousing to go on and on!

DIONYSUS I'm in cahoots alright, but it's with a *god!*

PENTHEUS Bring me my weapons, and will you please
SHUT UP!

DIONYSUS Hold on—
How would you like to see what they're doing up in the hills?

PENTHEUS Would I! I'd give anything to see it!

DIONYSUS But why so anxious?

PENTHEUS Well, uh, seeing them drunk, would be, uh, pretty ghastly . . .

DIONYSUS Ghastly or not, you'd still like to see it, is that it?

PENTHEUS Of course that's it! quietly, under the pines, lying still . . .

DIONYSUS You know they'll track you down though, even if you do come secretly!

PENTHEUS Yes, you're right, what you say is right, I'll go openly!

DIONYSUS Shall I take you then, will you really give it a try?

PENTHEUS Let's go right now, don't take any more time!

DIONYSUS Put on some women's clothes then.

PENTHEUS What *is* this, am I supposed to change from a man into a woman?

DIONYSUS They'd kill you if you were seen there as a man.

PENTHEUS Yes, you're right again, you're really very clever.

DIONYSUS It's something I picked up from Dionysus.

PENTHEUS Tell me what to do then, you're the one who's good at this.

DIONYSUS I'll go in your palace and dress you, come on.

PENTHEUS   But in what dress, in a woman's dress? I'd be
   humiliated!
DIONYSUS   Then you're not very anxious after all to see the
   maenads, are you?
PENTHEUS   What dress do you want me to put on?
DIONYSUS   First I'll put a long wig on your head.
PENTHEUS   Then what, what's the rest of my outfit?
DIONYSUS   A dress that's down to your ankles, and a nice hat for
   your head!
PENTHEUS   And is there anything else you will give me?
DIONYSUS   A wand for your hand and a spotted fawnskin.
PENTHEUS   I JUST CAN'T PUT A WOMAN'S DRESS ON!
DIONYSUS   Then fight the Bacchae, spill blood.
PENTHEUS   Yes, you're right, first we've got to go spy on them.
DIONYSUS   That's at least wiser than trying to catch evil with evil.
PENTHEUS   But how can I get through the city of Cadmus without
   being seen?
DIONYSUS   The streets we take will be deserted, and I'll lead you.
PENTHEUS   Anything's better than having these Bacchae laugh
   at me,
   but I'm going inside now, I want to think over your advice.
DIONYSUS   That's fair enough, and in any case, I'm always ready
   to help.
PENTHEUS   I'm going in, and I'll either march out, armed to the
   teeth,
   or take your advice.

[*Exit* PENTHEUS.]

DIONYSUS   Well ladies, we've got our man in the net,
   and he'll find the Bacchae, but it will cost him his life.
   Dionysus, it's up to you now. You're close now.
   Now we'll get our revenge. First, put him out of his mind,
   then pour a little insanity in, since in his right mind
   he'd never be able to put a woman's dress on,
   but once he goes out of his mind he'll put it on,
   and after those threats of his before, which were just terrible,
   I'll make him the laughingstock of Thebes,
   led through the city looking like a woman.
   I'm going, I'll deck him out in the clothes

324   he'll be wearing to Hades, slaughtered by his mother's hands,
and he'll recognize Dionysus, the son of Zeus,
who's out at last, the most terrible god of all,
and yet the kindest too, for humankind.

[*Exit* DIONYSUS.]

STROPHE

CHORUS   Do you mean I'll be putting down my white foot again
in those dances of ours that go all night
living it up, and in the dew of the air
I'll be tossing my neck,
like a fawn playing again
in the green pleasures of a meadow,
when she gets away
from the frightening hunt
and jumps woven nets
while the hunters speed up their dogs
with all that screaming,
when the running is so hard,
when she has to leap like the wind
over a river-plain,
who loves the darkness of the forest,
among the lonely tree shoots
where there are no men?
What's wisdom or glory
next to this gift the gods give men:
to hold your winning hand
over the heads of your enemies,
for glory is something we'll always love.

ANTISTROPHE

Divine power doesn't come on strong
at first, but it sure is there,
knocking down the man
who exalts his own arrogance,

who keeps it up, all for some crazy notion,
and never thinks of the gods,
the gods who hide very slyly
but time's long foot marches on
and they hunt down the heathen,
and it's wrong to think you're better than the law,
and it's wrong to act as if you were,
and it doesn't cost you much
to believe in this:
what's divine is strong,
what we've had for a long time,
based on nature,
is to be believed.

What's wisdom or glory
next to this gift the gods give men:
to hold your winning hand
over the heads of your enemies,
for glory is something we'll always love.

It's a lucky man who escapes a storm at sea
and gets to where he's going,
a lucky man who can chuck his troubles
and one man always gets more than another
in money and power,
and for every million people
there are a million dreams,
and some people end up rich,
others bankrupt,
but it's the man who has a good life day by day
who's the happy one, bless him.

[*Enter* DIONYSUS *from the palace, calling* PENTHEUS *out.*]

DIONYSUS   Come on out here, you eager beaver for things you're
    not supposed to see,
    always chasing after the wrong thing, yes I mean you, Pentheus,
    come on out here in front of your palace, let's see you
    now that you've got on your woman's dress, you mad Bacchant
    you,

326 spying on your own mother and her bunch—
oh my, if it isn't one of the daughters of Cadmus!

[*Enter* PENTHEUS, *dressed as a Bacchant.*]

PENTHEUS Why—
I think I see two suns
and two cities of Thebes, each with seven gates,
and you mister, you look like a bull going in front of me
and you seem to have grown horns on your head.
Were you an animal before too? You're certainly a bull now!
DIONYSUS It's a god that's walking with you, one who wasn't
gentle with you before
but he's friends with us now, and what you see now you're
supposed to see.
PENTHEUS What do I look like, don't I look like Ino,
don't I seem to stand like my own mother Agave?
DIONYSUS Yes, as I look at you I do seem to see them,
but wait, one of your curls has come out of place here,
it's not how I fixed it under your hat.
PENTHEUS I guess I knocked it out of place
when I was throwing myself back and forth in my Bacchic
frenzy.
DIONYSUS I'll fix it again for you, I'll be your maid,
just hold your head back.
PENTHEUS There—now you take care of it, I'm leaving everything
up to you.
DIONYSUS Now your girdle's come loose
and the pleats of your dress aren't hanging even at your ankles.
PENTHEUS Oh, you're right, my right foot's not even
but it's hanging right on the left side.
DIONYSUS You know, you'll think I'm your best friend
after the surprise of seeing how good the Bacchae really are.
PENTHEUS Which way should I hold my wand, in the right hand
like this,
or like this, which way seems more professional?
DIONYSUS You hold it in your right hand and at the same time
you lift your right foot, and good for you for changing your
mind.

PENTHEUS   Do you think I could lift up the whole of Mount Cithaeron
on my shoulders, with all the Bacchae on it too?
DIONYSUS   You could if you want to, and though you were crazy before,
you're now thinking like a sane man!
PENTHEUS   Will I heave up the cliffs with my arm or shoulders,
or should we bring crowbars?
DIONYSUS   You don't want to destroy the nymphs' shrines, do you,
and where Pan hangs out playing his pipe?
PENTHEUS   Oh no, you're right, women mustn't be beaten by force,
I'll hide myself under the pines.
DIONYSUS   Hide? You'll have to hide
if you come to the maenads spying and tricking them.
PENTHEUS   Yes, it's as if I can see them now, like birds in the bushes
all tangled up in their loving.
DIONYSUS   That's why you're going—to watch them,
and maybe you'll catch a glimpse of them, maybe they'll catch you!
PENTHEUS   Take me right through the center of Thebes,
me, the only man in this whole city who'd dare this!
DIONYSUS   Yes, you're the only one whom the city wears out, the only one,
and there's a hard job ahead of you,
so follow me, I'll guide you there very safely,
though somebody else will bring you back.
PENTHEUS   My mother, I'll bet you!
DIONYSUS   You will be noticed by everyone.
PENTHEUS   That's what I'm coming for!
DIONYSUS   You will be carried when you come back—
PENTHEUS   My usual luxury of course!
DIONYSUS   —in the arms of your mother.
PENTHEUS   Oh, you'll make me go soft!
DIONYSUS   Yes, you'll be very soft.
PENTHEUS   It's only what I deserve.
DIONYSUS   You're a strange man, a strange man, and it's a strange experience ahead of you,
but the glory you will get from it will rise up to the sky.

328 [*Exit* PENTHEUS.]

Hold out your hands, Agave, and you other daughters of
   Cadmus,
for I'm bringing this youngster to a great contest,
where I will be the winner and Bromius will be the winner,
and everything else will be shown in due course.

[*Exit* DIONYSUS.]

STROPHE

CHORUS Go you dogs of madness, quick, quick, go to the hills
where the daughters of Cadmus are having their riot, quick,
bite them rabid
against this madman who spies on maenads
in a woman's dress!

He'll be peeking from smooth rock or from a tree
and his mother will be the first to see
and she'll yell to the maenads, she'll yell:
"Hey Bacchae, who's that Peeping Tom
that's come all the way up these hills
to see the women of Thebes running around,
who, who was *his* mother?
He wasn't born from the blood of a woman,
maybe from some lady lion
or from one of the Gorgons of Libya!"

Come on, Justice, show yourself, come on and bring your sword,
killing him clean through his throat
that godless lawless unjust earthborn son
of Echion.

ANTISTROPHE

He's got the mind of a criminal, he's got a criminal's rage
over your orgies, Bacchus, and your mother's,
he has the heart of a lunatic,
he has the gall of a true crackpot to come
thinking he'll beat with force those who are unbeatable!

There's no sorrow in life
for the wise mind, for the honest man concerned with the gods,
for the man who knows his limit,
and in the wisdom I am hunting for so happily
there is no envy, there are other things,
great things, and they have always been known,

the beautiful things in life
from day to night, and to be pure in my reverence,
honoring gods and keeping away
from outlaws.

Come on, Justice, show yourself, come on and bring your sword,
killing him clean through his throat
that godless lawless unjust earthborn son
of Echion.

EPODE

Let's see you as a bull, Dionysus,
let's see you as a dragon with lots of heads,
let's see you as a lion burning fire,
and hey, Bacchus, come on, put a smile on your face
and throw your net over this Bacchae-hunter,
as he falls
under the herd of your murdering maenads!

[*Enter* MESSENGER–SERVANT.]

MESSENGER   Oh to think this house was once so well-off in Greece
  and that it was the old man from Sidon
  who put the seed of the dragon in this land of the snake,
  well how I weep for you, only a slave and yet
  good slaves share the misfortunes of their masters.
CHORUS   What's the matter, do you have any news of the Bacchae?
MESSENGER   Pentheus is dead, the son of Echion is dead.
CHORUS   Oh Bromius, you *are* a king, now we see what a great
    god you are!
MESSENGER   What are you saying, what is this, are you women glad
  at this terrible thing for my master?

330 CHORUS I'm a foreigner, and this is the way we rejoice abroad, and
hurray, I don't have to be afraid of going to prison anymore!
MESSENGER Do you think Thebes is so out of men that—
CHORUS It's Dionysus, it's Dionysus who rules me,
not Thebes!
MESSENGER Well, you might be forgiven, except that it isn't nice,
ladies—
to rejoice when disaster has struck!
CHORUS Tell me how he died, how an unjust man
who lived an unjust life died? Come on, tell us!
MESSENGER Well, when we got past the last houses of this land of
ours, Thebes,
and we crossed the river of Asopus,
we started up the huge rock of Cithaeron,
Pentheus and I—I was working for my master,
and that stranger, who was to be our guide for the spectacle,
and first we sat down in a grassland,
keeping our feet still and our tongues from moving
so that we'd see them but they wouldn't see us,
and there was a valley, with cliffs all around it and broken by
streams
and shaded very well by pines, and here the maenads sat
with their hands at work on things they enjoy,
some topping their shabby wands
with fresh leaves of ivy,
others like fillies that have just had their bridles removed,
chanting back and forth to each other some Bacchic music,
but poor old Pentheus, he couldn't see these women at all
so he said: "Hey, stranger, from where I'm standing
I can't see these phony maenads at all—
if I climb that hill, though, or that large pine over there
I could see the lewdness of these maenads a lot better,"
and then I saw the stranger do something very strange,
for then reaching the top branch of a towering pine tree
he pulled it and pulled it and pulled it down to the dark ground,
so that it was curved like a bow or like the curve of a wheel
after you turn it on a lathe to round off its edge,
and the stranger bent that mountain tree down to the ground

just like that with his own bare hands, which no man could do,
and then he set Pentheus down on those pine branches
and let the trunk slide up through his hands
very softly, making sure that it didn't throw him off,
and the tree straightened itself up into the sky
with my master sitting on top of it,
but the maenads saw him a lot better than he saw them,
and no sooner was he spotted up there
when BANG, the stranger was no longer anywhere around,
and a voice from out of the sky—it sounded like the voice of
    Dionysus—
cried out: "Well, girls, I've brought him to you, our orgy-mocker,
he mocks you and he mocks me and he mocks our orgies too,
    go get him!"
and just as he was speaking he fired a blast of terrible flames
up into the sky and down into the earth,
and the air itself was soundless, and that whole shaded valley
held every leaf silent, and you couldn't hear a peep from any of
    the animals,
but the Bacchae didn't quite catch what the voice had said,
and they shot up bobbing their heads all over the place,
so that he sounded off again, and this time the daughters of
    Cadmus
knew very well it was an order from their Bacchus,
and they soared out and I tell you their feet were as fast as doves
that keep gaining on each other as they race,
Pentheus' mother, Agave, and her sisters
and all the Bacchae, and they went through a torrent even
and over boulders and the god was breathing madness into
    their feet,
and when they saw my master just sitting up there on top of
    his tree,
they climbed up a huge rock opposite his position
and fired boulders at him and then they launched spears made
    of pine
and others shot their wands through the air at Pentheus,
but their aim was poor, and they didn't get anywhere,
and poor old Pentheus just sat up there, way out of reach

332   knowing that things were now hopeless,
and as a last resort they banged down oak branches that fell
    like thunder,
and then with wooden crowbars they pried at the roots of the
    tree itself,
and when all this work got them nowhere,
Agave said: "Come on, girls, everybody grab part of the trunk,
we've got to catch this little animal we've treed
or he'll blab all the secrets of our god!"
And then a thousand little hands went around that pine tree
and they tore it right out of the ground,
and from his lofty perch Pentheus fell all the way down to the
    ground
with all kinds of screams and cries,
knowing now he was near the end,
and his mother was the first one to drop on him,
beginning the slaughter like a true priestess,
but he tore off the hat he had over his hair
so she'd recognize him and wouldn't kill him—
poor Agave—and he touched her cheeks and he said:
"It's me, mother, it's your son, Pentheus!
You and Echion are my own parents!
Have pity on me, mother! Don't kill your own son
just because he did something wrong!"
But she was foaming at the mouth and her eyes were rolling
    around
in her head like a crazy woman, and she was completely out of
    her mind,
a woman possessed by Bacchus, not thinking of her son,
and she grabbed his left arm at the wrist
and placed her foot against his ribs, the poor thing,
and then she tore his shoulder off, not by her own strength,
    of course,
the god put that power in her hands,
and Ino was working on the other side of him,
pulling off his flesh, and Autonoë was at it, and all the Bacchae
were hard at it, though there was only one screaming sound,
they yelling for joy, Pentheus yelling with what breath he had
    left,

and one of the Bacchae had taken off an arm, another
a shoe with the foot still in it,
his ribs being stripped to the bone in little shreds,
and they were playing ball with parts of his body, their hands
    all blood,
and his body is now lying all over the place, part of it next to
    some rocks,
some of it deep inside the forest in some leaves—
it would be a hard job to find it—and his pitiful head
which his mother happened to find, she picked up
and stuck on the top of her wand, and she's carrying it
all over Mount Cithaeron as if it were the head of a mountain
    lion,
having left her sisters behind doing their maenad dances,
and she's coming inside these walls gloating over her horrible
    catch,
calling to Bacchus, her "fellow hunter," her "helper in the chase,"
"the triumphant one," though for all her triumph she wins only
    tears,
but I'm getting out of this miserable place
before Agave gets back,
yes, the best thing for a man is to restrain himself, and be
    reverent to the gods,
I think this is the wisest thing any man can do.
It's his best possession. [*Exit.*]

ASTROPHA

CHORUS   Let's all do a dance for Bacchus,
    let's all shout about the death of Pentheus,
    the man who was born from a dragon is dead,
    the man who put on a woman's dress is dead,
    the man who took one of our beautiful wands
    has taken it down to Hades,
    letting a bull lead him to disaster,
    Bacchae, ladies of Thebes,
    you have a tremendous victory, a beautiful victory,
    in your tears and in your weeping,

EURIPIDES

334   for it's a beautiful game, oh yes, when a mother dips her hands
in the dripping blood of her son,

but now I see the mother of Pentheus, I see you Agave,
crazy-eyes, I see you running home,
welcome to the party for our god!

[*Enter* AGAVE, *holding* PENTHEUS' *head on her wand. A few of her
followers await by the entrance.*]

STROPHE

AGAVE   Bacchae! Asians!
CHORUS   What's all the excitement, speak up!
AGAVE   Look at this new hunk of ivy
we've brought home from the mountain,
a good catch!
CHORUS   I see it, welcome to our party!
AGAVE   I trapped him myself without any equipment,
see, it's the cub of a mountain lion,
that's obvious, isn't it?
CHORUS   How far out of your way did you go?
AGAVE   Cithaeron—
CHORUS   Cithaeron what?
AGAVE   Cithaeron killed him.
CHORUS   Who hit him first?
AGAVE   I did, he's my prize,
"Lucky Agave" they call me at our assemblies.
CHORUS   What happened next?
AGAVE   The, uh, Cadmus', uh—
CHORUS   The what? Cadmus' what?
AGAVE   Daughters—
they touched the beast only after me, after me, after me,
oh what a great hunt,

ANTISTROPHE

but you get your share of the feast: here!
CHORUS   You poor dear, what are you talking about, my share?

AGAVE   This is a young one: **335**
　under the part of its head where the hair is
　there's a soft fuzz blooming on his cheeks.
CHORUS   Yes, with all that hair it does look like a beast.
AGAVE   Bacchus whipped up the maenads
　when they where hunting this one,
　Bacchus is great!
CHORUS   That's our king, Bacchus, a real hunter!
AGAVE   NOW do you praise me?
CHORUS   Why not, I praise you.
AGAVE   And soon the men of Thebes—
CHORUS   And of course your own son, Pentheus—
AGAVE   Yes, he too will praise his mother,
　she caught this lion, she bagged it.
CHORUS   A very unusual catch!
AGAVE   Very unusually caught!
CHORUS   Are you proud of yourself?
AGAVE   I'm so happy—
　I did something big on this hunt, something great!
　It's so obvious!

CHORUS   Well then, you miserable woman, show everyone in
　　town now
　your prize, show them what you've brought back.
AGAVE   Thebans! You who live in the land
　of the beautiful towers, Thebes, look what I've caught,
　not with any of those special spears you get in Thessaly,
　not with nets, we used our own lily white hands
　to catch this animal, we ladies of Thebes,
　so what good is all your bragging now,
　and all that silly gear you get from armorers,
　we caught this thing here with our bare hands,
　and we tore its limbs apart with our bare hands—
　but where's my father at—let him get a close look,
　and where's that son of mine, Pentheus?
　Have him set a ladder against the wall of the palace
　so he can nail up on the beam up there this head
　I brought home from some lion.

　[*Enter* CADMUS *and attendants carrying the remains of* PENTHEUS.]

336   CADMUS   Follow me, men, bring that horrible pile of Pentheus
and follow me out front of the palace.
That's the body, after hard work and endless searching,
or what I found of it scattered all over the valley
of Mount Cithaeron, not one bit of it in the same place
as the rest, and those woods just impossible,
for I heard all about what my daughters were doing
when I got back into town
away from the Bacchae, with old Teiresias,
and I turned right around for the mountain again
to get my son those maenads killed,
and I saw the mother of Actaeon there, Aristaeus' wife,
and I saw Ino up there too in those oak trees
and both of those poor demented creatures were still excited,
one of them telling me that Agave was coming here,
raving—well at least that was the truth,
I see her now, not a very pretty sight.

AGAVE   Daddy, can you ever be proud of us,
you who produced the best daughters any man ever did
by a long shot—I say daughters, but I mean really me,
me, who left my shuttle by the loom
and took off for better things, hunting big game with my
    hands now,
and see this here, I brought it home in my own arms,
it's my trophy, we'll hang it up at home—
come on, father, you take it once in your hands,
and call all your friends for a party and enjoy my trophy,
for now that we've done this, father,
we'll have to call you blessed.

CADMUS   Oh, what agony, it's beyond my power to grasp, there's
    no end to it,
you did this murder with your own hands,
a fine sacrifice to be tossing to the gods,
a great feast to be inviting me and the rest of Thebes to,
I pity you, what you've done, and I pity myself too,
and the god was right to do it to us, it was Bromius, King
    Bromius
who ruined us, one of our own family!

AGAVE   How grouchy old men are, how creepy when they look
    at you,

I hope my son is more like his mother, a good hunter,   **337**
when he goes hunting with other Theban boys,
though all that one ever does is quarrel with the gods,
and if he deserves a talking-to, father,
it's your job to give it to him,
and will somebody please call him out here where I can see him
and where he can see what a happy mother he's got!
CADMUS   Stop it! Stop it! When you find out what you've really
    done, all of you,
    your pain will be terrible, and only if you keep up this craziness
    until the day you die
    could you ever be well off—
AGAVE   What's wrong here? Why are you so miserable?
CADMUS   First lift your head up and look at the sky.
AGAVE   So—why do you want me to look up there though?
CADMUS   Does it look the same, or does it seem any different?
AGAVE   Why, it's brighter, it's clearer than before.
CADMUS   Do you still feel all shaken up inside?
AGAVE   I don't know what you mean by that, my head feels a little
    clearer though,
    it doesn't feel the same as it did before.
CADMUS   Can you hear me, can you give me a straight answer now?
AGAVE   I forgot what we were talking about before father.
CADMUS   Whose house did you marry into when you were married?
AGAVE   Why you gave me away to Echion, father.
CADMUS   And who was the son that you and Echion had?
AGAVE   Pentheus, Echion and I gave birth to Pentheus.
CADMUS   And whose head are you holding in your hands?
AGAVE   A lion's—that's what the hunters told me it was.
CADMUS   Look right at it, that's not much trouble, is it, to look
    right at it?
AGAVE   [screams] What am I looking at, what have I got in my
    hands?
CADMUS   Take a good look, make sure!
AGAVE   This is the worst thing I've ever seen!
CADMUS   Do you think it looks like a lion's head now?
AGAVE   It's Pentheus' head, I'm holding Pentheus' head!
CADMUS   I was crying long before you ever recognized him.
AGAVE   Who killed him, what is he doing in my hands?
CADMUS   What a horrible time to have to learn the truth!

338

AGAVE Tell me, my heart's pounding at what you're going to say!

CADMUS You did it, you killed him, you and those sisters of yours.

AGAVE Where was he killed, at home, where?

CADMUS Remember where those dogs once tore apart Actaeon?

AGAVE Cithaeron, but why did my poor son ever go up there?

CADMUS He went to mock god and to sneer at your orgies.

AGAVE Our orgies? what were we doing up there?

CADMUS You were crazy, everybody in town went crazy over
  Bacchus.

AGAVE Dionysus destroyed us all, only now do I understand it.

CADMUS In a way, you insulted him, you didn't think he was
  a god.

AGAVE Father, where's the body of this son I loved so much?

CADMUS I brought it here, after labriously locating the pieces.

AGAVE Is the body fixed properly?
  What did Pentheus ever do that he had to suffer for my
  foolishness?

CADMUS He was just like you, he didn't have any respect for
  the god.
  and that's why we were all taken care of with one blast,
  you and your sisters, and him, the whole family gone to pieces
  now,
  myself included, never having had any sons of my own,
  and now I see this boy that came out of your womb,
  you poor creature, murdered in such a vicious way.
  Child, you were someone our house looked up to,
  you held it together, and you were the son of one of my own,
  you meant terror to the city, nobody insulted your grandfather
  once they looked you in the eyes or you'd make him pay for it,
  and now I have to clear out of here, in shame,
  me—the great Cadmus! who planted the seed of the Theban
  people
  and reaped such a grand harvest,
  oh, my son, I loved you more than anyone else,
  and even though you are dead now I still count you my most
  loved friend,
  your hand that will never touch my chin anymore,
  and you'll never grab me and say: "Grandfather,
  who's bothering you? Is anyone insulting you, old man?

Who's getting on your nerves that you're so sad?
Tell me, Grandfather, and I'll fix the troublemaker for you!"
Well now I am really sad, and you're wretched,
your mother and her sisters pitiful,
and if there is still anyone around who snubs the gods
he can look at the death of this one, and start believing!

CHORUS   I'm sorry for you, Cadmus, though your grandson got
      only what he deserved,
   but I'm sorry that his death hurts you.

AGAVE   Father, you see how changed I am now,[1]
   [I see now that what I was carrying in my own hands
   was a curse, but how can I hold this body in my arms now,
   or press him to my breast in some tender way,
   or cry over him?
   Is there some cloth we can wrap him in?
   Are my hands the ones that should take care of him?
   But come, let's put his head back with his body
   and lay out the body as best we can—
   there is the face I once loved, how young it is,
   I'm covering over your head now with this cloth,
   I'm covering over these blood-soaked limbs of yours.

   [DIONYSUS *appears above the wall of the palace.*]

DIONYSUS   Everything that this man suffered he deserved to suffer,
   he deserved to be torn up on those rocks,
   trying to chain me, insulting me,
   that's why he was killed by the last person in the world
   who should have killed him, but as for the rest of you,
   I won't hide from you what this country has in store:
   some day you will all be driven into other lands, away from here,
   because of what you have done,
   and you, Agave, and your sisters, must leave this city: get out,
   you must pay for this murder of yours, leaving Thebes for good,
   for murderers have no place beside the graves of their victims,]
   and as for you, Cadmus, you will be changed into a snake,
   and your wife, Harmonia, the daughter of Ares, becomes a
      snake too,

---

[1] The lines in brackets have been added by the translator to fill a lacuna in
the Greek text.

340   an animal, and the oracle of Zeus says that you and your wife
will drive a chariot of oxen, leading a pack of foreigners
and with such an innumerable army you will destroy many
    cities,
but when they pillage the shrine of Apollo,
they will find their trip home a very bitter one,
but Ares will [save you, and he will] save Harmonia
and he will give both of you life among the blessed,
and I, Dionysus, tell this to you all—I who was not born of a
    mortal father,
but from Zeus—if you had only been wise before,
when you refused to be, you would be blessed now
and you would have the son of Zeus on your side.

AGAVE   Dionysus, we're begging you, we've sinned!

DIONYSUS   It's too late to know me now, you didn't when you had
    time to.

AGAVE   We know that now, but you're being too hard on us.

DIONYSUS   I am a god, I was deeply offended by you.

AGAVE   It isn't right that gods should get as angry as men.

DIONYSUS   My father, Zeus, arranged this a long time ago.

AGAVE   Father, it is all Fate, we are wretched exiles.

DIONYSUS   Why do you delay then, all these things have to be.

[*Exit* DIONYSUS.]

CADMUS   Oh my daughter, what terrible trouble we're in now,
all of us, you and your sisters and myself,
for I'm an old man and I have to go be an immigrant
and live among foreigners, doomed
to lead some mixed-up foreign army against Greece,
and my wife, Harmonia, the daughter of Ares,
I have to bring her against Greek altars and tombs
along with armed men, and both of us in the form of snakes
and my troubles will never stop, I won't even have the peace
of sailing down the stream of Death.

AGAVE   Oh father, I'll be an exile, I'll be taken away from you!

CADMUS   Why are you throwing your arms around me, you poor
    thing.
you're like a white swan with its tired old father.

AGAVE   Where can I go, I'm banished from my own country!

CADMUS   I don't know, child, your father's not much help anymore.
AGAVE   Then good-bye, my house, good-bye my city and land,
   I leave you, feeling miserable, an exile from the bed of my
     marriage!
CADMUS   Go on, child, try the house of Aristaeus.
AGAVE   Father, I just pity you.
CADMUS   I pity you, child,
   and I cry because of your sisters too.
AGAVE   Terribly, terribly
Dionysus did this outrage
to your house.
CADMUS   But he suffered some awful things from you, and the
   others.
Remember, his name wasn't honored in Thebes.
AGAVE   Good-bye, father.
CADMUS   Good-bye, my daughter,
   if there's some good you can find—
AGAVE   [turning to attendants waiting at entrance to the stage]
Those of you who are going to guide me,
take me to my sisters, we're fellow-exiles in our misery.
I want to go
where that filthy Cithaeron can't see me
and where I can't see it with my own eyes,
and where there's nothing to remind me of the wand.
I leave all that to other Bacchae.

[Exit, followed by CADMUS.]

CHORUS   The gods have many forms,
   the gods can bring many surprises,
   and they don't do what you usually expect,
   as this god who found a way for the unexpected.
   And that's how this whole thing happened.

The Rape of Psyche, Prud'hon

myth and poetry

JOHN KEATS (1795–1821)

After many difficulties, the god Eros (Cupid) and the mortal
woman Psyche are united in love. In Greek, the name *Psyche*
means both "butterfly" and "soul." The myth of Eros and
Psyche is a myth of the immortality of the soul. The human
soul, purified by suffering, bursts like the butterfly from the
cocoon, which is its earthly prison. The story is basically
Romantic, and it provides an ideal catalyst for this fine
Romantic ode by John Keats.

ode to psyche

O goddess! hear these tuneless numbers, wrung
  By sweet enforcement and remembrance dear,
And pardon that thy secrets should be sung
  Even into thine own soft-conchèd ear:
Surely I dreamt to-day, or did I see   5
  The winged Psyche with awakened eyes?
I wandered in a forest thoughtlessly,
  And, on the sudden, fainting with surprise,
Saw two fair creatures, couchèd side by side
  In deepest grass, beneath the whisp'ring roof   10   **343**

344   Of leaves and trembled blossoms, where there ran
            A brooklet, scarce espied:
    'Mid hushed, cool-rooted flowers, fragrant-eyed,
        Blue silver-white, and budded Tyrian,
    They lay calm-breathing on the bedded grass;   15
        Their arms embracèd, and their pinions too;
        Their lips touched not, but had not bade adieu,
    As if disjoinèd by soft-handed slumber,
    And ready still past kisses to outnumber
        At tender eye-dawn of aurorean love: 20
            The wingèd boy I knew;
    But who wast thou, O happy, happy dove?
            His Psyche true!

    O latest born and loveliest vision far
        Of all Olympus' faded hierarchy!   25
    Fairer than Phœbe's sapphire-regioned star,
        Or Vesper, amorous glow-worm of the sky;
    Fairer than these, though temple thou hast none,
            Nor altar heaped with flowers;
    Nor virgin-choir to make delicious moan   30
        Upon the midnight hours;
    No voice, no lute, no pipe, no incense sweet
        From chain-swung censer teeming;
    No shrine, no grove, no oracle, no heat
        Of pale-mouthed prophet dreaming.   35

    O brightest! though too late for antique vows,
        Too, too late for the fond believing lyre,
    When holy were the haunted forest boughs,
        Holy the air, the water, and the fire;
    Yet even in these days so far retired   40
        From happy pieties, thy lucent fans,
        Fluttering among the faint Olympians,
    I see, and sing, by my own eyes inspired.
    So let me be thy choir, and make a moan
            Upon the midnight hours;   45
    Thy voice, thy lute, thy pipe, thy incense sweet
        From swingèd censer teeming;

Thy shrine, thy grove, thy oracle, thy heat
   Of pale-mouthed prophet dreaming.

Yes, I will be thy priest, and build a fane   50
   In some untrodden region of my mind,
Where branchèd thoughts, new grown with pleasant
        pain,
   Instead of pines shall murmur in the wind:
Far, far around shall those dark-clustered trees
   Fledge the wild-ridgèd mountains steep by steep;   55
And there by zephyrs, streams, and birds, and bees,
   The moss-lain Dryads shall be lulled to sleep;
And in the midst of this wide quietness
A rosy sanctuary will I dress
With the wreathed trellis of a working brain,   60
   With buds, and bells, and stars without a name,
With all the gardener Fancy e'er could feign,
   Who breeding flowers, will never breed the same:
And there shall be for thee all soft delight
   That shadowy thought can win,   65
A bright torch, and a casement ope at night,
To let the warm Love in!

myth and modern fiction

JAMES BALDWIN (1924–   )

Myth and ritual are as important to the understanding of this contemporary story by James Baldwin as they are to the understanding of *The Bacchae*. Much of the success of a given work depends on the author's conscious or unconscious ability to express the universal themes embodied in myth. Here, Baldwin builds upon the myth and ritual of the scapegoat, a myth in which a human being is used as a sacrifice to assuage the guilt or impotence of an entire society.

going to meet the man

"What's the matter?" she asked.

"I don't know," he said, trying to laugh, "I guess I'm tired."

"You've been working too hard," she said. "I keep telling you."

"Well, goddammit, woman," he said, "it's not my fault!" He tried again; he wretchedly failed again. Then he just lay there, silent, angry, and helpless. Excitement filled him just like a toothache, but it refused to enter his flesh. He stroked her breast. This was his wife. He could not ask her to do just a little thing for him, just to help him out, just for a little while, the way he could ask a nigger girl to do it. He lay there, and he sighed. The image of a black girl caused a distant excitement in him, like a far-away light; but, again, the excitement was more like pain; instead of forcing him to act, it made action impossible.

"Go to sleep," she said, gently, "you got a hard day tomorrow."

"Yeah," he said, and rolled over on his side, facing her, one hand still on one breast. "Goddamn the niggers. The black stinking coons. You'd think they'd learn. Wouldn't you think they'd learn? I mean, *wouldn't* you?"

"They going to be out there tomorrow," she said, and took his hand away, "get some sleep."

He lay there, one hand between his legs, staring at the frail sanctuary of his wife. A faint light came from the shutters; the moon was full. Two dogs, far away, were barking at each other, back and forth, insistently, as though they were agreeing to make an appointment. He heard a car coming north on the road and he half sat up, his hand reaching for his holster, which was on a chair near the bed, on top of his pants. The lights hit the shutters and seemed to travel across the room and then went out. The sound of the car slipped away, he heard it hit gravel, then heard it no more. Some liver-lipped students, probably, heading back to that college—but coming from where? His watch said it was two in the morning. They could be coming from anywhere, from out of state most likely, and they would be at the court-house tomorrow. The niggers were getting ready. Well, they would be ready, too.

He moaned. He wanted to let whatever was in him out; but it wouldn't come out. Goddamn! he said aloud, and turned again, on his side, away from Grace, staring at the shutters. He was a big, healthy man and he had never had any trouble sleeping. And he wasn't old enough yet to have any trouble getting it up—he was only forty-two. And he was a good man, a God-fearing man, he had tried to do his duty all his life, and he had been a deputy sheriff for several years. Nothing had ever bothered him before, certainly not getting it up. Sometimes, sure, like any other man, he knew that he wanted a little more spice than Grace could give him and he would drive over yonder and pick up a black piece or arrest her, it came to the same thing, but he couldn't do that now, no more. There was no telling what might happen once your ass was in the air. And they were low enough to kill a man then, too, everyone of them, or the girl herself might do it, right while she was making believe you made her feel so good. The niggers. What had the good Lord Al-

mighty had in mind when he made the niggers? Well. They were
pretty good at that, all right. Damn. Damn. Goddamn.

This wasn't helping him to sleep. He turned again, toward Grace
again, and moved close to her warm body. He felt something he
had never felt before. He felt that he would like to hold her, hold
her, hold her, and be buried in her like a child and never have to
get up in the morning again and go downtown to face those faces,
good Christ, they were ugly! and never have to enter that jail
house again and smell that smell and hear that singing; never again
feel that filthy, kinky, greasy hair under his hand, never again
watch those black breasts leap against the leaping cattle prod,
never hear those moans again or watch that blood run down or the
fat lips split or the sealed eyes struggle open. They were animals,
they were no better than animals, what could be done with people
like that? Here they had been in a civilized country for years and
they still lived like animals. Their houses were dark, with oil cloth
or cardboard in the windows, the smell was enough to make you
puke your guts out, and there they sat, a whole tribe, pumping out
kids, it looked like, every damn five minutes, and laughing and talking and playing music like they didn't have a care in the world, and
he reckoned they didn't, neither, and coming to the door, into the
sunlight, just standing there, just looking foolish, not thinking of
anything but just getting back to what they were doing, saying,
Yes suh, Mr. Jesse. I surely will, Mr. Jesse. Fine weather, Mr. Jesse.
Why, I thank you, Mr. Jesse. He had worked for a mail-order house
for a while and it had been his job to collect the payments for the
stuff they bought. They were too dumb to know that they were
being cheated blind, but that was no skin off his ass—he was just
supposed to do his job. They would be late—they didn't have the
sense to put money aside; but it was easy to scare them, and he
never really had any trouble. Hell, they all liked him, the kids used to
smile when he came to the door. He gave them candy, sometimes,
or chewing gum, and rubbed their rough bullet heads—maybe the
candy should have been poisoned. Those kids were grown now. He
had had trouble with one of them today.

"There was this nigger today," he said; and stopped; his voice
sounded peculiar. He touched Grace. "You awake?" he asked. She
mumbled something, impatiently, she was probably telling him to
go to sleep. It was all right. He knew that he was not alone.

"What a funny time," he said, "to be thinking about a thing like that—you listening?" She mumbled something again. He rolled over on his back. "This nigger's one of the ringleaders. We had trouble with him before. We must have had him out there at the work farm three or four times. Well, Big Jim C. and some of the boys really had to whip that nigger's ass today." He looked over at Grace; he could not tell whether she was listening or not; and he was afraid to ask again. "They had this line you know, to register"—he laughed, but she did not—"and they wouldn't stay where Big Jim C. wanted them, no, they had to start blocking traffic all around the court house so couldn't nothing or nobody get through, and Big Jim C. told them to disperse and they wouldn't move, they just kept up that singing, and Big Jim C. figured that the others would move if this nigger would move, him being the ring-leader, but he wouldn't move and he wouldn't let the others move, so they had to beat him and a couple of the others and they threw them in the wagon—but *I* didn't see this nigger till I got to the jail. They were still singing and I was supposed to make them stop. Well, I couldn't make them stop for me but I knew he could make them stop. He was lying on the ground jerking and moaning, they had threw him in a cell by himself, and blood was coming out his ears from where Big Jim C. and his boys had whipped him. Wouldn't you think they'd learn? I put the prod to him and he jerked some more and he kind of screamed—but he didn't have much voice left. "You make them stop that singing," I said to him, "you hear me? You make them stop that singing." He acted like he didn't hear me and I put it to him again, under his arms, and he just rolled around on the floor and blood started coming from his mouth. He'd pissed his pants already." He paused. His mouth felt dry and his throat was as rough as sandpaper; as he talked, he began to hurt all over with that peculiar excitement which refused to be released. "You all are going to stop your singing, I said to him, and you are going to stop coming down to the court house and disrupting traffic and molesting the people and keeping us from our duties and keeping doctors from getting to sick white women and getting all them Northerners in this town to give our town a bad name—!" As he said this, he kept prodding the boy, sweat pouring from beneath the helmet he had not yet taken off. The boy rolled around in his own dirt and water and blood and tried to scream again as

the prod hit his testicles, but the scream did not come out, only
a kind of rattle and a moan. He stopped. He was not supposed to
kill the nigger. The cell was filled with a terrible odor. The boy was
still. "You hear me?" he called. "You had enough?" The singing
went on. "You had enough?" His foot leapt out, he had not known
it was going to, and caught the boy flush on the jaw. *Jesus,* he
thought, *this ain't no nigger, this is a goddamn bull,* and he
screamed again, "You had enough? You going to make them stop
that singing now?"

But the boy was out. And now he was shaking worse than the
boy had been shaking. He was glad no one could see him. At the
same time, he felt very close to a very peculiar, particular joy;
something deep in him and deep in his memory was stirred, but
whatever was in his memory eluded him. He took off his helmet. He
walked to the cell door.

"White man," said the boy, from the floor, behind him.

He stopped. For some reason, he grabbed his privates.

"You remember Old Julia?"

The boy said, from the floor, with his mouth full of blood, and
one eye, barely open, glaring like the eye of a cat in the dark, "My
grandmother's name was Mrs. Julia Blossom. *Mrs.* Julia Blossom.
You going to call our women by their right names yet.—And those
kids ain't going to stop singing. We going to keep on singing until
every one of you miserable white mothers go stark raving out of
your minds. Then he closed the one eye; he spat blood; his head
fell back against the floor.

He looked down at the boy, whom he had been seeing, off and
on, for more than a year, and suddenly remembered him: Old
Julia had been one of his mail-order customers, a nice old woman.
He had not seen her for years, he supposed that she must be dead.

He had walked into the yard, the boy had been sitting in a swing.
He had smiled at the boy, and asked, "Old Julia home?"

The boy looked at him for a long time before he answered.
"Don't no Old Julia live here."

"This is her house. I know her. She's lived here for years."

The boy shook his head. "You might know a Old Julia someplace
else, white man. But don't nobody by that name live here."

He watched the boy; the boy watched him. The boy certainly
wasn't more than ten. *White man.* He didn't have time to be
fooling around with some crazy kid. He yelled, "Hey! Old Julia!"

But only silence answered him. The expression on the boy's face did not change. The sun beat down on them both, still and silent; he had the feeling that he had been caught up in a nightmare, a nightmare dreamed by a child; perhaps one of the nightmares he himself had dreamed as a child. It had that feeling—everything familiar, without undergoing any other change, had been subtly and hideously displaced: the trees, the sun, the patches of grass in the yard, the leaning porch and the weary porch steps and the cardboard in the windows and the black hole of the door which looked like the entrance to a cave, and the eyes of the pickaninny, all, all, were charged with malevolence. *White man.* He looked at the boy. "She's gone out?"

The boy said nothing.

"Well," he said, "tell her I passed by and I'll pass by next week." He started to go; he stopped. "You want some chewing gum?"

The boy got down from the swing and started for the house. He said, "I don't want nothing you got, white man." He walked into the house and closed the door behind him.

Now the boy looked as though he were dead. Jesse wanted to go over to him and pick him up and pistol whip him until the boy's head burst open like a melon. He began to tremble with what he believed was rage, sweat, both cold and hot, raced down his body, the singing filled him as though it were a weird, uncontrollable, monstrous howling rumbling up from the depths of his own belly, he felt an icy fear rise in him and raise him up, and he shouted, he howled, "You lucky we *pump* some white blood into you every once in a while—your women! Here's what I got for all the black bitches in the world—!" Then he was, abruptly, almost too weak to stand; to his bewilderment, his horror, beneath his own fingers, he felt himself violently stiffen—with no warning at all; he dropped his hands and he stared at the boy and he left the cell.

"All that singing they do," he said. "All that singing." He could not remember the first time he had heard it; he had been hearing it all his life. It was the sound with which he was most familiar— though it was also the sound of which he had been least conscious— and it had always contained an obscure comfort. They were singing to God. They were singing for mercy and they hoped to go to heaven, and he had even sometimes felt, when looking into the eyes of some of the old women, a few of the very old men, that they were singing for mercy for his soul, too. Of course he had never thought of their heaven or of what God was, or could be, for them; God was the same for everyone, he supposed, and heaven was where good people went—he supposed. He had never thought much about what it meant to be a good person. He tried to be a good person and treat everybody right: it wasn't his fault if the niggers had taken it into their heads to fight against God and go against the rules laid down in the Bible for everyone to read! Any preacher would tell you that. He was only doing his duty: protecting white people from the niggers and the niggers from themselves. And there were still lots of good niggers around—he had to remember that; they weren't all like that boy this afternoon; and the good niggers must be mighty sad to see what was happening to their people. They would thank him when this was over. In that way they had, the best of them, not quite looking him in the eye, in a low voice, with a little smile: We surely thanks you, Mr. Jesse. From the bottom of our hearts, we thanks you. He smiled. They hadn't all gone crazy. This trouble would pass.—He knew that the young people had changed some of the words of the songs. He had scarcely listened to the words before and he did not listen to them now; but he knew that the words were different; he could hear that much. He did not know if the faces were different, he had never, before this trouble began, watched them as they sang, but he certainly did not like what he saw now. They hated him, and this hatred was blacker than their hearts, blacker than their skins, redder than their blood, and harder, by far, than his club. Each day, each night, he felt worn out, aching, with their smell in his nostrils and filling his lungs, as though he were drowning— drowning in niggers; and it was all to be done again when he woke. It would never end. It would never end. Perhaps this was what the singing had meant all along. They had not been singing black folks into heaven, they had been singing white folks into hell.

Everyone felt this black suspicion in many ways, but no one knew how to express it. Men much older than he, who had been responsible for law and order much longer than he, were now much quieter than they had been, and the tone of their jokes, in a way that he could not quite put his finger on, had changed. These men were his models, they had been friends to his father, and they had taught him what it meant to be a man. He looked to them for courage now. It wasn't that he didn't know that what he was doing was right—he knew that, nobody had to tell him that; it was only that he missed the ease of former years. But they didn't have much time to hang out with each other these days. They tended to stay close to their families every free minute because nobody knew what might happen next. Explosions rocked the night of their tranquil town. Each time each man wondered silently if perhaps this time the dynamite had not fallen into the wrong hands. They thought that they knew where all the guns were; but they could not possibly know every move that was made in that secret place where the darkies lived. From time to time it was suggested that they form a posse and search the home of every nigger, but they hadn't done it yet. For one thing, this might have brought the bastards from the North down on their backs; for another, although the niggers were scattered throughout the town—down in the hollow near the railroad tracks, way west near the mills, up on the hill, the well-off ones, and some out near the college—nothing seemed to happen in one part of town without the niggers immediately knowing it in the other. This meant that they could not take them by surprise. They rarely mentioned it, but they *knew* that some of the niggers had guns. It stood to reason, as they said, since, after all, some of them had been in the Army. There were niggers in the Army right now and God knows they wouldn't have had any trouble stealing this half-assed government blind—the whole world was doing it, look at the European countries and all those countries in Africa. They made jokes about it—bitter jokes; and they cursed the government in Washington, which had betrayed them; but they had not yet formed a posse. Now, if their town had been laid out like some towns in the North, where all the niggers lived together in one locality, they could have gone down and set fire to the houses and brought about peace that way. If the niggers had all lived in one place, they could have kept the fire in one place. But the way this town was laid out, the fire could hardly be controlled. It would spread all over town—and the niggers would probably be helping it to spread. Still, from time to time, they spoke of doing it, anyway; so that now there was a real fear among them that somebody might go crazy and light the match.

They rarely mentioned anything not directly related to the war that they were fighting, but this had failed to establish between them the unspoken communication of soldiers during a war. Each

man, in the thrilling silence which sped outward from their ex-
changes, their laughter, and their anecdotes, seemed wrestling, in
various degrees of darkness, with a secret which he could not articulate to himself, and which, however directly it related to the war,
related yet more surely to his privacy and his past. They could no
longer be sure, after all, that they had all done the same things.
They had never dreamed that their privacy could contain any
element of terror, could threaten, that is, to reveal itself, to the
scrutiny of a judgment day, while remaining unreadable and in-
accessible to themselves; nor had they dreamed that the past, while
certainly refusing to be forgotten, could yet so stubbornly refuse to
be remembered. They felt themselves mysteriously set at naught, as
no longer entering into the real concerns of other people—while
here they were, outnumbered, fighting to save the civilized world.
They had thought that people would care—people didn't care; not
enough, anyway, to help them. It would have been a help, really,
or at least a relief, even to have been forced to surrender. Thus
they had lost, probably forever, their old and easy connection with
each other. They were forced to depend on each other more and,
at the same time, to trust each other less. Who could tell when one
of them might not betray them all, for money, or for the ease of
confession? But no one dared imagine what there might be to confess. They were soldiers fighting a war, but their relationship to
each other was that of accomplices in a crime. They all had to keep
their mouths shut.

I stepped in the river at Jordan.

Out of the darkness of the room, out of nowhere, the line came
flying up at him, with the melody and the beat. He turned word-
lessly toward his sleeping wife. *I stepped in the river at Jordan.*
Where had he heard that song?
"Grace," he whispered. "You awake?"
She did not answer. If she was awake, she wanted him to sleep.
Her breathing was slow and easy, her body slowly rose and fell.

I stepped in the river at Jordan.
The water came to my knees.

He began to sweat. He felt an overwhelming fear, which yet
contained a curious and dreadful pleasure.

> *I stepped in the river at Jordan.*
> *The water came to my waist.*

It had been night, as it was now, he was in the car between his
mother and his father, sleepy, his head in his mother's lap, sleepy,
and yet full of excitement. The singing came from far away, across
the dark fields. There were no lights anywhere. They had said
good-bye to all the others and turned off on this dark dirt road.
They were almost home.

> *I stepped in the river at Jordan,*
> *The water came over my head,*
> *I looked way over to the other side,*
> *He was making up my dying bed!*

"I guess they singing for him," his father said, seeming very
weary and subdued now. "Even when they're sad, they sound like
they just about to go and tear off a piece." He yawned and leaned
across the boy and slapped his wife lightly on the shoulder, allowing his hand to rest there for a moment. "Don't they?"

"Don't talk that way," she said.

"Well, that's what we going to do," he said, "you can make up
your mind to that." He started whistling. "You see? When I begin
to feel it, I gets kind of musical, too."

Oh, Lord! Come on and ease my troubling mind!

He had a black friend, his age, eight, who lived nearby. His
name was Otis. They wrestled together in the dirt. Now the
thought of Otis made him sick. He began to shiver. His mother put
her arm around him.

"He's tired," she said.

"We'll be home soon," said his father. He began to whistle again.

"We didn't see Otis this morning," Jesse said. He did not know
why he said this. His voice, in the darkness of the car, sounded
small and accusing.

"You haven't seen Otis for a couple of mornings," his mother said.

That was true. But he was only concerned about *this* morning.

"No," said his father, "I reckon Otis's folks was afraid to let him show himself this morning."

"But Otis didn't do nothing!" Now his voice sounded questioning.

"Otis *can't* do nothing," said his father, "he's too little." The car lights picked up their wooden house, which now solemnly approached them, the lights falling around it like yellow dust. Their dog, chained to a tree, began to bark.

"We just want to make sure Otis *don't* do nothing," said his father, and stopped the car. He looked down at Jesse. "And you tell him what your Daddy said, you hear?"

"Yes sir," he said.

His father switched off the lights. The dog moaned and pranced, but they ignored him and went inside. He could not sleep. He lay awake, hearing the night sounds, the dog yawning and moaning outside, the sawing of the crickets, the cry of the owl, dogs barking far away, then no sounds at all, just the heavy, endless buzzing of the night. The darkness pressed on his eyelids like a scratchy blanket. He turned, he turned again. He wanted to call his mother, but he knew his father would not like this. He was terribly afraid. Then he heard his father's voice in the other room, low, with a joke in it; but this did not help him, it frightened him more, he knew what was going to happen. He put his head under the blanket, then pushed his head out again, for fear, staring at the dark window. He heard his mother's moan, his father's sigh; he gritted his teeth. Then their bed began to rock. His father's breathing seemed to fill the world.

That morning, before the sun had gathered all its strength, men and women, some flushed and some pale with excitement, came with news. Jesse's father seemed to know what the news was before the first jalopy stopped in the yard, and he ran out, crying, "They got him, then? They got him?"

The first jalopy held eight people, three men and two women and three children. The children were sitting on the laps of the grown-ups. Jesse knew two of them, the two boys; they shyly and uncomfortably greeted each other. He did not know the girl.

"Yes, they got him," said one of the women, the older one, who

wore a wide hat and a fancy, faded blue dress. "They found him **357**
early this morning."

"How far had he got?" Jesse's father asked.

"He hadn't got no further than Harkness," one of the men said. "Look like he got lost up there in all them trees—or maybe he just got so scared he couldn't move." They all laughed.

"Yes, and you know it's near a graveyard, too," said the younger woman, and they laughed again.

"Is that where they got him now?" asked Jesse's father.

By this time there were three cars piled behind the first one, with everyone looking excited and shining, and Jesse noticed that they were carrying food. It was like a Fourth of July picnic.

"Yeah, that's where he is," said one of the men, "declare, Jesse, you going to keep us here all day long, answering your damn fool questions. Come on, we ain't got no time to waste."

"Don't bother putting up no food," cried a woman from one of the other cars, "we got enough. Just come on."

"Why, thank you," said Jesse's father, "we be right along, then."

"I better get a sweater for the boy," said his mother, "in case it turns cold."

Jesse watched his mother's thin legs cross the yard. He knew that she also wanted to comb her hair a little and maybe put on a better dress, the dress she wore to church. His father guessed this, too, for he yelled behind her, "Now don't you go trying to turn yourself into no movie star. You just come on." But he laughed as he said this, and winked at the men; his wife was younger and prettier than most of the other women. He clapped Jesse on the head and started pulling him toward the car. "You all go on," he said, "I'll be right behind you. Jesse, you go tie up that there dog while I get this car started."

The cars sputtered and coughed and shook; the caravan began to move; bright dust filled the air. As soon as he was tied up, the dog began to bark. Jesse's mother came out of the house, carrying a jacket for his father and a sweater for Jesse. She had put a ribbon in her hair and had an old shawl around her shoulders.

"Put these in the car, son," she said, and handed everything to him. She bent down and stroked the dog, looked to see if there was water in his bowl, then went back up the three porch steps and closed the door.

"Come on," said his father, "ain't nothing in there for nobody to steal." He was sitting in the car, which trembled and belched. The last car of the caravan had disappeared but the sound of singing floated behind them.

Jesse got into the car, sitting close to his father, loving the smell of the car, and the trembling, and the bright day, and the sense of going on a great and unexpected journey. His mother got in and closed the door and the car began to move. Not until then did he ask, "Where are we going? Are we going on a picnic?"

He had a feeling that he knew where they were going, but he was not sure.

"That's right," his father said, "we're going on a picnic. You won't ever forget *this* picnic—!"

"Are we," he asked, after a moment, "going to see the bad nigger —the one that knocked down old Miss Standish?"

"Well, I reckon," said his mother, "that we *might* see him."

He started to ask, *Will a lot of niggers be there? Will Otis be there?*—but he did not ask his question, to which, in a strange and uncomfortable way, he already knew the answer. Their friends, in the other cars, stretched up the road as far as he could see; other cars had joined them; there were cars behind them. They were singing. The sun seemed, suddenly very hot, and he was, at once very happy and a little afraid. He did not quite understand what was happening, and he did not know what to ask—he had no one to ask. He had grown accustomed, for the solution of such mysteries, to go to Otis. He felt that Otis knew everything. But he could not ask Otis about this. Anyway, he had not seen Otis for two days; he had not seen a black face anywhere for more than two days; and he now realized, as they began chugging up the long hill which eventually led to Harkness, that there were no black faces on the road this morning, no black people anywhere. From the houses in which they lived, all along the road, no smoke curled, no life stirred —maybe one or two chickens were to be seen, that was all. There was no one at the windows, no one in the yard, no one sitting on the porches, and the doors were closed. He had come this road many a time and seen women washing in the yard (there were no clothes on the clotheslines) men working in the fields, children playing in the dust; black men passed them on the road other mornings, other days, on foot, or in wagons, sometimes in cars, tipping their hats, smiling, joking, their teeth a solid white against their skin, their eyes as warm as the sun, the blackness of their skin like dull fire against the white of the blue or the grey of their torn clothes. They passed the nigger church—dead-white, desolate, locked up; and the graveyard, where no one knelt or walked, and he saw no flowers. He wanted to ask, *Where are they? Where are they all?* But he did not dare. As the hill grew steeper, the sun grew colder. He looked at his mother and his father. They looked straight ahead, seeming to be listening to the singing which echoed and echoed in this graveyard silence. They were strangers to him now. They were looking at something he could not see. His father's lips had a strange, cruel curve, he wet his lips from time to time, and swallowed. He was terribly aware of his father's tongue, it was as though he had never seen it before. And his father's body suddenly seemed immense, bigger than a mountain. His eyes, which were grey-green, looked yellow in the sunlight; or at least there was a light in them which he had never seen before. His mother patted her hair and adjusted the ribbon, leaning forward to look into the car mirror. "You look all right," said his father, and laughed. "When that nigger looks at you, he's going to swear he throwed his life away for nothing. Wouldn't be surprised if he don't come back to haunt you." And he laughed again.

The singing now slowly began to cease; and he realized that they were nearing their destination. They had reached a straight, narrow, pebbly road, with trees on either side. The sunlight filtered down on them from a great height, as though they were under-water; and the branches of the trees scraped against the cars with a tearing sound. To the right of them, and beneath them, invisible now, lay the town; and to the left, miles of· trees which led to the high mountain range which his ancestors had crossed in order to settle in this valley. Now, all was silent, except for the bumping of the tires against the rocky road, the sputtering of motors, and the sound of a crying child. And they seemed to move more slowly. They were beginning to climb again. He watched the cars ahead as they toiled patiently upward, disappearing into the sunlight of the clearing. Presently, he felt their vehicle also rise, heard his father's changed breathing, the sunlight hit his face, the trees moved away from them, and they were there. As their car crossed the clearing, he looked around. There seemed to be millions, there were certainly hundreds of people in the clearing, staring toward something he could not see. There was a fire. He could not see the flames, but he smelled the smoke. Then they were on the other side of the clearing, among the trees again. His father drove off the road and parked the car behind a great many other cars. He looked down at Jesse.

"You all right?" he asked.

"Yes sir," he said.

"Well, come on, then," his father said. He reached over and opened the door on his mother's side. His mother stepped out first. They followed her into the clearing. At first he was aware only of confusion, of his mother and father greeting and being greeted, himself being handled, hugged, and patted, and told how much he had grown. The wind blew the smoke from the fire across the clearing into his eyes and nose. He could not see over the backs of the people in front of him. The sounds of laughing and cursing and wrath—and something else—rolled in waves from the front of the mob to the back. Those in front expressed their delight at what they saw, and this delight rolled backward, wave upon wave, across the clearing, more acrid than the smoke. His father reached down suddenly and sat Jesse on his shoulders.

Now he saw the fire—of twigs and boxes, piled high; flames made pale orange and yellow and thin as a veil under the steadier light of the sun; grey-blue smoke rolled upward and poured over their heads. Beyond the shifting curtain of fire and smoke, he made out first only a length of gleaming chain, attached to a great limb of the tree; then he saw that this chain bound two black hands together at the wrist, dirty yellow palm facing dirty yellow palm. The smoke poured up; the hands dropped out of sight; a cry went up from the crowd. Then the hands slowly came into view again, pulled upward by the chain. This time he saw the kinky, sweating, bloody head—he had never before seen a head with so much hair on it, hair so black and so tangled that it seemed like another jungle. The head was hanging. He saw the forehead, flat and high, with a kind of arrow of hair in the center, like he had, like his father had; they called it a widow's peek; and the mangled eye brows, the wide nose, the closed eyes, and the glinting eye lashes and the hanging lips, all streaming with blood and sweat. His hands were straight above his head. All his weight pulled downward from his hands; and he was a big man, a bigger man than his father, and black as an African jungle Cat, and naked. Jesse pulled upward; his father's hands held him firmly by the ankles. He wanted to say something, he did not know what, but nothing he said could have been heard, for now the crowd roared again as a man stepped forward and put more wood on the fire. The flames leapt up. He thought he heard the hanging man scream, but he was not sure. Sweat was pouring from the hair in his armpits, poured down his sides, over his chest, into his navel and his groin. He was lowered again; he was raised again. Now Jesse knew that he heard him scream. The head went back, the mouth wide open, blood bubbling from the mouth; the viens of the neck jumped out; Jesse clung to his father's neck in terror as the cry rolled over the crowd. The cry of all the people rose to answer the dying man's cry. He wanted death to come quickly. They wanted to make death wait: and it was they who held death, now, on a leash which they lengthened little by little. *What did he do?* Jesse wondered. *What did the man do? What did he do?*—but he could not ask his father. He was seated on his father's shoulders, but his father was far away. There were two older men, friends of his father's, raising and lowering the chain; everyone, indiscriminately, seemed to be responsible for the fire. There was no hair left on the nigger's privates, and the eyes, now, were wide open, as white as the eyes of a clown or a doll. The smoke now carried a terrible odor across the clearing, the odor of something burning which was both sweet and rotten.

He turned his head a little and saw the field of faces. He watched his mother's face. Her eyes were very bright, her mouth was open: she was more beautiful than he had ever seen her, and more strange. He began to feel a joy he had never felt before. He watched the hanging, gleaming body, the most beautiful and ter-rible object he had ever seen till then. One of his father's friends rushed up and in his hands he held a knife: and Jesse wished that he had been that man. It was a long, bright knife and the sun seemed to catch it, to play with it, to caress it—it was brighter than the fire. And a wave of laughter swept the crowd. Jesse felt his father's hands on his ankles slip and tighten. The man with the knife walked toward the crowd, smiling slightly; as though this were a signal, silence fell; he heard his mother cough. Then the man with the knife walked up to the hanging body. He turned and

362   smiled again. Now there was a silence all over the field. The hanging head looked up. It seemed fully conscious now, as though the fire had burned out terror and pain. The man with the knife took the nigger's privates in his hand, one hand, still smiling, as though he were weighing them. In the cradle of the one white hand, the nigger's privates seemed as remote as meat being weighed in the scales; but seemed heavier, too, much heavier, and Jesse felt his scrotum tighten; and huge, huge, much bigger than his father's, flaccid, hairless, the largest thing he had ever seen till then, and the blackest. The white hand stretched them, cradled them, caressed them. Then the dying man's eye looked straight into Jesse's eyes— it could not have been as long as a second, but it seemed longer than a year. Then Jesse screamed, and the crowd screamed as the knife flashed, first up, then down, cutting the dreadful thing away, and the blood came roaring down. Then the crowd rushed forward, tearing at the body with their hands, with knives, with rocks, with stones, howling and cursing. Jesse's head, of its own weight, fell downward toward his father's head. Someone stepped forward and drenched the body with kerosene. Where the man had been, a great sheet of flame appeared. Jesse's father lowered him to the ground.

"Well, I told you," said his father, "you wasn't never going to forget *this* picnic." His father's face was full of sweat, his eyes were very peaceful. At that moment Jesse loved his father more than he had ever loved him. He felt that his father had carried him through a mighty test, had revealed to him a great secret which would be the key to his life forever.

"I reckon," he said. "I reckon."

Jesse's father took him by the hand and, with his mother a little behind them, talking and laughing with the other women, they walked through the crowd, across the clearing. The black body was on the ground, the chain which had held it was being rolled up by one of his father's friends. Whatever the fire had left undone, the hands and the knives and the stones of the people had accomplished. The head was caved in, one eye was torn out, one ear was hanging. But one had to look carefully to realize this, for it was, now, merely, a black charred object on the black, charred ground. He lay spread-eagled with what had been a wound between what had been his legs.

"They going to leave him here, then?" Jesse whispered.

"Yeah," said his father, "they'll come and get him by and by. I reckon we better get over there and get some of that food before it's all gone."

"I reckon," he muttered now to himself, "I reckon." Grace stirred and touched him on the thigh: the moonlight covered her like glory. Something bubbled up in him, his nature again returned to him. He thought of the boy in the cell; he thought of the man in the fire; he thought of the knife and grabbed himself and stroked himself and a terrible sound, something between a high laugh and a howl, came out of him and dragged his sleeping wife up on one elbow. She stared at him in a moonlight which had now grown cold as ice. He thought of the morning and grabbed her, laughing and crying, crying and laughing, and he whispered, as he stroked her, as he took her, "Come on, sugar, I'm going to do you like a nigger, just like a nigger, come on, sugar, and love me just like you'd love a nigger." He thought of the morning as he labored and she moaned, thought of morning as he labored harder than he ever had before, and before his labors had ended, he heard the first cock crow and the dogs begin to bark, and the sound of tires on the gravel road.

commentary:
myth and the
discovery of self

The mythic flight is a particularly extraordinary one, because it is not something that is willed, but something that simply happens and because it is not always a conscious act. Man's mentality "does not invent myths," writes C. G. Jung, "it experiences them."[1]

Mythology is an immensely complex subject. In order to begin to understand it—and only a beginning can be made here—a distinction must be drawn between story and myth. We grow up thinking of myths as the stories of particular gods and heroes, and, indeed, these stories are mythic. They are not, however, the myths themselves, but from them, the basic myths can be extracted. The stories of Attis, Osiris, Dionysus, and Jesus, for example, are all mythic stories belonging to particular cultures. When we consider these stories together, a basic myth of death and resurrection emerges, in which Attis, Osiris, Dionysus, and Jesus become a single World Hero. The story of Jesus belongs to the Christians, but the myth of death and resurrection belongs to humanity. While someone (or some group) invented the Osiris story or attached mythic importance to it, the basic myth itself is, in essence, a "product of the unknown," and it attracts us whether we wish it to or not. Myth is the narrative or image of the world soul, of ultimate reality. It is "the penultimate truth, of which all experience is the temporal reflection," writes Ananda Coomaraswamy. "The mythical

[1] Carl Gustav Jung and C. Kerényi, *Essays on a Science of Mythology: The Myth of the Divine Child and the Mysteries of Eleusis* (Princeton: Bollingen Series, 1971), p. 73.

narrative is of timeless and placeless validity, true nowhere and everywhere."[2]

This sense of the reality of myth is essential. The word *Myth* comes from the Greek root μ (*mu*) meaning to make a sound. "In the beginning was the Word, and the Word was with God, and the Word was God," says the Gospel. Even in this sense, myth is basic to our existence. For Mircea Eliade, it is:

> . . . 'true history,' because it always deals with *realities*. The cosmogenic myth is 'true' because the existence of the World is there to prove it; the myth of the origin of death is equally true because man's mortality proves it, and so on.[3]

Bronislaw Malinowski sees myth as "not an explanation in satisfaction of a scientific interest, but a narrative resurrection of a primeval reality, told in satisfaction of deep religious wants, moral cravings, social submissions, assertions, even practical requirements."[4] Alan Watts calls myth "an imagery in terms of which we make sense out of life."[5] And, as we have seen, Joseph Campbell calls the symbols of myth the "telling metaphors of the destiny of man, man's hope, man's faith, and man's dark mystery." All of these definitions assume a reality within myth.

There are numerous ways in which myth is real. It is obvious, for instance, that myths explain natural phenomena. Sir James Frazer demonstrated this in *The Golden Bough*. It is also obvious that they explain religious practices. Myths are the narrative form of rituals. Thus, quite literally, the stories of Hyacinth and Narcissus, for example, embody a myth of death and fertility that is the correlative of the ritual sacrifice of youths for purposes of crop fertility.

There are, however, other less obvious areas in which myth is real and alive, as, for instance, in the achievement of group and individual identity and in the achievement of art.

[2] Ananda Coomaraswamy, *Hinduism and Buddhism* (New York: The Philosophical Library, 1943), p. 6.

[3] Mircea Eliade, *Myth and Reality* (New York: Harper & Row, Publishers, 1968), p. 6.

[4] Bronislaw Malinowski, "Myth in Primitive Psychology," in *Magic, Science and Religion* (Glencoe: The Free Press, 1948), p. 101.

[5] Alan Watts, "Western Mythology," in Joseph Campbell, ed., *Myths, Dreams and Religion* (New York: E. P. Dutton & Co., Inc., 1970), p. 14.

366   A useful first step is to suggest, as Joseph Campbell does in the selection included here, that myth is related to dream. Myths are the dreams of man—they are safety valves, ways he has of expressing his fears and desires and of putting the ineffable into images. Like dreams, myths also have their superficial level—aspects that can be traced to the immediate and recent experiences and neuroses of the group in question—but they also have their innermost level, which is evident from the existence of certain motifs in the mythic stories of nearly all cultures.

Myths are both psychological and sociological. They express our group psyche and help to define what we are. As Theodore Roszak suggests, myth "at its deepest level is that collectively created thing which crystallizes the great central values of a culture." For example, the central myth for the creators of Chartres and Mont Saint-Michel was Christianity. For the classical Greek, as indicated by *The Bacchae*, it might well have been—in spite of the more staid Olympian religion—the mysteries of nature associated with the earth cults of Dionysus and Demeter. For our culture, says Roszak, the basic myth has been that of objective consciousness—the absolute faith in rationalism—which we are only now beginning to question.

Myth is associated with the individual as well as with cultures. The hero of myth, in his many forms, is the personification, not only of the soul of a culture but of the Self within each of us—the Self that longs to be identified. The hero is each of us on the passage through life. By simply living, the individual shares in the myth of man, which the hero expresses by his actions. As with our own lives, the life of the hero follows an established pattern. For example, we all experience the trauma of birth. This miraculous event —and it is miraculous in spite of the scientific "explanations" we have for it—is embodied in the myth of the miraculous conception and birth of the hero found in such stories as those of Jesus, Buddha, Theseus, and Dionysus. In nearly all societies, human beings, having been cared for by their parents longer than is the case with other animals, are suddenly expected, at some pre-established age, to make the transition from childhood to adulthood. Thus, we have myths and rituals of initiation that take narrative form in such stories as David's killing of Goliath, King Arthur's removal of the sword, and Theseus' acquisition of the sword and sandals. Our adult life—the period in which we struggle on our own for subsistence—lies **367** behind the trial and quest myth contained in stories like that of the Holy Grail or the labors of Heracles. The mystery of death is narrated by the myth of the hero's extraordinary death (by dismemberment, castration, hanging, crucifixion) and his descent to the Underworld. In the Underworld, he confronts death. In his resurrection or rebirth, he expresses the universal hope of overcoming that ultimate obstacle to achieving safety in the eternal cycles of nature. We long to be returned, like Jesus, Attis, and Osiris to the regenerative flow of the cosmos. The myth of the hero is the record of man's desire to discover his real Self in relation to all things.

These individual and group expressions of Self are not conscious ones—we have no choice in the matter. As Jung has written, "it is a question neither of belief nor knowledge, but of the agreement of our thinking with the primordial images of the unconscious."[6] Nowhere is this magical, unconscious, and ever-living aspect of myth better revealed than in literature. Frye suggests the mythic importance of literature in "The Archetypes of Literature." The Baldwin story illustrates many of Frye's points and many of the points already made in this commentary. The myth that is present behind "Going to Meet the Man" is that of the scapegoat—the myth of the ritual sacrifice for fertility found in the numerous stories of the dying god-hero (Jesus, Attis, Osiris, Dionysus, Adonis). It is present in this story, not because the author decided to write a story about an ancient myth, but rather, because his unconscious Self provided him with this inherited human memory—this myth—as a means of bringing a local event into the realm of universality. The success of any artist can be measured by his ability to be a "medium" between men and the unknown. This, along with the ability to use the tools of his art, is the meaning of what we call talent and of what older cultures called the grace or gift of God.

The final step in understanding myth involves the part played by the conscious flight. If the myth of the Hero is the story of our universal unconscious search for Self, it is also the myth of the individual's conscious search for personal identity. The person who strives to find psychic wholeness must first come to grips with the

[6] Carl Gustav Jung, *Modern Man in Search of a Soul* (New York: Harcourt, Brace & World, 1936), p. 129.

368   mythic reality that is alive within and all around him. He must, in at least a small way, become a magician, a mystic, and a fantasy-maker: he must develop a mythical consciousness. To do this is to rejoin the real forces from which our age of reason and technocracy has done so much to remove us. To achieve a mythical conscious-ness is to rediscover the whole Self, which can only be realized in relation to the unknown that we have denied for so long. To achieve a mythical consciousness is to recognize, as the revolutionary of the spirit would have us do, the mythical reality of all that makes up life, and to proclaim one's existence as real only in terms of that reality. Jung has said that:

> The need for mythic statements is satisfied when we frame a view of the world which adequately explains the meaning of human existence in the cosmos, a view which springs from our psychic wholeness, from the cooperation between the conscious and unconscious. Meaninglessness inhibits fullness of life and is therefore equivalent to illness. Meaning makes a great many things endurable—perhaps everything.[7]

The mythic flight is the movement from the alienated "I" to the true Self, which is in union with and expressed by all that is existence.

[7] Carl Gustav Jung, *Memories, Dreams, Reflections* (New York: Vintage Books, 1963), p. 340.

suggestions for further reading

INTRODUCTION:
THE REVOLUTION OF THE SPIRIT

Burrow, Trigant, *Science and Man's Behavior*. New York, Philosophical Library, Inc., 1953.
> In this book, Burrow deals with the philosophical questions involved in determining the relationship between science and human psychology.

de Chardin, Teilhard, *The Phenomenon of Man*. New York, Harper Torchbooks, 1965.
> An extraordinary work by a scientist-priest whose aim is to prove that there can and does exist a synthesis of the material and spiritual worlds.

Pauwels, Louis, and Bergier, Jacques, *The Morning of the Magicians*. New York, Avon Books, 1972.
> In this remarkable book, an editor-writer and a nuclear physicist envision a union of science and the occult—a union that they call "fantastic realism."

Roszak, Theodore, *The Making of a Counter Culture*. Garden City, New York, Doubleday Anchor Books, 1969.
> A study of the revolutionary ideas of the new "children of technocracy," whose goals are no longer to be found in the American work ethic but rather, in the thoughts of such people as Herbert Marcuse, Norman O. Brown, Alan Watts, and Allen Ginsberg.

Watts, Alan, *The Book: On the Taboo Against Knowing Who You Are*. New York, Collier Books, 1968.
> This is one of the most popular of the recent discussions that deal with the search for Self and with the difficulties encountered in that search.

Young, John Z., *Doubt and Certainty in Science*. New York, Oxford University Press, 1960.
> This is a work concerned with modern man, science, the unknown, and the relationship between them.

PART ONE
MAGIC:
SHAMANS AND WITCHES

Campbell, Joseph, *The Masks of God: Primitive Mythology*. New York, Viking Compass Books, 1970.
>   This is the first of a definitive four-volume study of world mythology, which is the most complete and thorough study of this subject available to the modern reader. It contains one chapter—Chapter Six, entitled "Shamanism"—which is of particular interest to our study here.

Castaneda, Carlos, *The Teachings of Don Juan: A Yaqui Way of Knowledge*. New York, Ballantine Books, 1969.

————, *A Separate Reality: Further Conversations with Don Juan*. New York, Pocket Books, 1971.

————, *Journey to Ixtlan: The Lessons of Don Juan*. New York, Simon & Schuster, 1972.
>   In each of these three books the author, an anthropologist, describes his experiences with the Yaqui Indian shaman, Don Juan. Castaneda met and lived with Don Juan on three separate occasions over a period of ten years, and in each book he has recorded his experiences with Don Juan.

Eliade, Mircea, *Shamanism: Archaic Techniques of Ecstasy*, trans. by Willard R. Trask. New York, Bollingen Foundation, 1964.
>   A thorough and scientific examination of shamanism—especially its ecstatic aspects—by a leading authority on comparative religion.

Frank, Jerome, *Persuasion and Healing*. New York, Schocken Books, 1961.
>   A study of faith healing in nonindustrialized cultures.

Gardiner, Gerald, *Witchcraft Today*. London, Jarrolds Publishers Ltd., 1968.
>   Gardiner claims here that witchcraft is as common in England today as it was in the fifteenth century, and that it is a survival of pagan cults.

Hart, Roger, *Witchcraft*. London, Wayland (Publishers) Ltd., 1971.   **373**
An historical survey of witchcraft.

Hone, Margaret E., *The Modern Textbook of Astrology*. London,
L.N. Fowler & Co. Ltd., 1951.
A comprehensive study of an ancient subject that has only
recently gained serious attention.

Kiev, Ari, *Magic, Faith and Healing*. New York, The Free Press,
1964.
A study of magic and healing in primitive cultures of the past
and present.

Kluckholm, Clyde, *Navaho Witchcraft*. Boston, Beacon Press, 1944.
Kluckholm, an anthropologist whose lifelong interest was his
study of the Navaho Indians, here considers their psychic development. He does so through a study of the particular form
of witchcraft that they practice.

LaVey, Anton Szandor, *The Satanic Bible*. New York, Avon Books,
1969.
The "word" of Satan as transcribed by the man his followers
call the "Black Pope"—the high priest of the "Church of Satan."

Leek, Sybil, *Diary of a Witch*. New York, Signet Books, 1968.
The autobiography of a contemporary "white" witch. The book
is also an attempt to change the general opinion of witches by
describing their beneficial effects on an American town.

Lissner, Ivar, *Man, God and Magic*, trans. by J. M. Brownjohn. London, Jonathan Cape Ltd., 1961.
An ethnologist, Lissner suggests here that our primitive ancestors "degenerated," through the influence of magic and
witchcraft, from monotheism to polytheism.

Macfarlane, Alan, *Witchcraft in Tudor and Stuart England*. New
York, Harper Torchbooks, 1970.
A study of African witchcraft and its relation to witchcraft in
Tudor and Stuart England.

Murray, Margaret, *The God of the Witches*. Garden City, New
York, Doubleday Anchor Books, 1960.

374   A classic study of Satanism, based on actual pagan cults and practices.

Neihardt, John G., *Black Elk Speaks*. New York, Pocket Books, 1972.
The life of a Sioux Indian holy man told by him through the author—a beautifully lyrical book filled with descriptions of shamanic visions.

Parrinder, Geoffrey, *Witchcraft*. Middlesex, England, Pelican Books, 1958.
A standard work on the general subject of witchcraft by a leading scholar in the field.

Rosen, Barbara, *Witchcraft*. London, Edward Arnold (Publishers) Ltd., 1969.
A useful collection of material related to the subject of witchcraft.

Santillana, Giorgio de, *Hamlet's Mill*. Boston, Gambit, Inc., 1969.
A remarkable and highly imaginative book on astrology.

Thompson, Stith, *Tales of the North American Indians*. Bloomington, Indiana, Indiana University Press, 1966.
The most complete and scholarly paperback collection of stories of the American Indians.

Tindall, Gillian, *A Handbook on Witches*. London, Panther Books Ltd., 1967.
Answers obvious and not so obvious questions about witchcraft.

Williams, Charles, *Witchcraft*. New York, Meridian Books, 1960.
Witchcraft as seen by a religious man who is best known for his interest in the subject of fantasy.

Wilson, Colin, *The Occult*. New York, Vintage Books, 1973.
A definitive history of magic and related fields from earliest times to the present.

Literary Works

Coleridge, Samuel Taylor, *Complete Poetical Works*, E. H. Coleridge, ed. New York, Oxford University Press, 1912.

Euripides, *Medea*, trans. by Rex Warner. London, John Lane Ltd., 1944.

Fowler, Gene, *Fires*. Berkeley, California, Thorp Springs Publishers, 1971.

Frost, Robert, *The Poetry of Robert Frost*, Edwin Connery Lathem, ed. New York, Holt, Rinehart and Winston, Inc., 1969.

Hawthorne, Nathaniel, *The Scarlet Letter and Other Tales of the Puritans*, Harry Levin, ed. Cambridge, Massachusetts, The Riverside Press, 1961.

Hughes, Ted, *Crow*. New York, Harper & Row, Publishers, 1971.

Marlowe, Christopher, *Doctor Faustus*, Sylvan Barnet, ed. New York, Signet Books, 1969.

Melville, Herman, *Moby Dick*, Alfred Kazin, ed. Cambridge, Massachusetts, The Riverside Press, 1956.

Yeats, William Butler, *The Collected Poems*. New York, The Macmillan Company, 1956.

PART TWO
MYSTICISM

Bucke, Richard M., *Cosmic Consciousness.* New York, E.P. Dutton & Co., Inc., 1959.
> Bucke here considers the great mystical questions concerning the union of man's consciousness with the cosmos.

Coomaraswamy, Ananda, *Buddha and the Gospel of Buddhism.* New York, G.P. Putnam's Sons, 1916.
> A fine collection of Buddhist stories, with perceptive commentary by a leading expert on religions and mythologies.

Ebon, Martin, *They Knew the Unknown.* New York, Signet Books, 1972.
> Case histories of famous people who "explored the reality behind our senses."

I Ching: The Book of Changes, trans. into English by Cary F. Baynes, from the German translation by Richard Wilhelm, with foreword by C. G. Jung. Routledge and Kegan Paul Ltd., 1951, 2 vols.
> This ancient Chinese book of oracles dates to the fourth millenium B.C. and is based on the lunar calendar.

James, Joseph, *The Way of Mysticism.* London, Jonathan Cape Ltd., 1950.
> A definition and survey of the general subject of mysticism.

James, William, *The Varieties of Religious Experience.* New York, Mentor Books, 1968.
> A famous work that deals with the psychology of the religious experience.

Jung, Carl Gustav, *Memories, Dreams, Reflections.* New York, Vintage Books, 1963.
> In this autobiography, Jung focuses on his inner life. (See, especially, the part entitled "Septem Sermones ad Mortuous," pp. 378–90.)

Krishnamurti, J., *Commentaries on Living.* Wheaton, Illinois, Quest Books, 1967, 3 vols.

————, *The First and Last Freedom*. Wheaton, Illinois, Quest Books, 1968.
> In these two books, as in most of his works, Krishnamurti speaks of a new freedom—a freedom that can only exist without society, without forms, and without any systems of belief.

Shah, Indries, *The Magic Monastery*. New York, E.P. Dutton & Co., Inc., 1972.

————, *The Sufis*, with introduction by Robert Graves. Garden City, New York, Doubleday Anchor Books, 1971.
> In these two books, Indries Shah provides great insight into the Islamic mystics.

Spraggett, Allen, *The Bishop Pike Story*. New York, Signet Books, 1970.
> An "inside" look at the dramatic and enigmatic events in the life of the well-known bishop and spiritualist.

Suzuki, D. T., *Mysticism: Christian and Buddhist*. New York, Harper & Row, Publishers, 1957.

————, *Zen Buddhism*, William Barrett, ed. Garden City, New York, Doubleday Anchor Books, 1956.
> Two important books by an authoritative scholar of Oriental mysticism in general and of Zen Buddhism in particular.

The Mystic Vision: Papers from the Eranos Yearbooks. Yearbook No. 6, Bollingen Series XXX. (Princeton, New Jersey, Princeton University Press, 1968.)
> The Eranos Yearbooks are published on a regular basis by followers of Jungian psychology, and, in this volume, mysticism is approached from that point of view. (See, especially, Eric Neumann's article entitled "Mystical Man.")

The Secret of the Golden Flower: A Chinese Book of Life, trans. by Richard Wilhelm, with foreword and commentary by C. G. Jung. New York, Harcourt, Brace and World, 1962.
> An ancient Chinese book expounding the mystical wisdom of yoga.

Thurston, Herbert, *The Physical Phenomena of Mysticism*, J. H. Crehan, ed. Chicago, Henry Regnery Company, 1952.

378   A study of one fascinating aspect of the mystical experience that is neglected in most works on the subject.

Underhill, Evelyn, *Mysticism: A Study in the Nature and Development of Man's Spiritual Consciousness.* London, Methuen and Co. Ltd., 1911.
Man's spiritual consciousness as viewed by a Catholic mystic. A basic book for the student of mysticism.

————, *Practical Mysticism.* New York, Dutton Paperbacks, 1943.
An attempt to bring an understanding of mysticism, through the practical approach, to the layman.

Von Hugel, Friedrich, *The Mystical Element of Religion.* London, J.M. Dent & Sons Ltd., 1908, 2 vols.
A consideration of the mystical element present in all forms of religion.

Watts, Alan, *This Is It and Other Essays.* New York, Collier Books, 1967.
All of Alan Watts's books present novel and vital approaches to the unknown. A serious figure of the counter culture, Watts here stresses the importance of mystical experience in a technocratic world.

Yeats, William Butler, *A Vision.* New York, Collier Books, 1966.
This book, Yeats's attempt to create a modern myth, presents his controversial "system" for viewing the world, its people, and its history.

Yogananda, Paramhansa, *Autobiography of a Yogi.* London, Rider & Co., 1963.
This book conveys the mystical essence of Hinduism, despite the author's claims to miraculous powers.

Zaehner, R. C., *Mysticism: Sacred and Profound.* New York, Oxford University Press, 1961.
A study of mystical experiences, including those produced by drugs.

Literary Works

The Bhagavad Gita, trans. by Ann Stanford. New York, Herder and Herder, Inc., 1970.

Blake, William, *Life of William Blake: With Selections from his Poems and Other Writings,* Alexander Gilchrist, ed. London, Macmillan and Co., 1880, 2 vols.

Eliot, T. S., *The Complete Poems and Plays: 1909–1950.* New York, Harcourt Brace & Co., 1952.

Hesse, Hermann, *Siddhartha,* trans. by Hilda Resner. New York, New Directions Paperbacks, 1957.

John of the Cross, *Poems of Saint John of the Cross,* trans. by Roy Campbell. London, Harvill Press Ltd., 1952.

Kerouac, Jack, *Dharma Bums.* New York, The Viking Press, Inc., 1958.

Merton, Thomas, *Selected Poems,* with introduction by Mark Von Doren. New York, New Directions Paperbacks, 1967.

———, *The Way of Chuang Tzu.* New York, New Directions Paperbacks, 1969.

Neihardt, John G., *Black Elk Speaks.* New York, Pocket Books, 1972.

Snyder, Gary, *Myths and Texts.* New York, Totem Press, 1960.

Thompson, Francis, *Selected Poems of Francis Thompson,* with biographical note by Wilfred Meynell. London, Methuen and Co. Ltd., 1909.

Whitman, Walt, *Leaves of Grass,* 1855.

Yeats, William Butler, *The Collected Plays.* New York, The Macmillan Company, 1962.

PART THREE
FANTASY

Chesterton, G. K., "The Ethics of Elfland," in W. H. Auden, ed., *G. K. Chesterton: A Selection from his Non-Fictional Prose* (London, Faber & Faber Ltd., 1970), pp. 174–90.
    A lively essay by the well-known fantasy writer.

Cox, Harvey, *The Feast of Fools: A Theological Essay on Festivity and Fantasy*. Cambridge, Massachusetts, Harvard University Press, 1969.
    An exploration of the religious side of fantasy.

Hall, Mary Harrington, "A conversation with Ray Bradbury and Chuck Jones: The Fantasy-Makers." *Psychology Today*, Vol. 1, No. 11 (April, 1968), pp. 28–37, 70.
    This interview with Ray Bradbury and Chuck Jones is included here, as both men are important writers of science fiction.

Jung, Carl Gustav, "The Phenomenology of the Spirit in Fairytales," in *Four Archetypes* (Princeton, New Jersey, Bollingen Series/ Princeton University Press, 1970), pp. 83–132.
    A psychological study of the "wise old man" type of character as portrayed in fairy tale. The essay also contains Jung's own interpretations of several fairy tales.

Sartre, Jean Paul, *The Psychology of Imagination*. New York, Philosophical Library, Inc., 1948.
    A study of the powers of fantasy by the French Existentialist philosopher.

Science Fiction: The Future, Dick Allen, ed. New York, Harcourt Brace Jovanovich, 1971.
    A valuable science fiction anthology containing essays as well as stories.

Tolkien, J. R. R., "On Fairy-Stories," in *The Tolkien Reader* (New York, Ballantine Books, 1966), pp. 3–84.
    An unusual and controversial definition of fantasy and related forms by the author of the trilogy, *The Lord of the Rings*.

Literary Works

The Annotated Mother Goose, William and Ceil Baring-Gould, eds. New York, Meridian Press, 1972.

Carroll, Lewis, *Alice's Adventures in Wonderland and Through the Looking-Glass.* New York, St. Martin's Press, 1971.

Fitzgerald, F. Scott, "The Diamond as Big as the Ritz," in *Babylon Revisited and Other Tales* (New York, Charles Scribner's Sons, 1960), pp. 75–113.

Grahame, Kenneth, *The Wind in the Willows,* with introduction by Mary Ellman. New York, Signet Books, 1969.

Grimm, Jacob Ludwig Carl, and Wilhelm Carl, *Household Stories from the Collections of the Brothers Grimm,* trans. by Lucy Crane. London, Macmillan & Co., Ltd., 1882.

Huxley, Aldous, *Brave New World.* New York, Bantam Books, 1967.

Lewis, C. S., *Out of the Silent Planet.* New York, The Macmillan Company, 1963.

Lovecraft, H. P., *Dagon and Other Macabre Tales,* August Derleth, ed. Sawk City, Wisconsin, Arkham House, 1965.

Macdonald, George, *Phantasies and Lilith,* C. S. Lewis, ed. Grand Rapids, Michigan, W.B. Eerdmans Publishing Company, 1964.

Orwell, George, *Animal Farm.* New York, Harcourt, Brace & Co., 1954.

———, *1984.* New York, Harcourt, Brace & Co., 1949.

Poe, Edgar Allan, *The Selected Poetry and Prose of Edgar Allan Poe,* with introduction by T. A. Mabbott. New York, Modern Library, Inc., 1951.

Scully, James, *The Marches.* New York, Holt, Rinehart and Winston, Inc., 1967.

Smith, Stevie, *The Best Beast.* New York, Ballantine Books, 1966.

Tolkien, J. R. R., *The Tolkien Reader.* New York, Ballantine Books, 1966.

———, *The Lord of the Rings.* Boston, Houghton Mifflin Company, 1967.

382   Vonnegut, Kurt Jr., *Welcome to the Monkey House*. New York, The Delacorte Press, 1968.

Wells, H. G., *The Time Machine*. New York, Random House, Inc., 1931.

PART FOUR
MYTH

Bodkin, Maud, *Archetypal Patterns in Poetry: Psychological Studies of Imagination*. London, Oxford Paperbacks, 1963.
An explanation, through literature, of Jung's theories of archetypes and the collective unconscious.

Campbell, Joseph, *The Hero with a Thousand Faces*. Cleveland, Bollingen Series/Meridian Press, 1956.
A dramatic and perceptive view of the composite "world hero" and his monomyth.

————, *The Masks of God*. New York, Viking Compass Books, 1970, 4 vols.
The most complete and thorough study of world mythology available to the modern reader.

Coomaraswamy, Ananda, *Hinduism and Buddhism*. New York, Philosophical Library, Inc., 1943.
A study of the myths and doctrines of Hinduism and Buddhism.

Eliade, Mircea, *Myth and Reality*. New York, Harper Torchbooks, 1968.
In this work, the author makes clear the importance of myth to modern man.

Frazer, Sir James, *The New Golden Bough*, Theodore Gaster, ed. New York, Mentor Books, 1964.
The classic work on myth, ritual, and magic by a leading cultural anthropologist of the early twentieth century.

Frye, Northrop, *Anatomy of Criticism*. New York, Atheneum Publishers, 1970.
This book expounds the basic theories of the literary world's most prestigious "myth critic."

————, *Fables of Identity: Studies in Poetic Mythology*. New York, Harcourt, Brace and World, 1963.
A further expression of Frye's theories, accompanied by valuable explanations of their practical literary application.

384 Henderson, Joseph L., and Oakes, Maud, *The Wisdom of the Serpent: The Myths of Death, Rebirth and Resurrection.* New York, Collier Books, 1971.
A Jungian analysis of death and resurrection through the use of mythic symbols and literature.

Jung, Carl Gustav, *The Archetypes and the Collective Unconscious,* trans. by R. F. C. Hull. New York, Pantheon Books, Inc., 1959.
This work outlines Jung's theories on mythic approaches to literature—theories that are now basic to all such approaches.

———, *Modern Man in Search of a Soul.* New York, Harvest Books, 1936.
Here, Jung discusses the spiritual gap suffered by modern man, and he provides illustrations of the "living quality of myth."

———, and Kerenyi, C., *Essays on a Science of Mythology: The Myth of the Divine Child and the Mysteries of Eleusis.* Princeton, New Jersey, Bollingen Series/Princeton University Press, 1971.
Jung and Kerenyi here develop a theory of myth.

———, and others, *Man and His Symbols.* New York, Dell Books, 1971.
In this book, the renowned psychiatrist and four of his associates deal with man's unconscious in terms particularly intended for the lay public.

Leeming, David A., *Mythology: The Voyage of the Hero.* Philadelphia, J.B. Lippincott Company, 1973.
A collection, with commentaries, of mythic stories from various cultures.

Malinowski, Bronislaw, *Magic, Science and Religion.* Glencoe, The Free Press, 1948.
A classic study of the ways in which the present and the unknown are strongly related to one another.

Mythologies of the Ancient World, S. N. Kramer, ed. Garden City, New York, Doubleday Anchor Books, 1961.
A handbook of ancient mythological stories.

Myths, Dreams and Religion, Joseph Campbell, ed. New York, Dutton Paperbacks, 1970.

A valuable collection of essays on myth by Campbell, Alan Watts, Norman O. Brown, and others.

Watts, Alan, *Myth and Ritual in Christianity*. Boston, Beacon Paperbacks, 1968.
One of Watts's early works in which he brings the Christian myth to life.

Literary Works

Baldwin, James, *Going to Meet the Man*. New York, Dell Books, 1971.

Burrows, David J., and others, *Myths and Motifs in Literature*. New York, The Free Press, 1973.

Euripides, *The Bacchae*, trans. by Charles Boer, in Albert Cook, and Edwin Dolin, eds., *An Anthology of Greek Tragedy* (New York, The Bobbs-Merrill Co., Inc., 1972), pp. 351–400.

Gasarch, Pearl and Ralph, *Fiction: The Universal Elements*. New York, Van Nostrand Reinhold Company, 1972.

Graves, Robert, *The Greek Myths*. Baltimore, Penguin Books, Inc., 1955, 2 vols.

Homer, *The Iliad*, trans. by Richard Lattimore. Chicago, Phoenix Books, 1961.

—————, *The Odyssey*, trans. by Robert Fitzgerald. Garden City, New York, Doubleday Anchor Books, 1963.

Keats, John, *Complete Poetical Works*, Horace E. Scudder, ed. Boston, Houghton Mifflin Company, no date.

The Epic of Gilgamesh, trans. by N. K. Sanders. Baltimore, Penguin Books, Inc., 1967.

The Holy Bible, King James Version, 1611. New York, American Bible Society, 1962.

The Scapegoat: Ritual and Literature, John B. Vickery, and J. M. Sellery, eds., Boston, Houghton Mifflin Company, 1972.

The World of the Short Story: Archetypes in Action, Oliver Evans, and Harry Finestone, eds. New York, Alfred A. Knopf, Inc., 1971.

386   HARCOURT BRACE JOVANOVICH, INC.   For "The Archetypes of Litera-
ture" from *Fables of Identity* by Northrop Frye, copyright, 1951, by Har-
court Brace Jovanovich, Inc; and for "Heavenly Consciousness" and "The
Primal Spirit and the Conscious Spirit" from *The Secret of the Golden
Flower,* A Chinese Book of Life, translated into German by Richard Wil-
helm and into English by Cary F. Baynes. Both reprinted by permission of
Harcourt Brace Jovanovich, Inc.
HARPER & ROW, PULISHERS, INC.   For "Crow's Fall" in *Crow* by Ted
Hughes. Copyright © 1971 by Ted Hughes. Originally appeared in *The
New Yorker;* and for an excerpt from *Witchcraft in Tudor and Stuart
England* by Alan Macfarlane. Both reprinted by permission of Harper &
Row, Publishers, Inc.
HOLT, RINEHART AND WINSTON, INC.   For "Two Witches" from *The
Poetry of Robert Frost* edited by Edwin Connery Lathem. Copyright 1923,
© 1969 by Holt, Rinehart and Winston, Inc. Copyright 1951 by Robert
Frost; and for "Facing Up" from *The Marches* by James Scully. Copyright
© 1960, 1961, 1962, 1963, 1965, 1966, 1967 by James Scully. Both re-
printed by permission of Holt, Rinehart and Winston, Inc.
OLWYN HUGHES   For the review of *Shamanism: Archaic Techniques of
Ecstasy* by Ted Hughes from *The Listener,* Oct. 29, 1964. Reprinted by
permission of Olwyn Hughes.
INDIANA UNIVERSITY PRESS   For "The Arrow Chain" from *Tales of the
North American Indians* by Stith Thompson. Reprinted by permission of
Indiana University Press.
ALFRED A. KNOPF, INC.   For "The Frog Prince." Copyright © 1966 by
Stevie Smith. Reprinted from *The Best Beast,* by Stevie Smith, by permis-
sion of Alfred A. Knopf, Inc.
HOPE LERESCHE & STEELE   For "What is Mysticism?" from *Practical
Mysticism* by Evelyn Underhill. Reprinted by permission of Hope Leresche
& Steele.
MACMILLAN PUBLISHING CO., INC.   For "Sailing to Byzantium" from
Collected Poems by William Butler Yeats. Copyright 1928 by Macmillan
Publishing Co., Inc., renewed 1956 by Georgie Yeats; and for "The Shadowy
Waters" from *Collected Plays* by William Butler Yeats. Copyright 1934,
1952 by Macmillan Publishing Co., Inc. Both reprinted with permission of
Macmillan Publishing Co., Inc.
MACMILLAN & COMPANY, LIMITED   For "Down the Rabbit-Hole" from
Alice's Adventures in Wonderland by Lewis Carroll. Reprinted by permis-
sion of Macmillan London & Basingstoke.
NEW DIRECTIONS PUBLISHING CORPORATION   For "Om" from *Sidd-
hartha* by Herman Hesse, translated by Hilda Rosner. Copyright 1951 by
New Directions Publishing Corporation; and for "Elegy for the Monastery
Barn" from *Selected Poems* by Thomas Merton. Copyright © 1957 by The
Abbey of Gethsemani. Both reprinted by permission of New Directions
Publishing Corporation.
PENGUIN BOOKS LTD.   For "The Frog Prince" from *The Frog Prince and
Other Poems* by Stevie Smith (Longmans 1966). Copyright © Stevie Smith,
1966. Reprinted by permission of Penguin Books Ltd.
HILDA N. PETRI   For an excerpt from *Black Elk Speaks* by John Neihardt.
Reprinted by permission of Hilda N. Petri.
PRINCETON UNIVERSITY PRESS   For "From Psychology to Metaphysics"
and "The Shapeshifter" from *The Hero with a Thousand Faces* by Joseph
Campbell, Bollingen Series XVII (copyright 1949 by Bollingen Foundation),

COPYRIGHTS AND ACKNOWLEDGMENTS

reprinted by permission of Princeton University Press: pp. 255–260, 381–382. **387**

RANDOM HOUSE   For excerpts from *Memories, Dreams, Reflections,* by C. G. Jung, recorded and edited by Aniela Jaffe, translated by Richard and Clara Winston. Copyright © 1963 by Random House, Inc.; and for "Beat Zen, Square Zen, Zen" from *This Is It and Other Essays,* by Alan W. Watts. Copyright © 1958, 1960 by Alan W. Watts. Both reprinted by permission of Pantheon Books, a Division of Random House, Inc.

ROUTLEDGE & KEGAN PAUL LTD   For an excerpt from *Witchcraft in Tudor and Stuart England* by Alan Macfarlane; and for "Heavenly Consciousness" and "The Primal Spirit and the Conscious Spirit" from *The Secret of the Golden Flower,* A Chinese Book of Life, translated by Richard Wilhelm. Both are reprinted by permission of Routledge & Kegan Paul Ltd.

CHARLES SCRIBNER'S SONS   For "The Diamond As Big As the Ritz" (copyright 1922 Smart Set Company, Inc.; renewal copyright 1950 Frances Scott Fitzgerald Lanahan), which first appeared in *Smart Set,* and is reprinted by permission of Charles Scribner's Sons from *Tales of the Jazz Age* by F. Scott Fitzgerald.

ST. MARTIN'S PRESS, INCORPORATED   For "Down the Rabbit-Hole" from *Alice's Adventures in Wonderland* by Lewis Carroll. Reprinted by permission of St. Martin's Press, Inc.

THORP SPRINGS PRESS   For "Shaman Song #12" from *Fires* by Gene Fowler. Copyright © 1971 by Gene Fowler. Reprinted by permission of Thorp Springs Press.

UNIVERSITY OF CALIFORNIA PRESS   For an excerpt from *The Teachings of Don Juan: A Yaqui Way of Knowledge* by Carlos Castaneda. Originally published by the University of California Press; reprinted by permission of The Regents of the University of California.

A.P. WATT & SON   For an excerpt from "The Ethics of Elfland" from *G. K. Chesterton: A Selection from his Non-Fictional Prose,* selected by W. H. Auden. Reprinted by permission of Miss Dorothy E. Collins and A.P. Watt & Son, and for "Sailing to Byzantium" from *The Collected Poems of W. B. Yeats* and "The Shadowy Waters" from *The Collected Plays of W. B. Yeats.* Reprinted by permission of Mr. M. B. Yeats, the Macmillan Company of Canada Ltd., and A.P. Watt & Son.

WAYLAND (PUBLISHERS) LTD.   For an excerpt from *Witchcraft* by Roger Hart. Reprinted by permission of Wayland (Publishers) Ltd.

Picture Credits

page 12   A ceremonial mask from the island of New Zealand (New Guinea). Copyright British Museum, Natural History Division

page 37   *The Sorcerer.* Courtesy of the American Museum of Natural History

page 57   *The Witches' Sabbath.* Photograph by SCALA New York/Florence; Lazaro Galdiano Museum, Madrid

page 72   *The Bewitched Groom.* Germanisches Nationalmuseum, Nuremburg

page 102   *Meditation, Stage 3.* From *The Secret of the Golden Flower,* translated from the Chinese into German and explained by Richard Wilhelm with commentary by Carl Jung. English translation by Cary F. Baynes. Reproduced by permission of Harcourt Brace Jovanovich, Inc.

COPYRIGHTS AND ACKNOWLEDGMENTS